SHADES OF

KASHMIR

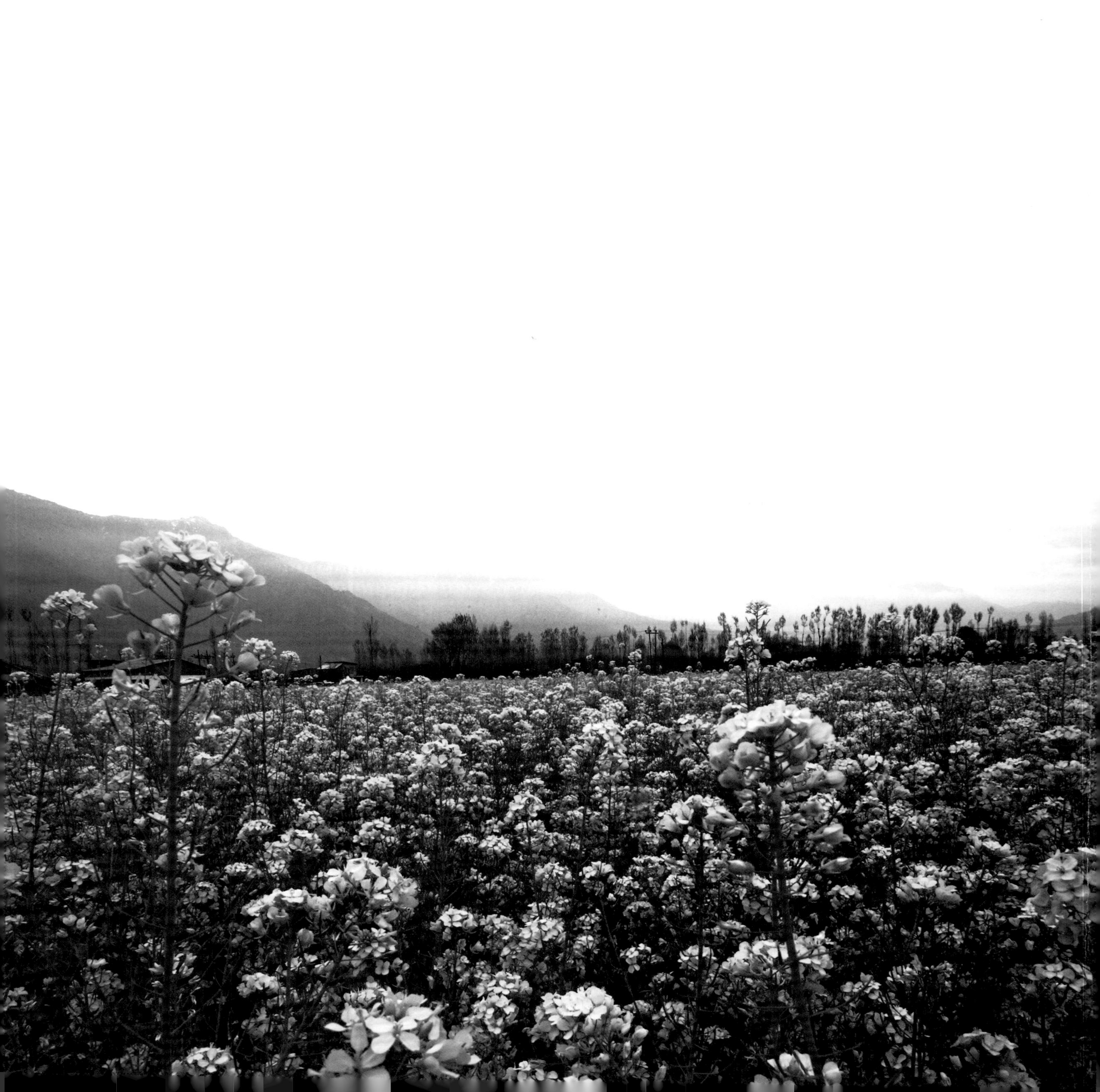

SHADES OF

KASHMIR

LANDSCAPE • DAILY LIFE • PEOPLE • PROTEST

SHOME BASU

Foreword by HAPPYMON JACOB

NIYOGI BOOKS

Overseas Distribution

USA and Canada
ACC Distribution
email: sales@accdistribution.com
www.accdistribution.com

United Kingdom, Ireland, Europe and Africa
Kodansha Europe Ltd.
email: info@kodansha.eu
www.kodansha.eu

Cambodia, Burma, Laos and Thailand
Paragon Asia Co. Ltd.
email: info@paragonasia.com
www.paragonasia.com

Published by
NIYOGI BOOKS
D-78, Okhla Industrial Area, Phase-I
New Delhi-110 020, INDIA
Tel: 91-11-26816301, 49327000
Fax: 91-11-26810483, 26813830
email: niyogibooks@gmail.com
website: www.niyogibooksindia.com

Editor: Jayalakshmi Sengupta
Design: Shashi Bhushan Prasad

ISBN: 978-93-83098-86-6
Publication: 2015

Printed at: Niyogi Offset Pvt. Ltd., New Delhi, India

DEDICATED TO

ARUNABHA BASU

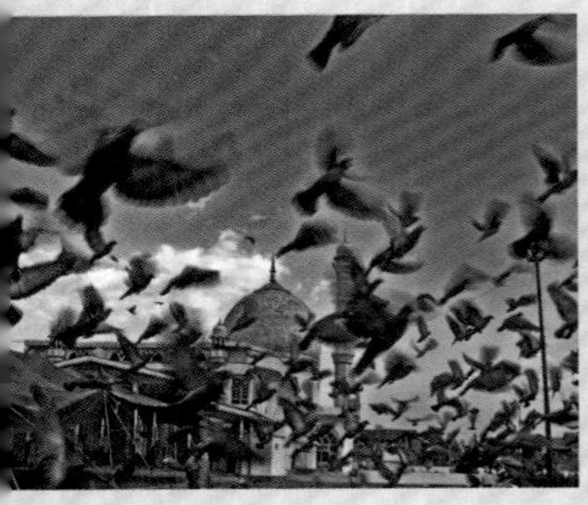

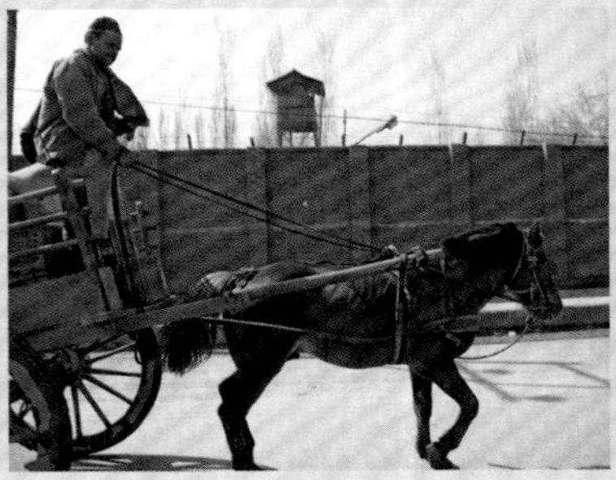

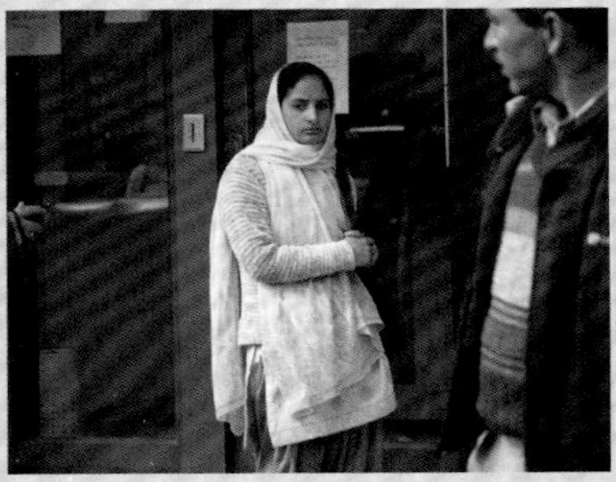

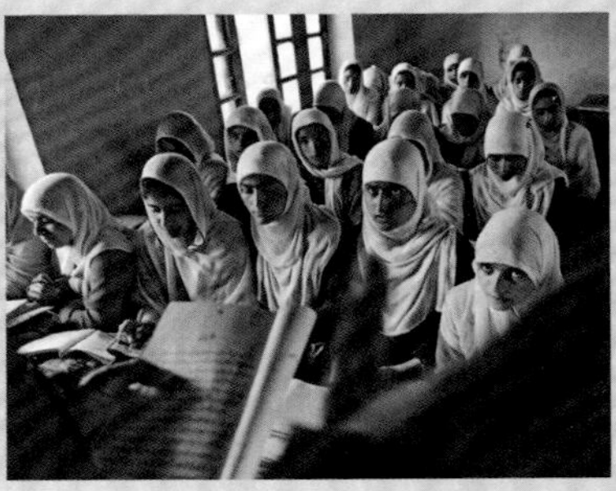

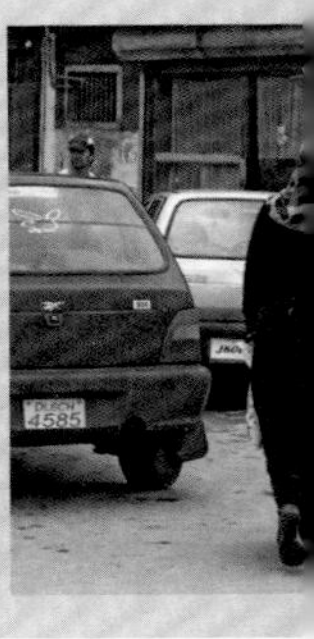

CONTENTS

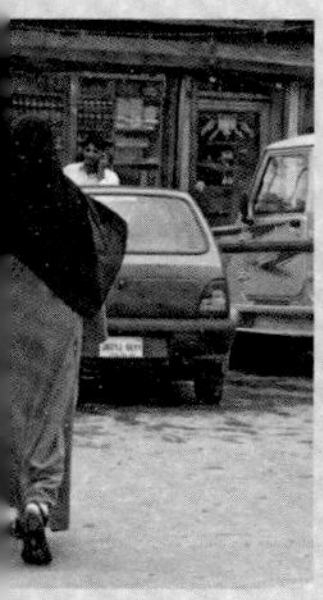
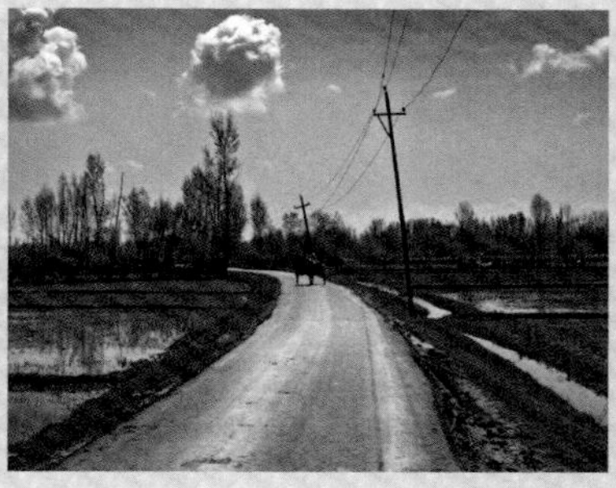
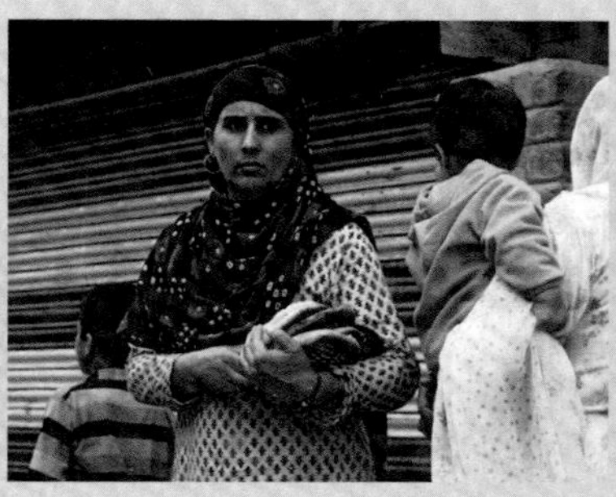
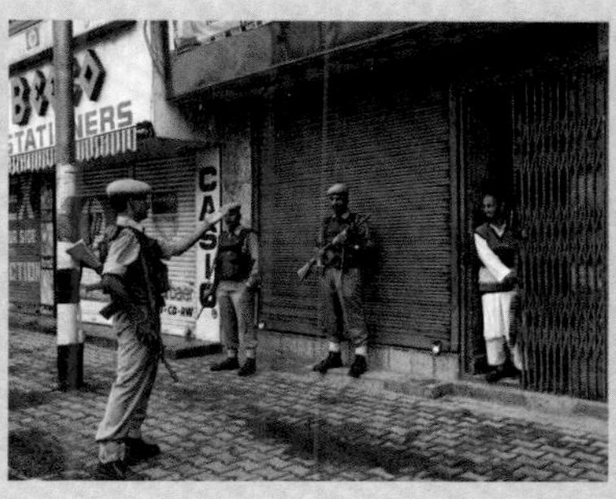
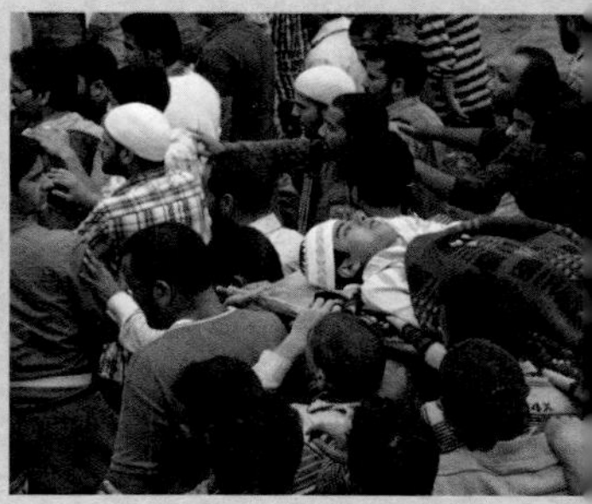

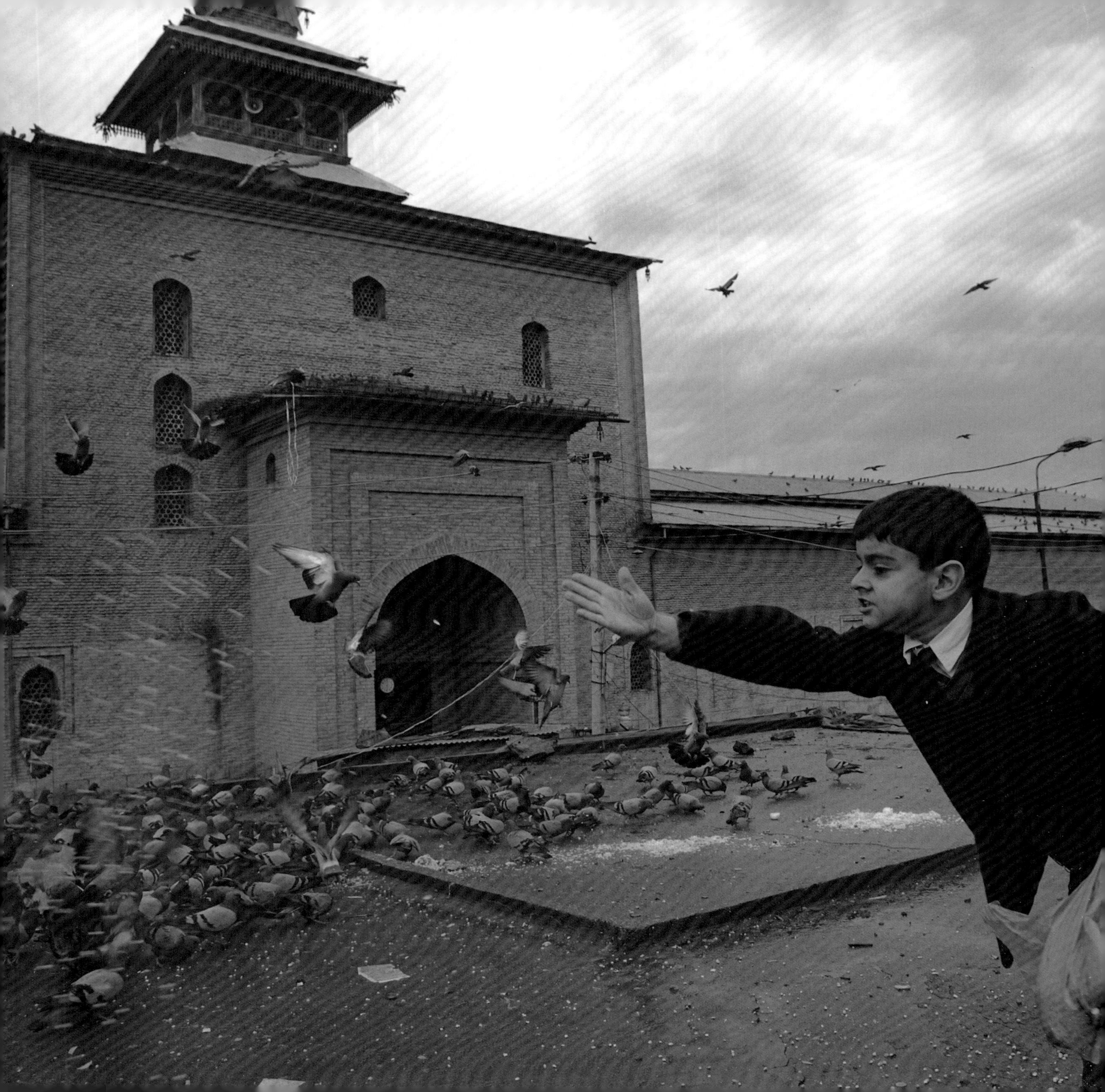

FOREWORD

Professionally and by training, I am a political scientist and have primarily learned to look at things around me from the lens of politics. Where there is no apparent politics, I am taught to look below the surface, beneath the misleading veneer of the apparent and immediate, to understand the subtle dynamics of politics. However, there are occasions when I venture out to understand life in an unstructured manner, through lenses other than those of a political scientist. Those are indeed the occasions, I must confess, when I have understood social realities better. Kashmir, for me, has been one of those segments of reality that I often tried to engage in, without the structures and strictures imposed by my discipline. I did not want to merely theorise Kashmir, I wanted to understand it, for what it really was, in its bare essence.

That's precisely what we talked about when I met Shome Basu, a year ago at the residence of a French Diplomat, Jeremie Robert, in New Delhi, where both of us had been invited to savour some fine French cheese and wine. At first, when we started talking about Kashmir, we had seemingly competing narratives: I thought his arguments were 'theoretically unsound' and he, I am sure, must have thought of my version to be devoid of 'human touch'. What can photographs do in telling us about the intricacies and complexities of a decade-long intractable conflict such as the one in Kashmir? How can a photographer look beyond the immediate and appreciate the layers and layers of conflict that has gone into constructing his subject? As we spoke into the night, aided by the uninterrupted supply of French wine and cheese, and Jeremie's courteous and warm company, I realised that our versions of Kashmir were not far apart. Our mutual suspicion gave way to mutual admiration for the kind of work that the other has been doing—I realised there was something very significant about the kind of work Shome was engaged in.

I came across Shome's Kashmir photographs in the weeks and months that followed and I started taking a liking to his work. Its only a few months ago that I took a good look at his Kashmir photos when Shome asked me to write a foreward for this book. This time around I took a serious look at his photos, without the methodological and theoretical biases of a political scientist. And I can state with great certainty today that Shome and I tell the same story of Kashmir—only our tools of craft make us narrate them differently. We are looking at the same world out there in Kashmir. Our 'objects' of analysis are the same: the very same people, their agonies and their daily lives.

What strikes me about this imaginatively put together collection of images from Kashmir is the ease with which it captures the many shades of the conflict in Kashmir. Where I struggle with words and phrases to narrate the many stories about Kashmir, Shome's camera does a great job of beautifully capturing those very stories with no words uttered. If you think that's nothing more than great craftsmanship, take a deeper look. Just as not all writers empathise with their objects of enquiry, not all photographers feel the agonies of those whose images they capture. Craftsmanship enables good shots, but cannot imbue empathy in the work.

Other than empathy, Shome's images evoke a number of other emotions within us: anguish, fear, guilt, helplessness, anticipation and beauty. Helplessness has multiple effects on us. On the one hand, looking at these images you feel helpless that you cannot do anything to alleviate their tragedy and suffering, that you are an inadequate, silent spectator. On the other hand, images, especially the powerful and evocative ones, transport you to the world captured in the image and then take you back into your own; you come face-to-face with a tragedy, you can hardly do anything about it. You are there, but you are not.

The background of Shome's images are mostly dark, dilapidated buildings, rundown roads, raised hands, pointed fingers, funeral processions, covered faces of young stone-throwers, waiting mothers, and old men staring blankly at you. There is resistance, anger, mourning and pain. Cries of 'We want freedom' come alive on the dirty walls of downtown Srinagar. There is an overdose of youth in these images: youngsters with stones and with guns in their hands. There is this one photo where an elderly woman looks through the hole of a damaged window, probably waiting for her son/daughter to return home, peeping through the window to see if the Indian soldiers are in the streets down, before stepping out to buy some essentials. To me she seemed to be just waiting for freedom.

Shome's work is conflict photography at its best, something for which he literally shed his blood. He takes you closer to the unimaginable images we normally would want to avoid seeing. As the acclaimed war photographer Adam Ferguson puts it: 'You see movies, you read books, you can imagine anything. But when you are in front of something, it's not like the movies'. It takes you from the abstract to the real, as close as short of real can get.

Shome wants us to see how the humanity in us has neglected the bloody conflict in Kashmir, that there are people suffering from the excesses of the armed forces and militants while we engage in idle talks about achieving greater power status. The images in this book bring you the forgotten nooks of the Kashmir Valley and neglected gazes of the Kashmiri people. The conflict comes at you more powerfully, speaks to you directly and strikes a chord in your inner self.

There is also a certain wonder in Shome's gaze. His choice of faces and places, to my mind, conveys that he is bewildered by what he sees, as it would be the case with me as well. For that matter, any outsider would see what is portrayed in these images as arresting as they are 'extraordinary'. But not for the Kashmiri observer—for him this is daily life, the hazards of life in Kashmir, and they are perhaps so used to the 'extraordinariness' that they would see all of this to be pretty ordinary. But then its Shome's ability to wonder at the 'extraordinary' that makes an unmistakable political statement, that 'there is something rotten in the state of Kashmir'.

Kashmir means different things to different people. To some it's their favourite summer getaway, for others it's a scary place to be posted to, and for still others it's the boiling pot of military strategy, statecraft and spy-games. For the Kashmiris, it's their promised land where promises have not been kept. Let me hasten to add here that the book also does justice to all of these perspectives. Despite the heavy dose of conflict images, you would get to see most of these perspectives represented in this collection.

This book is being published in the backdrop of Kashmir's tragic history. What is unique and tragic at the same time about the Kashmir conflict is how a lack of political maturity and wisdom has resulted in widespread alienation of Kashmir from the rest of India. This was taken advantage of by vested interests in the late 1980s, thus giving the internal dissension bilateral and international dimensions. Pakistan's covert activities in Kashmir lasted for about 15 years. Pakistan has been transforming the contours of its positions on the Kashmir question, much to the relief of New Delhi. However, the internal dimension of the Kashmir conflict continues to simmer, and occasionally erupts, despite the temporary lull, which again has to be attributed to the lack of political maturity and wisdom on the part of India's political class. The tragedy of Kashmir lies in the fact that while the conflict over Kashmir seems to be taking a backseat, the conflict in Kashmir does not seem to be seriously addressed. An opportunity lost it may be, to bring succor to the people of Kashmir, but even more clearly it is an act of injustice.

Contemporary Kashmir, which seems to represent a political-legal vacuum, where normal laws, rights, constitutional remedies, and governmental accountability applicable to other parts of the country are absent, fits well with Agamben's depiction of a 'state of exception'. Giorgio Agamben, a widely regarded European Philosopher, argues, in his book *State of Exception* that 'the voluntary creation of a permanent state of emergency (though perhaps not declared in the technical sense) has become one of the essential practices of contemporary states, including the so-called democratic ones.' While still very much within the Indian sovereign space, Kashmir is a 'state of exception', not merely characterised by the application of extraordinary legal provisions, but also embedded in the popular political imagination in India. Kashmiris are increasingly condemned to live in a state of exception and emergency by the ever-increasing use of extra-constitutional means of coercion. As a result, entire categories of citizens are kept out of ordinarily applicable rights and privileges.

It often takes massive protests on the streets of Kashmir and the deaths of scores of Kashmiris, for the 'collective conscience' of the nation to wake up and ask what has gone wrong there. Sometimes, even when it witnesses what happens in Kashmir, the country's 'collective conscience' is far from morally outraged. Most people simply believe that the emergency provisions in force should continue and that they will one day stabilise Kashmir.

This volume, fruit of Shome's decade-long journeys to the Valley, comes at a very crucial period in Kashmir history. Today the Kashmir conflict is ripe for resolution. Even though there is no bilateral deal on Kashmir yet, the Indo-Pak rivalry over the issue is characteristically different today than during the 1990s. In other words, Kashmir is not as contentious as it used to be. There is also a very significant kind of change taking place in the state politics of J&K. Indeed, most of the mainstream and dissident parties have now unveiled blueprints of their preferred solution to the problem. The New Delhi-Islamabad, Srinagar-New Delhi, and Jammu-Srinagar tracks of dialogue have been yielding positive results. Many of these dialogue tracks were frozen when the official peace process broke down in the wake of the Mumbai terror attacks in November 2008. Indeed, the two countries have already begun a new round of dialogues on a variety of outstanding bilateral issues.

The only logical conclusion of such a process is to correct the historical wrongs committed in Kashmir. The process in this regard is perhaps ongoing, but there is a need to accelerate it and for it to continue to be informed by the significant lessons of history. Persuaded by this line of argument, the Government of India has undertaken many initiatives in the recent years. Prime Minister Manmohan Singh, for example, organised a number of round table conferences with Kashmiri leadership even though the major actors form the dissident camp did not attend them. They were a good beginning, nevertheless. These round table conferences were followed up by the establishment of five working groups on the various aspects of the Kashmir issue, namely, 'Centre's relations with the State, furthering the relations across the Line of Control (LoC), giving a boost to the State's economic development, rehabilitating the destitute families of militants and reviewing the cases of detainees and ensuring good governance.' While the Centre did not implement any of the recommendations contained in those reports, it remains a good initiative.

Finally, during the 2010 agitations in Kashmir, the Ministry of Home, then headed by Palaniappan Chidambaram, announced the formation of a three-member group of interlocutors for Kashmir. Even though the credentials of the members of the group and their mandate were severely criticised by a lot of people, including me in the pages of *Greater Kashmir* and *The Hindu*, the very fact that the government appointed three members of civil society rather than retired bureaucrats was proof that it wished to address the Kashmir question politically. In other words, a good start had been made. The political courage to take the next step is what is required now.

People like Shome will continue to think of Kashmir, Kashmiris and their struggles, and tell us the untold stories, show us the unknown nooks of Kashmir's azadi struggle. People like him continue to help us rediscover the humanity in us.

Happymon Jacob
Faculty, School of International Studies, Jawaharlal Nehru University (JNU), New Delhi

Prior to joining JNU in 2008, he held teaching positions at the University of Jammu in J&K and the Jamia Millia Islamia University in New Delhi, and research positions at the Centre for Air Power Studies, Delhi Policy Group and Observer Research Foundation, all based in New Delhi. He has been participating in some of the most influential India-Pakistan track-two dialogues: 'Chaophraya Dialogue', 'Pugwash India-Pakistan Dialogue' and the 'Ottawa Dialogue on India-Pakistan Nuclear Relations'.

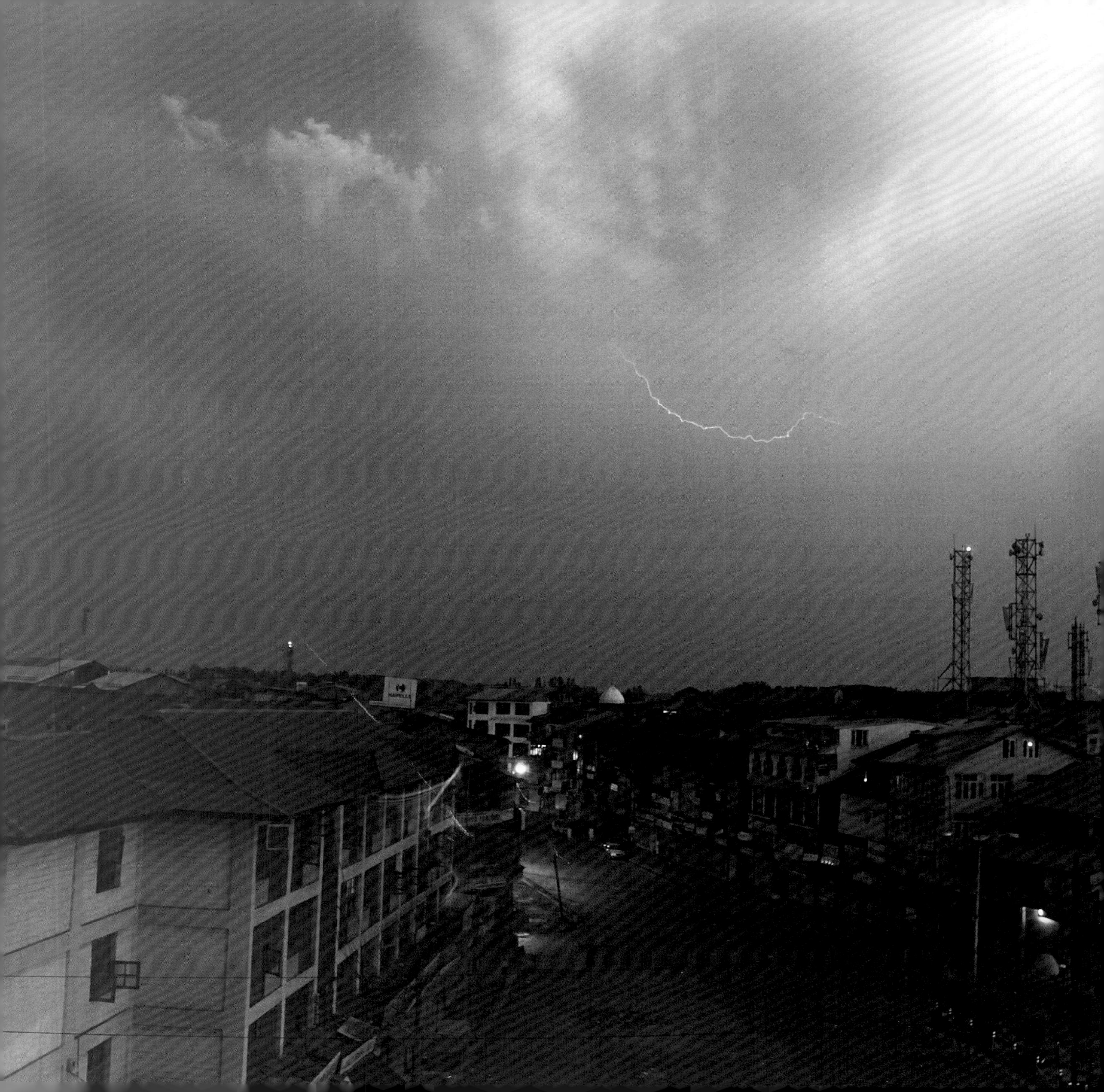

PREFACE

At the Delhi Airport I am subjected to scornful looks from the security personnel: I am late, I am wearing a kafia (the popular chequered Arabic scarf), and I am boarding an airplane bound for Srinagar. As I am the last passenger to board the flight, I am privy to some more scrutiny by the twenty-odd faces already seated in the plane.

'Welcome sir,' said the airhostess and greeted me with stereotypical politeness and a practiced smile. I looked for my aisle seat, something I generally do not prefer—but since I had reached the airport rather late, the airline staff had given me to understand I had a limited choice for seats. But looking around I found most of them still unoccupied.

The flight took off on time. After about thirty-five minutes, when the aircraft turned sharply from Pathankot, I could not resist myself anymore—pulling off the seat belt I jumped to an empty window seat—and was amazed at what I saw unfolding...The fold mountains spread before my eyes like crumpled bedsheets, with patches of green, brown, black and white prints on them. From an altitude of 39,000 ft, the Himalayas and the Pir Panjal looked like never-ending coverlets with soft, cotton, pillow-like clouds hovering over them. It was heavenly. 'God's own land!' I gasped.

Soon the gorges, ridges and the caves disappeared and a pristine valley welcomed me with its green fields and a blue sky and tiny dots of tin-roofed huts. We got ready at last to land at the Srinagar International Airport.

At the tarmac, from the windows, one could see men in khakis and olive fatigues, with INSAS and AKs and heavy bulletproof jackets guarding their chests; their eyes, peering out from under their helmets, searching and examining every corner. They would not hesitate to kill anyone who rose against them or the nation, I surmised. WELCOME TO KASHMIR.

Even at first glance, Srinagar felt quite foreign. There was very little India in Srinagar. Even the architecture looked more like that of Central Asia, and so did the Kashmiris. This feeling was further intensified when a plain-clothed cop walked over to me at the luggage belt and asked if I were a foreigner.

He must have been intimidated by my dark Afro-Asian looks. I denied by answering in Hindi, after which he gave me a gate-pass. I smirked and told myself, 'A foreigner indeed'—even though I was under the same sky of the Republic of India, of which I was a bonafide citizen. Ali Md, waited for me at the gate. The moment he saw me he came and greeted me with open arms. We proceeded to his new vehicle—an olive Scorpio, with an old PRESS sticker.

There had been a hartal and several curfews since 12 June 2010, for nearly three months, ever since a young boy in Kashmir had been gunned down by the security forces for reasons that did not deserve such a brutal punishment. The Valley was again on fire; a fire that no government could extinguish. Instead, it killed more protesters every day and aggravated the situation.

On my way to my hotel, near Lal Chowk at the heart of the city, I could see hundreds of uniformed men with stern faces, peeping out of their bunkers; their trigger-ready fingers, I imagined, waiting for any tell-tale sign of unrest. I stopped at Maisuma—a Jammu Kashmir Liberation Front (JKLF) stronghold and the den of its supremo, Yasin Mailk. I got down with my cameras and walked towards Standard Hotel from where two roads forked out. Both the lanes were fenced with barbed wires; brand new ones as I noticed from the lustre of the galvanised coating. The CRPF personnel, on alert, asked me about my credentials. With great reluctance I answered; I knew I was in the zone where the law of the gun ruled, due to the enforcement of the Armed Forces Special Powers Act (AFSPA).

AFSPA had been implemented in the states of Northeast India in 1958, (after being declared disturbed areas) due to the uprising of militias asking for freedom; in Kashmir it took its course during the militancy in 1990. Some Kashmiris have been asking for freedom from the day they received statehood in vOctober 1947.

If we leave all of this and Kashmir's ever-turbulent geo-politic status aside, the flip side of Kashmir is its beauty. My first visit to the Valley had been in mid-eighties as a young school boy on vacation with parents and family. The initial experience was not great. Travel sickness and hours of bus ride from

Jammu had taken a toll on me. I had at one point blacked out from acute dizziness but fortunately my uncle who was a doctor was there to look after me.

Even while suffering a severe headache, when the battered bus had pulled at the huge queue of the one-way traffic entering the Jawahar Tunnel (Banihal Pass), everything around looked like heaven. A stone-faced army man with his rifle and bayonet was guarding the entrance to Kashmir. He must have watched me regain consciousness, for he smiled and even offered me a toffee.

It was an experience I shall never forget: climbing up to the Shankaracharya Temple; rowing in a shikara in the Dal Lake; shopping at Lal Chowk; dad suffering chilblains at Pahalgam; my aunt and sister getting themselves photographed in traditional Kashmiri wear; my first puff from a hookah—all permanently etched in my memory. I even remember going around in a maroon ambassador from a hotel beside the Broadway cinema hall in the Badami Bagh Cantonment area.

My recollections of a picturesque Kashmir looked frayed against what I was witnessing after nearly two decades. The Broadway cinema hall did not exist but the alcohol shop opposite it still sold Scotch. I stood motionless amidst the vibrant physical beauty around me, at the Srinagar city. Even though as exotic as ever, militancy had engulfed the Valley and insurgency had left its stamp. Still nothing would let me erase the images of Henri Cartier Bresson's women praying on the hills of Srinagar or Raghuveer Singh's colour plates. I willed myself to see Kashmir through that lens, but the environment refused to grant me that beautiful canvas.

On my way to the Hazratbal shrine, I was again reminded of Bresson; but the import of the moment dawned on me as I crossed the barbed wire, and when I was subjected to frisking and questioning by the security personnel. I recalled Salman Rushdie's *The Prophet's Hair*.

Stories of the Hazratbal siege, during the days of active militancy in October 1993, had saddened us when we read about it in the papers. Hazratbal had turned into a high-security zone overnight, due to its political implications and Kashmir had become a forbidden land to all, for many years after that. But here I was amidst it, to chronicle human life and human pain as they were, through my eyes; I was there as a photo journalist to cover the human stories of this amazingly beautiful place, ravaged by incessant turmoil.

In Homage to Catalonia, the experiential non-fiction book, George Orwell had remarked, with regard to his participation against the Fascists: 'How many operations in this war, on the Government side, were not mucked up, I wonder?' This was applicable to all lands asking for change and freedom. Kashmir was no exception.

Meanwhile, Srinagar had become a fortress within a fort and there were horror stories galore, enough to make you sick. One had to watch out for the dark alleys and the dead bodies. And yet, I never gave up on my quest to look for its beauty. I was a little weary of shooting the dead bodies and the crying people after a while. I remembered when I had been to Chasmashai, as a child—while I drank the spring water and my aunt and sister regaled in their traditional Kashmiri dress and jewellery—my father, with his twin lens Rolleiflex, went on capturing the magic of that place. Who knew, then, that one day I would be back to look for the same, and find a deserted Chasmashai.

It seemed like straddling two worlds at the same time—that of my childhood memories and the stark reality of the moment. Susie Linfield observed in her book *The Cruel Radiance: Photography and Political Violence* that photographs of violence and suffering were not necessarily bloody photographs or war photographs. My profession demanded making a commentary on the contemporary times through my lens. The best I could do was to keep them artful, even while being true to the horror of the moment.

I restricted myself to clicking in black and white even as the world around me kept screaming in colours. This helped me retain my focus and a grip on the reality. I felt unfortunate, though that I could not capture the 'paradise' as Emperor Shah Jahan had experienced it, or for that matter even as Bresson and Singh, when they travelled up north.

One remembers Christopher Hitchens and his writings on protests, aimed at Kashmir. 'It is impossible to satisfy a "Rage Boy" and his ilk. It's stupid to try', he had said. While that may be true, can we really ignore the reasons behind that rage in Kashmir? The notion of 'peace' brings about curious sensations in young Kashmiris who have grown up only amidst disturbance, tension and riot all their life. Dissident Kashmiris can only react with great anguish to the failing negotiations between India and Pakistan regarding their status. They reflect the emotions expressed in Albert Camus' thought provoking treatise *The Rebel: An Essay on Man in Revolt*.

Protest after protest, and I was more than exhausted seeing the sadness beneath. Unfortunately, it was impossible for the camera to reach those darker recesses and the lens could not capture very much beyond the protests. But if I critique my own body of work on Kashmir today—that was created in order to chronicle the turbulence of Kashmir—my visits over a decade, with trove of photographs, were nothing but a first draft of history.

Natural beauty like that of the lakes, gardens or hills will remain as long as a natural catastrophes do not destroy them. But the times chronicled through my pictures is that of a festering wounded phase in Kashmir that should neither be ignored nor forgotten. They should remind one of the saying: 'I die every day as I have to live for tomorrow.'

PAGE 8: The Jama Masjid or the 'big mosque' is the best and the worst attraction in the Valley. Housed at the volatile area of the Nowahatta, this mosque has a spectacular view. Children studying at the local English medium missionary schools feed pigeons here by day. But as evening settles down the place turns into a war zone where pro-freedom protestors pelt Indian security forces with stones

PAGE 14: A chilly monsoon night in uptown Srinagar during curfew hours

PAGE 20: Timeless trees standing witness to an era gone by

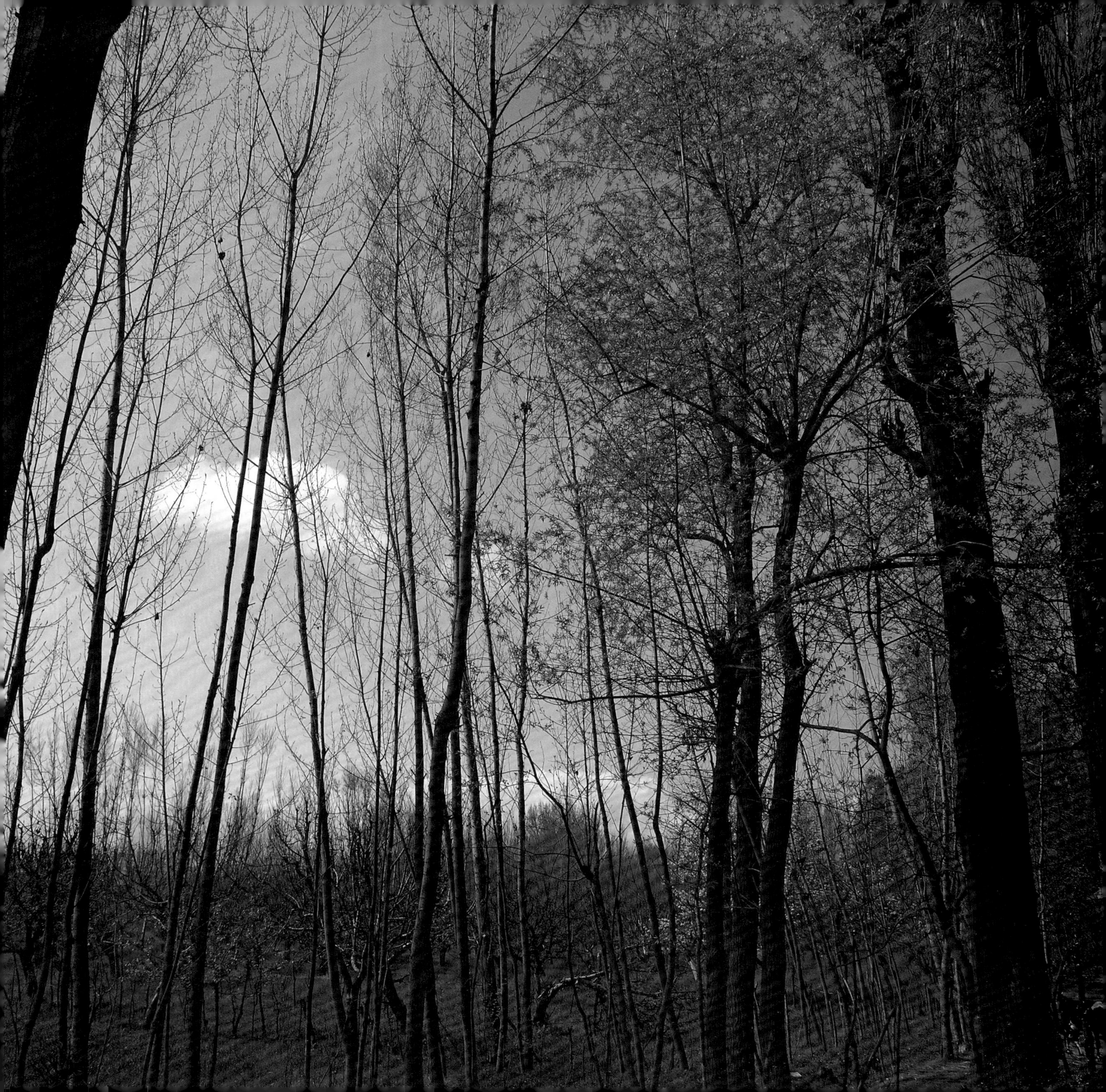

TIMELINE

- **1989:** End of Soviet occupation of Afghanistan releases a great deal of militant energy and weapons in Kashmir. Pakistan provides arms and training to both indigenous and foreign militants in Kashmir, adding to the smouldering fire of discontent in the Valley.
- **1990:** In January, Jagmohan is appointed the Governor. Farooq Abdullah resigns. On 20 January, an estimated 100 people are killed when a large group of unarmed protesters are fired upon by the Indian troops at the Gawakadal bridge. This incident spurs an insurgency in the Valley with thousands pouring into the road and several getting killed in police firing. On 13 February, Lassa Kaul, director of Srinagar Doordarshan, is killed by the militants as AIR symbolised 'voice of the government'. Though the JKLF tries to explain that the killings of Pandits were not communal, the murders cause a scare among the minority Hindu community. The rise of new militant groups, some warnings in anonymous posters and some unexplained killings of innocent members of the community contribute to an atmosphere of insecurity for the Kashmiri Pandits. Most of the estimated 162,500 Hindus in the Valley, including the entire Kashmiri Pandit community, flee the Valley in March.
- **1990 and after:** An official estimate of 10,000 desperate Kashmiri youth cross over to Pakistan for training and procurement of arms. Indigenous and foreign militant groups besides pro-India renegade militants proliferate through the 1990s. An estimated half a million Indian security forces is deployed in the Kashmir Valley with increasing violence and human right violations from all sides leading to massive civilian casualties.
- **1999:** Kargil War
- **14–16 July 2001:** General Pervez Musharraf and Atal Behari Vajpayee meet for peace talks.
- **October 2001:** Kashmir Assembly in Srinagar attacked (38 people dead).
- **December 2001:** Attack on Indian Parliament in New Delhi.
- **2 May 2003:** India and Pakistan restore diplomatic ties.
- **11 July 2003:** Delhi-Lahore bus service resumed.
- **24 September 2004:** Prime Minister Manmohan Singh and President Musharraf meet in New York during UN General Assembly.
- **July 2006:** Second round of Indo-Pakistani peace talks start.
- **June 2010:** Following the killing of a young Kashmiri Tufail Ahmad Mattoo, protest demonstrations continue in Kashmir for months.
- **June 2011:** Indian forces kill three Pakistani soldiers in firing across the Line of Control in retaliation to Pakistani firing.
- **June 2012:** The Chief Minister of Indian-administered Jammu and Kashmir, Omar Abdullah, says that the security situation there is not yet conducive to the revoking of the Armed Forces Special Powers Act (AFSPA) in the state.
- **June 2012:** Indian President Pranab Mukherjee visits Indian-administered Jammu and Kashmir within two months of taking up office. Despite the threat of protests from separatists, sees insurgency in Jammu and Kashmir. The visit passes off without serious incident.

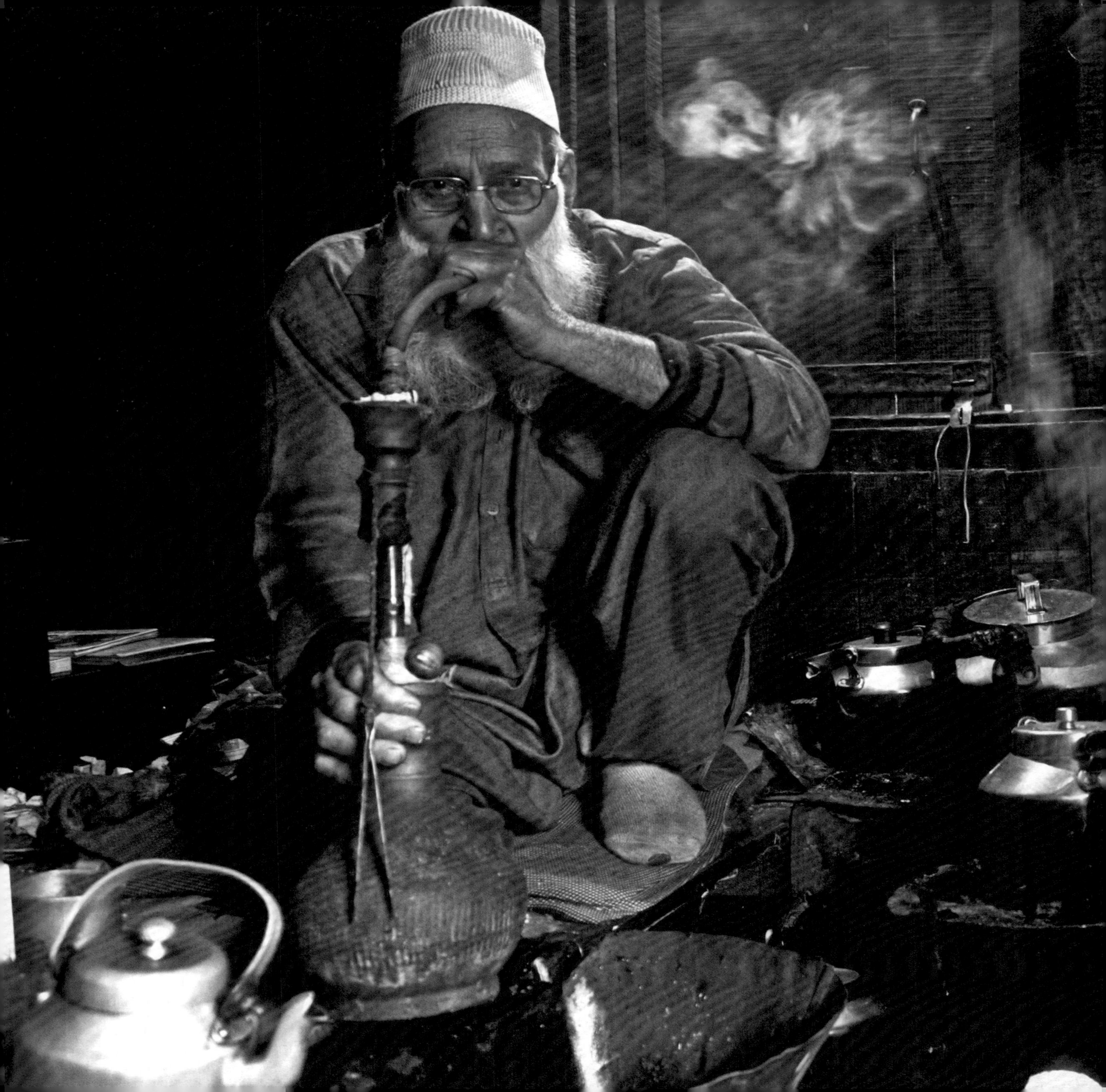

DAILY LIFE

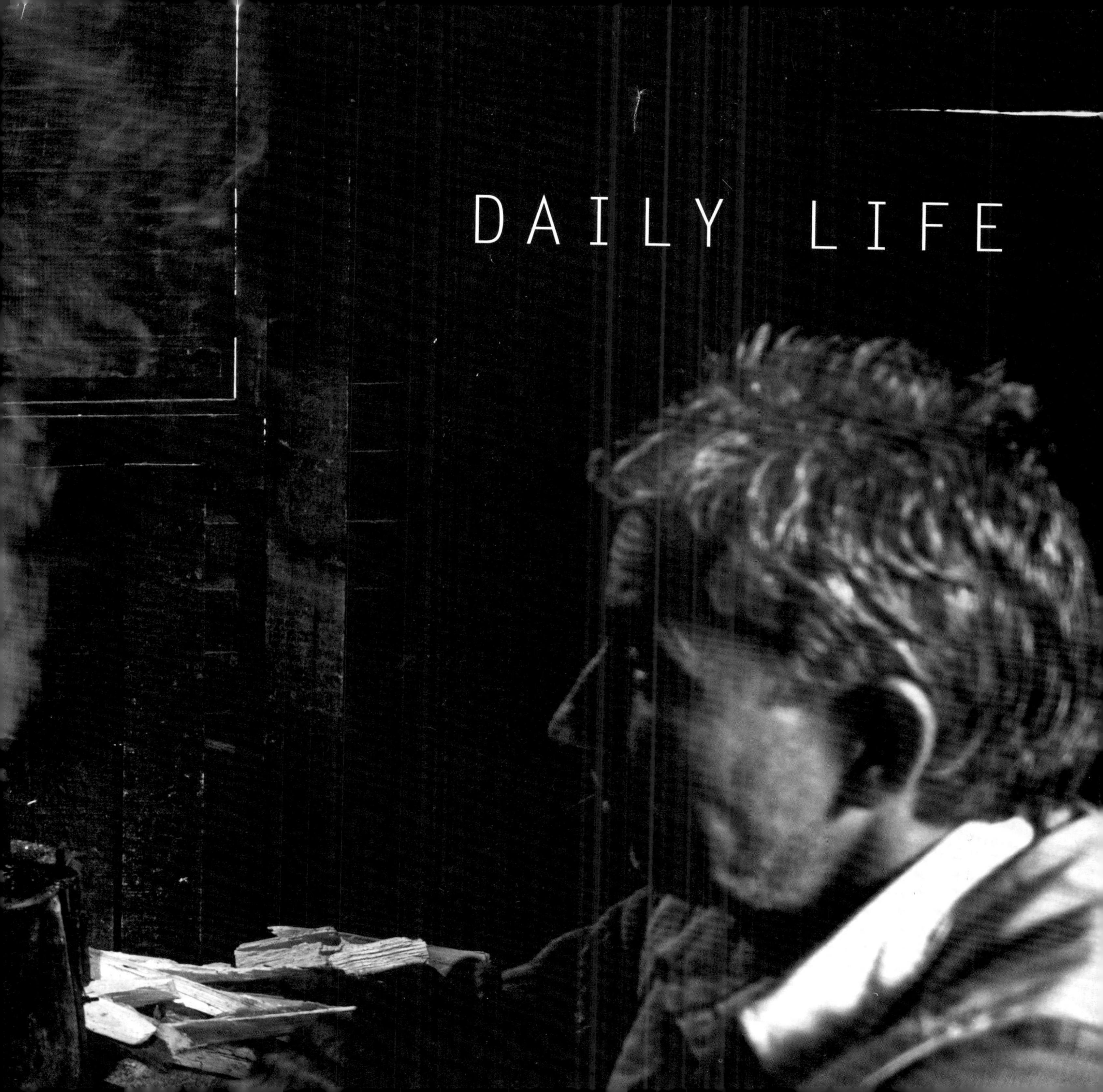

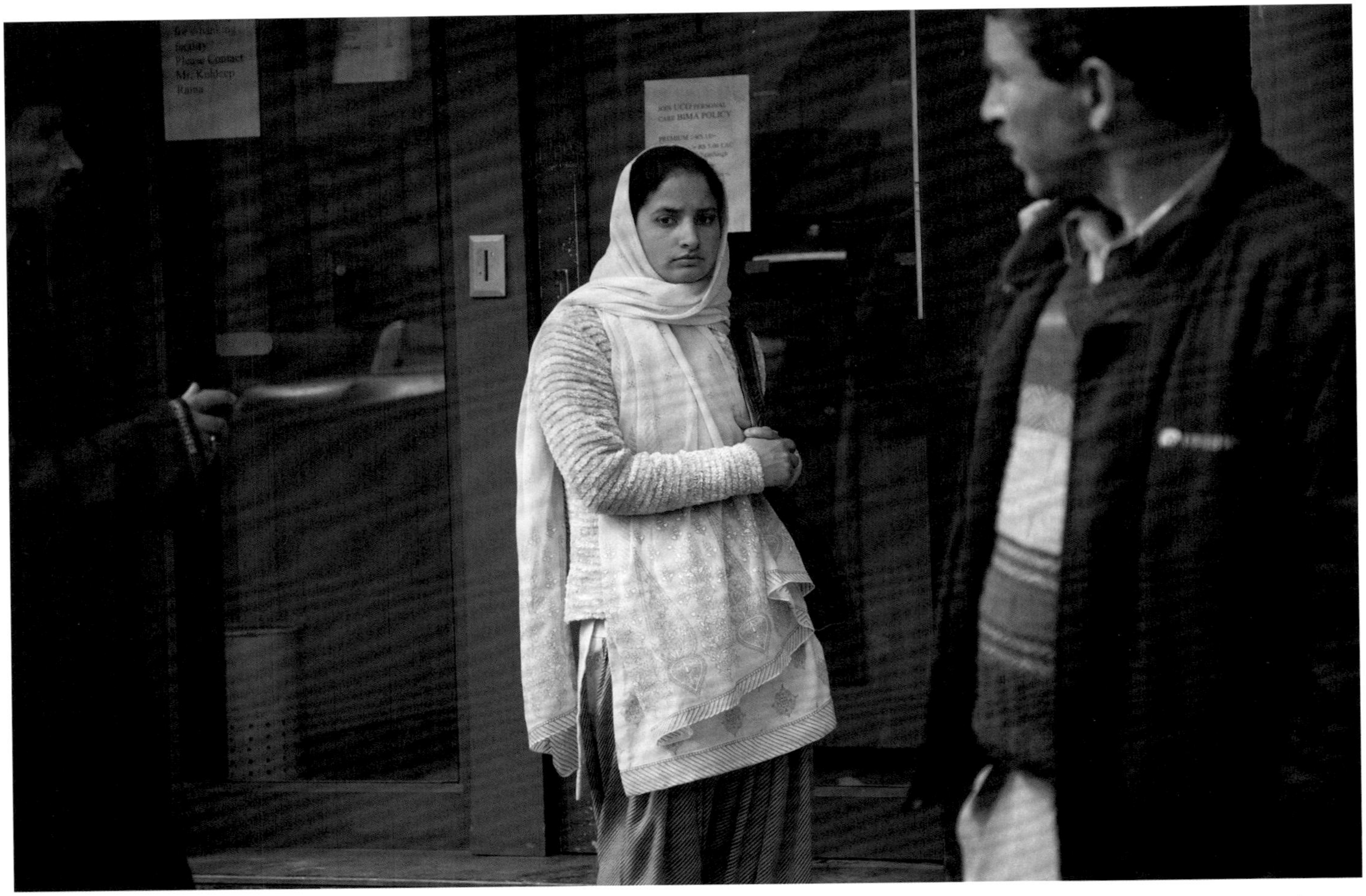

A lady at an ATM of an Indian bank in the Valley. In the days of militancy national banks could not operate in the Valley, creating severe disgruntlement among civilians

PAGE 22-23: Malik's tea stall on the National Highway 1A, between Taral and Srinagar, cannot be missed. Malik lost both his sons during the heydays of militancy. Now in his eighties, he lives with his ailing wife serving tea and butter buns to locals and tourists

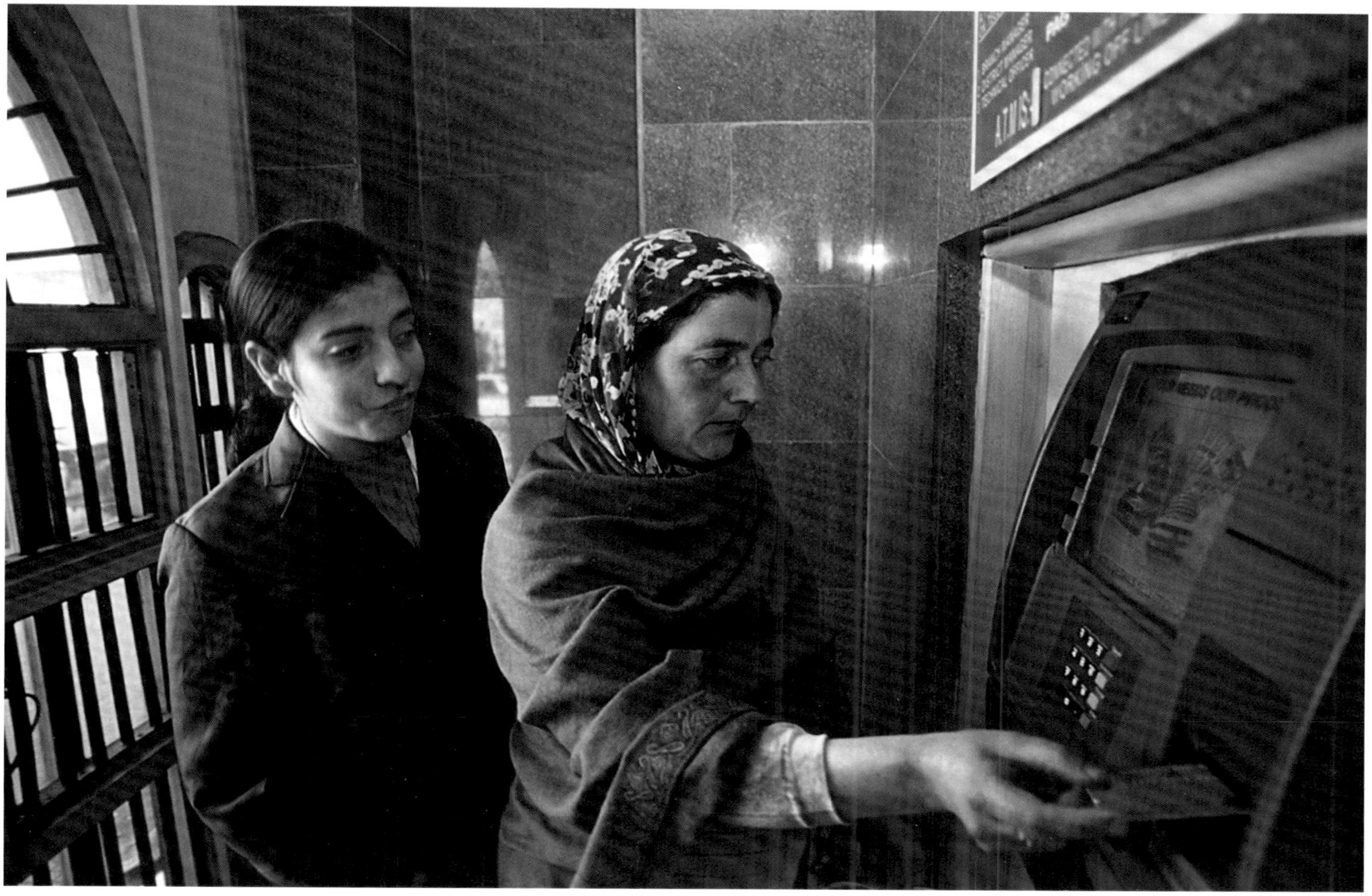

Today, ATM machines operated by Indian banks are in abundance. For those apprehensive of unforeseen strikes and closing of daily life, they are a boon

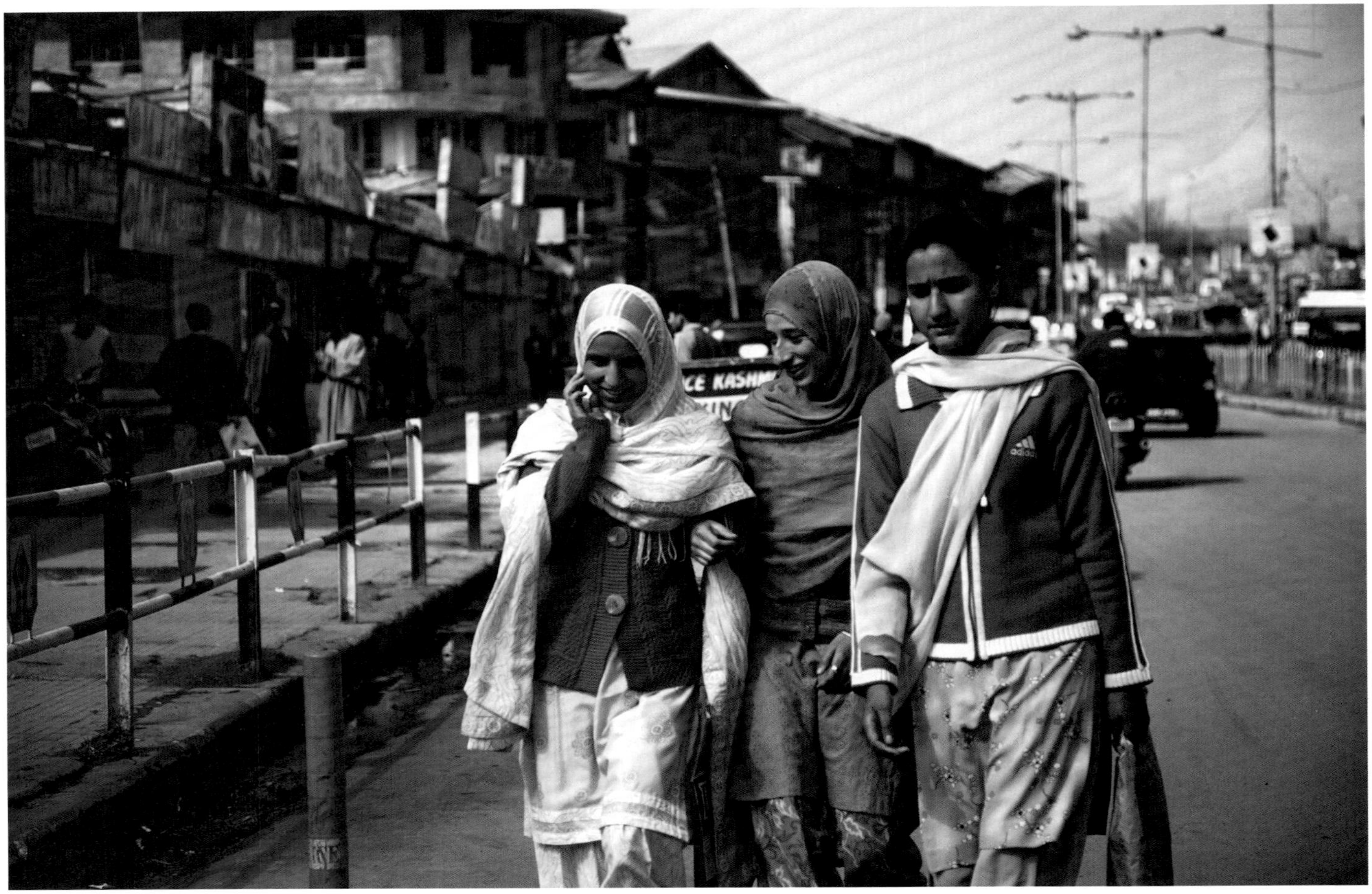

Young women have to wear a headscarf as a mandatory dress code or else the militia threatens them and even attacks them with acid or grenades

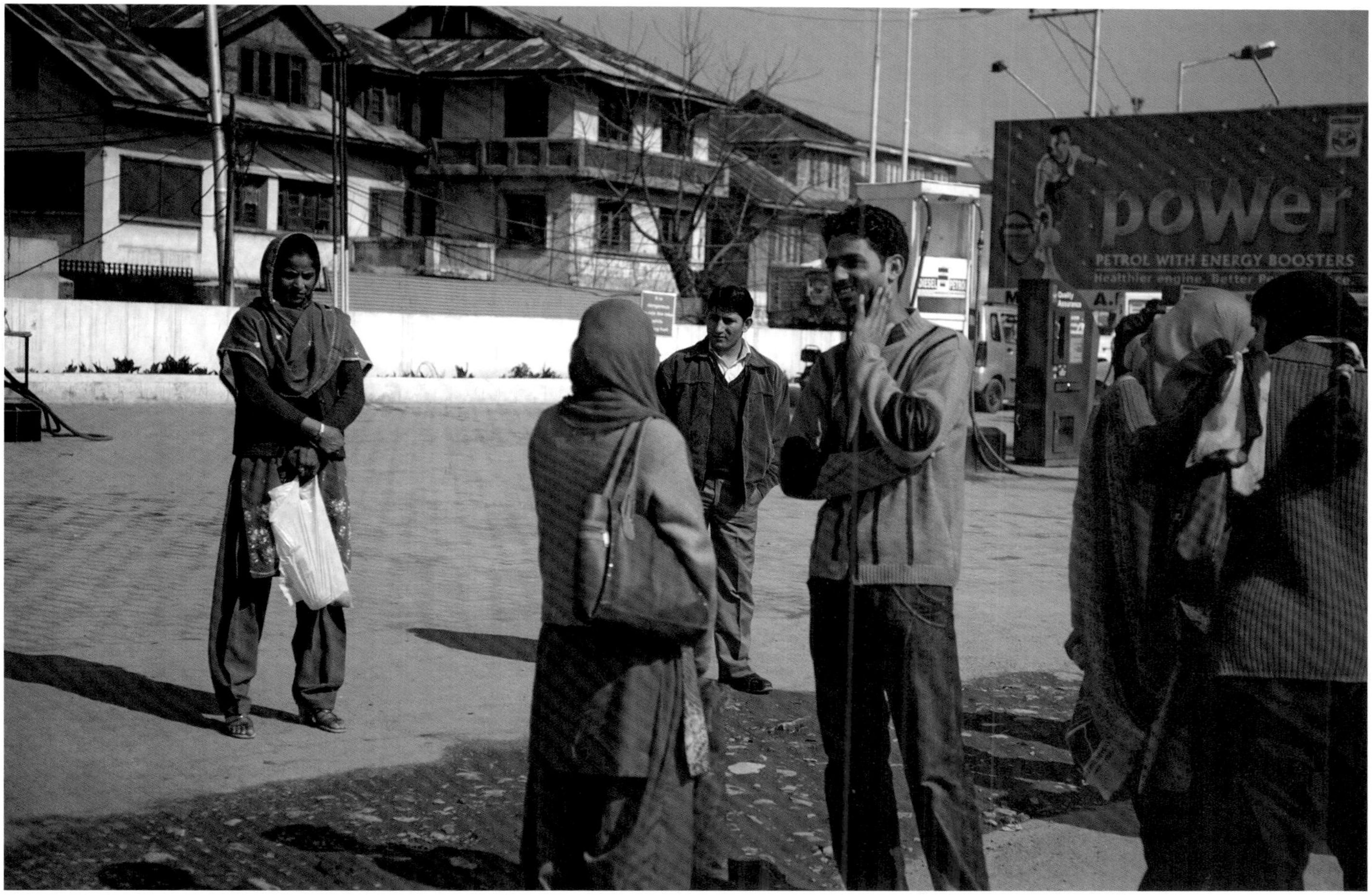

An advertisement of 'power' reminds one of the raw power play in Kashmir

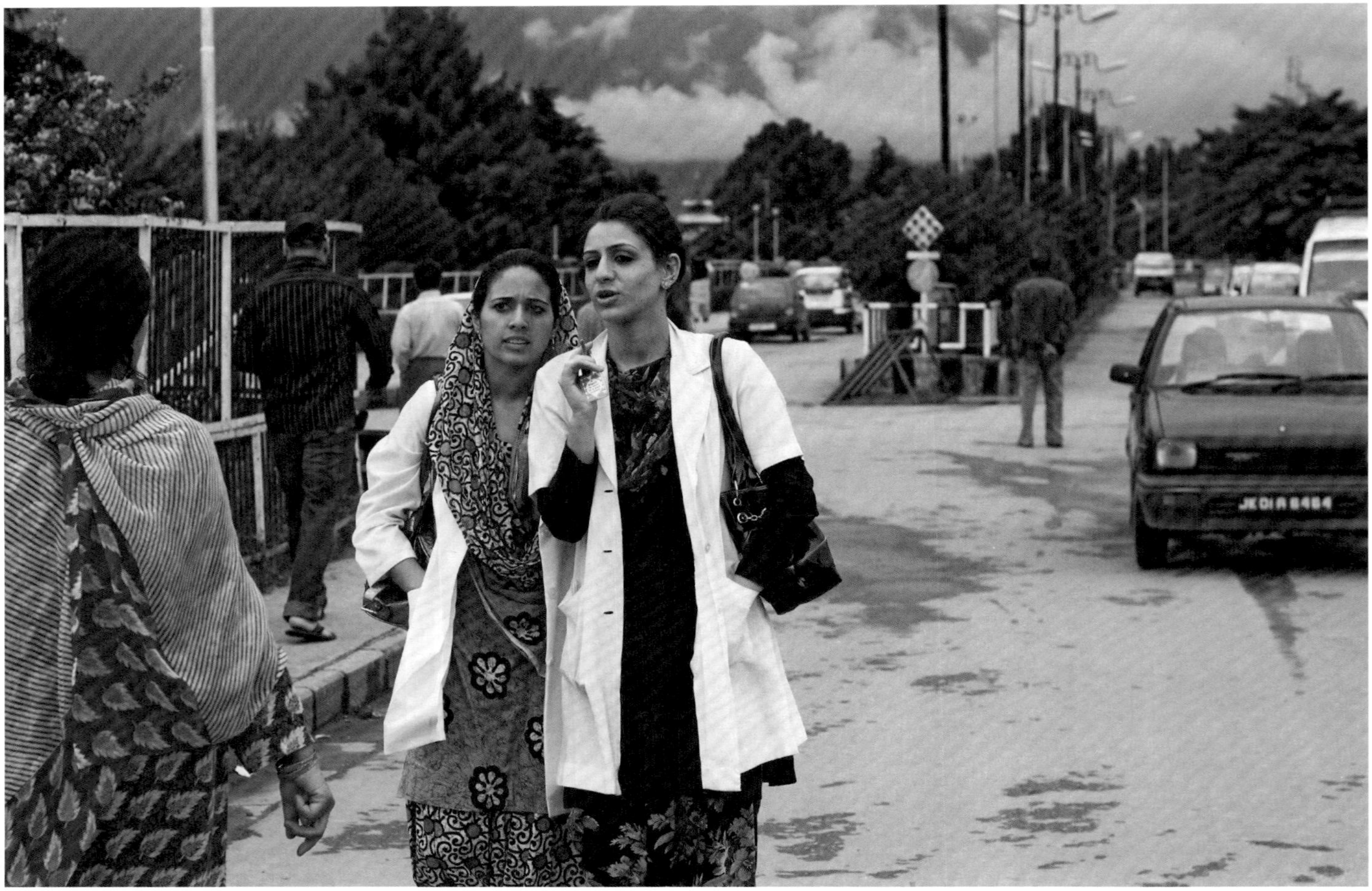

Doctors during changing of shifts at the government hospital in Soura. Doctors have a stressful job doing their rounds at the emergency rooms taking care of bullet wounds and riot victims

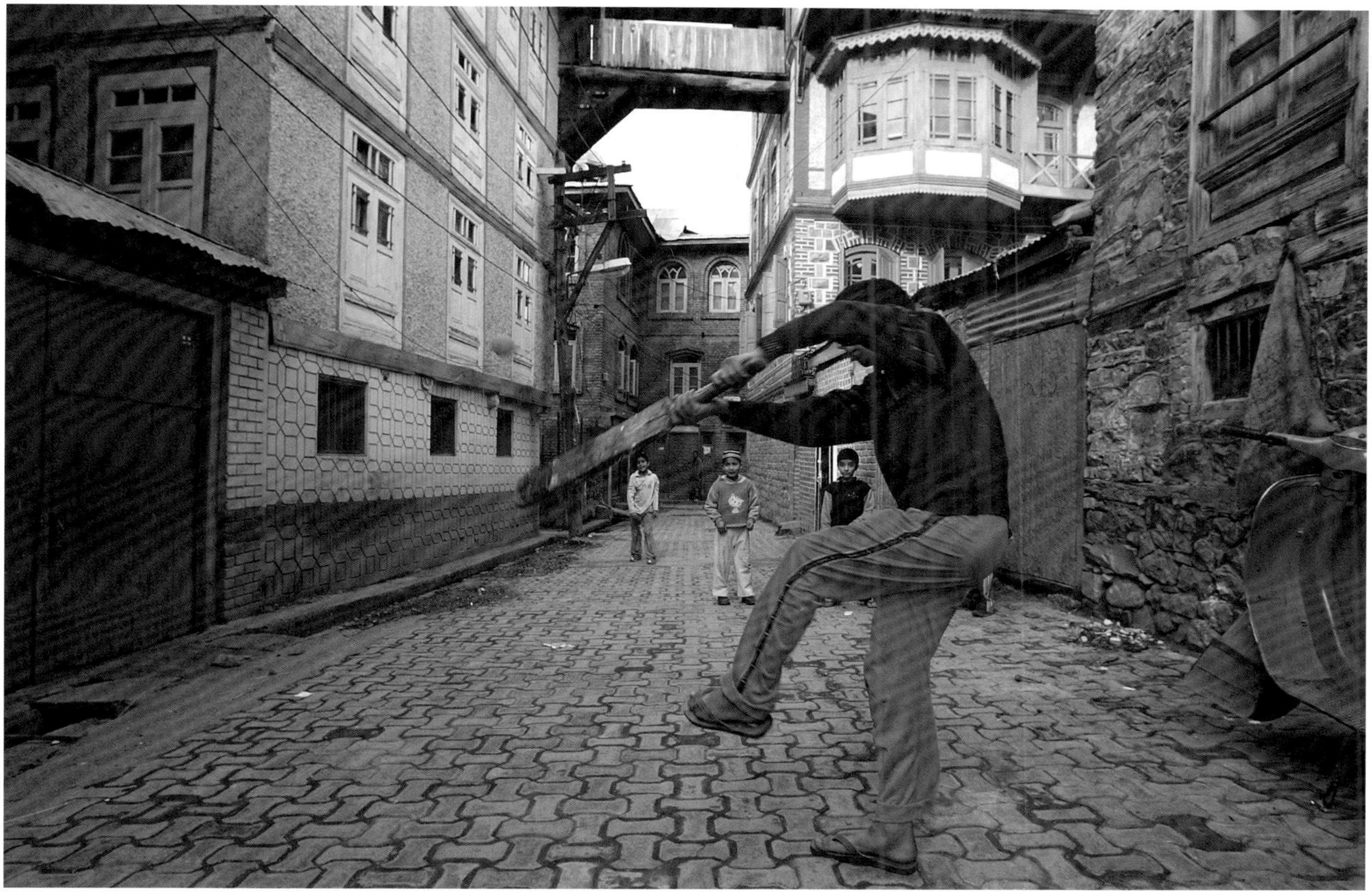

Children playing cricket in the alleys of Habba Kadal. Once a Hindu dominated area it wears a deserted look today with very few Hindus residing here. During India vs Pakistan cricket matches, many may be seen cheering for Pakistan

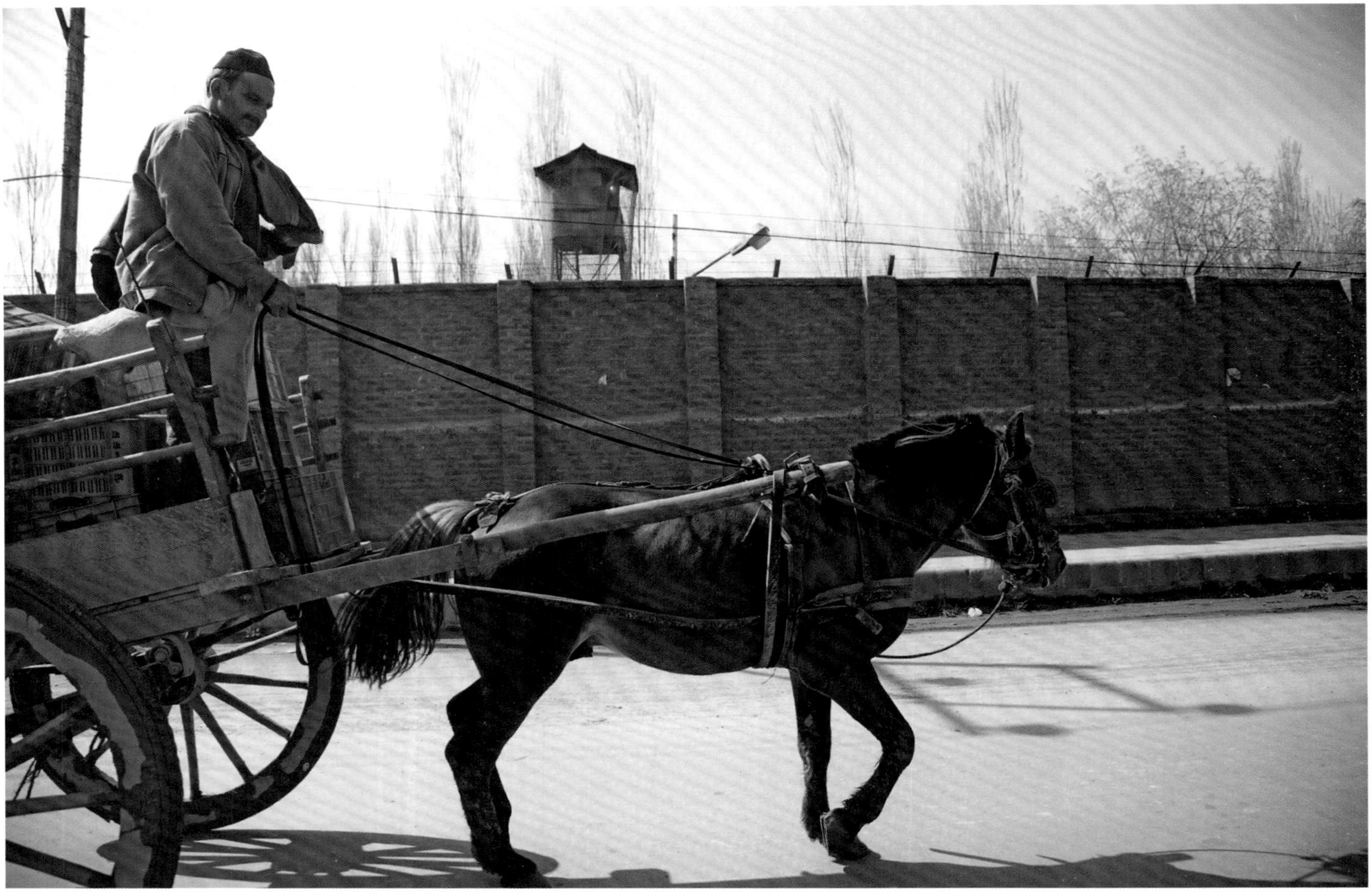

Rashtrya Rifles (RR) was raised to take care of the LOC with Pakistan and control militancy in the Valley. A horse carriage crosses such an army camp in the outskirts of Srinagar

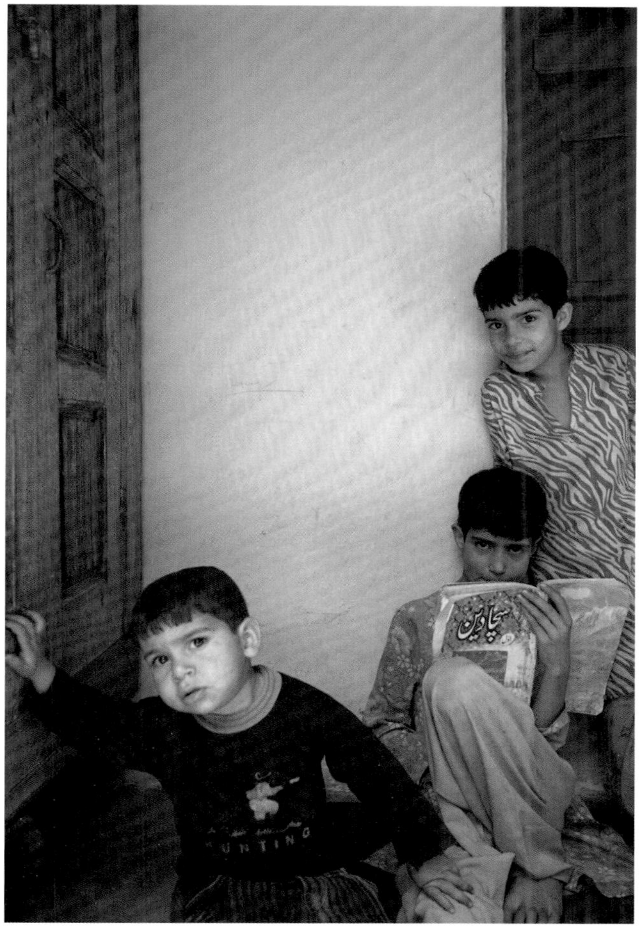

Children studying at their home in Sopore. Once a hub of rising militancy it is still one of the most volatile zones in Kashmir

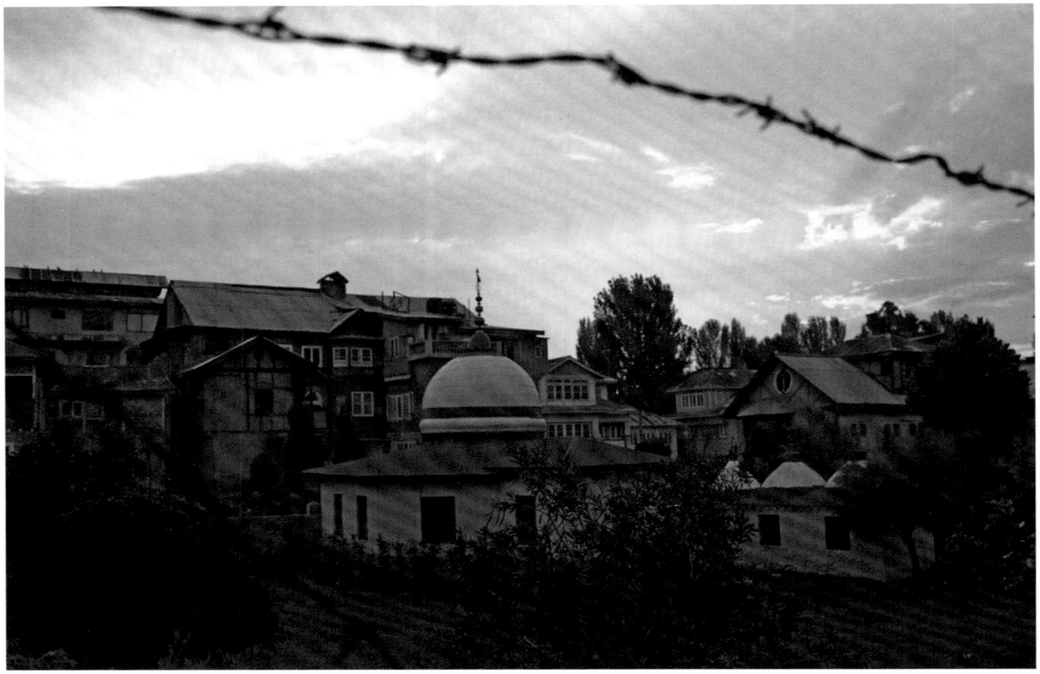

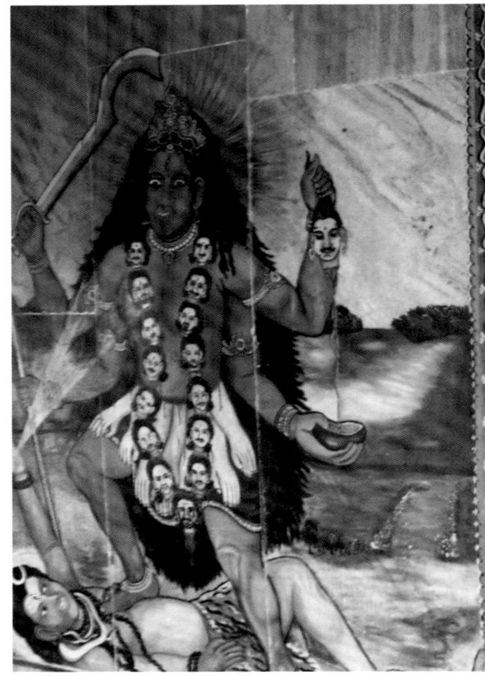

In the heart of Srinagar, at Lal Chowk, is a place called Abi Guzar. A temple showcases the dominance of the Hindus once, but only a few Hindu families reside here today due to heavy threat perception

FACING PAGE: The Shiva temple at the Shankaracharya shrine on the hills of Zabarwan. This Shiva lingam is very ancient and revered by the Hindus around the world. It is a high-security zone as both the government-owned Doordarshan and All India Radio transmission towers are located beside the shrine. The possibility of a militant attack is very high here and so, of late, photography has also been prohibited

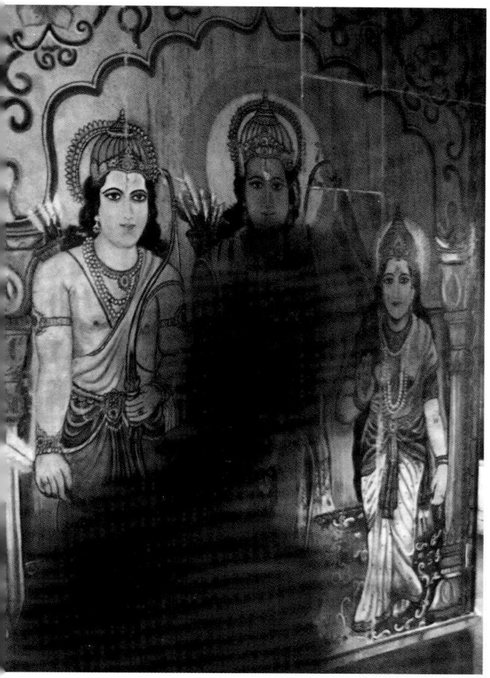

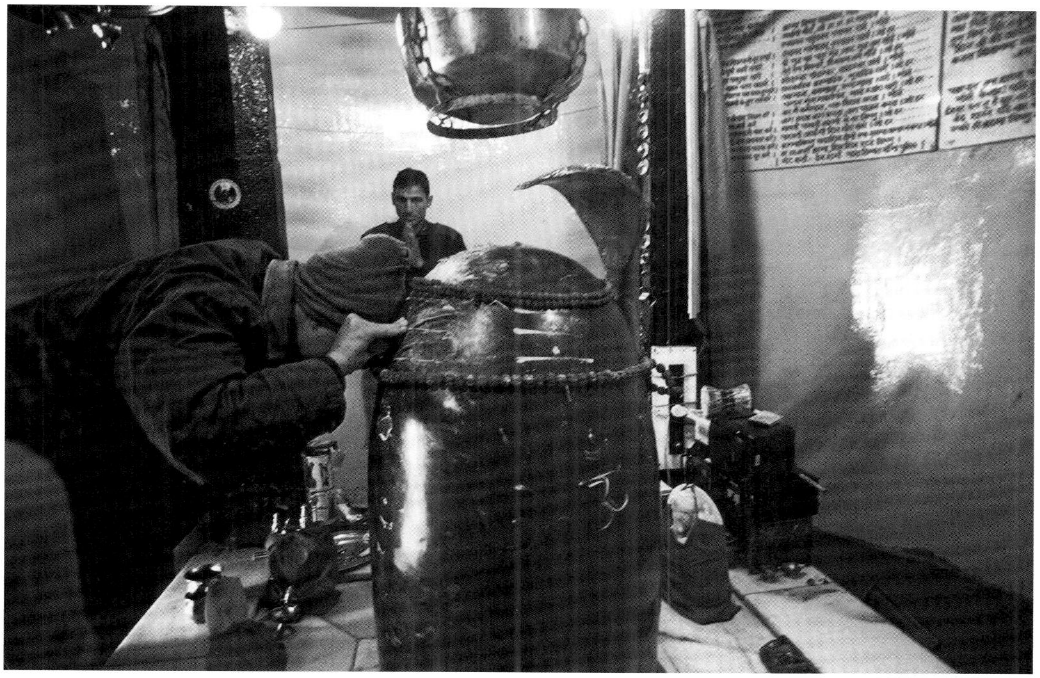

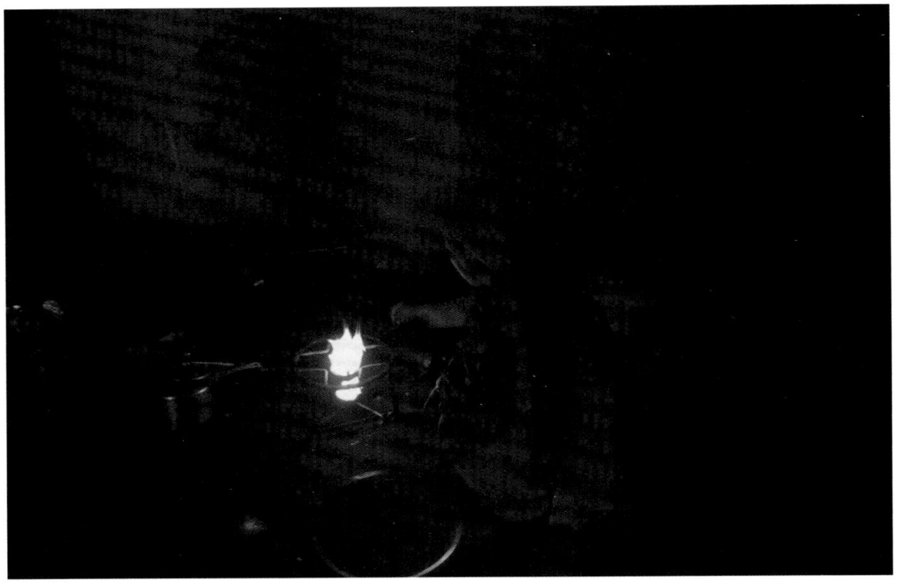

A woman cooking lamb in Drass. She has witnessed the 1999 war with Pakistan and survived the bad days. She still fears sudden uprisings and complains of shelling that go unreported

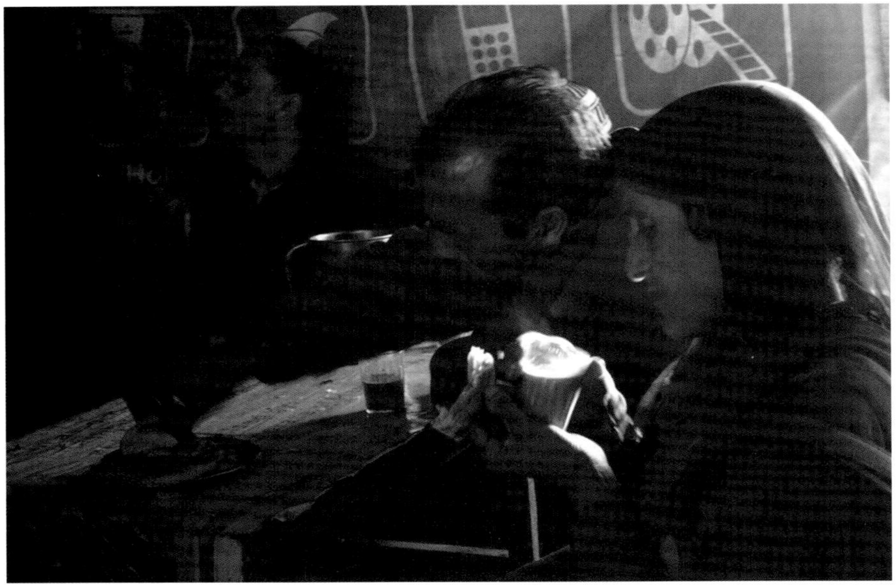

Kashmiri labour couple sipping ginger tea before going to work. It's a new culture

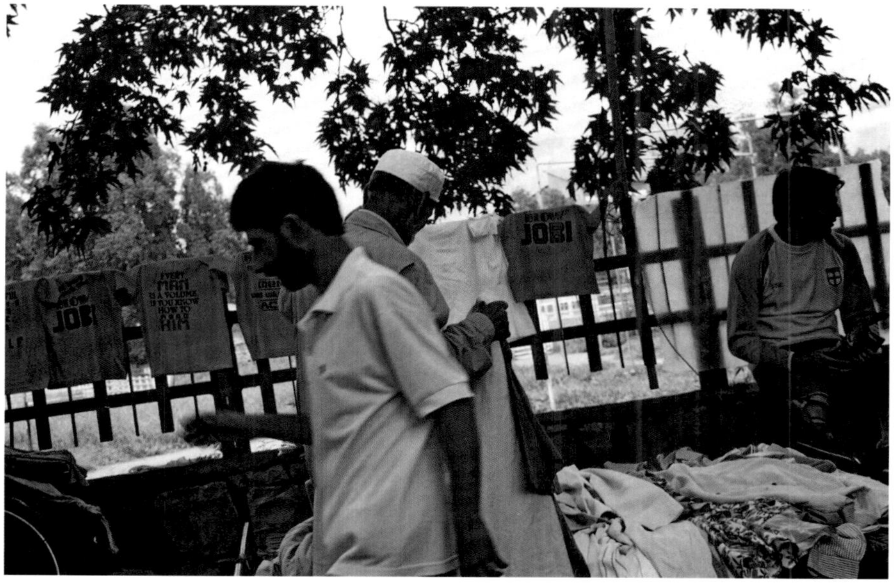

T-shirts sold at a street market

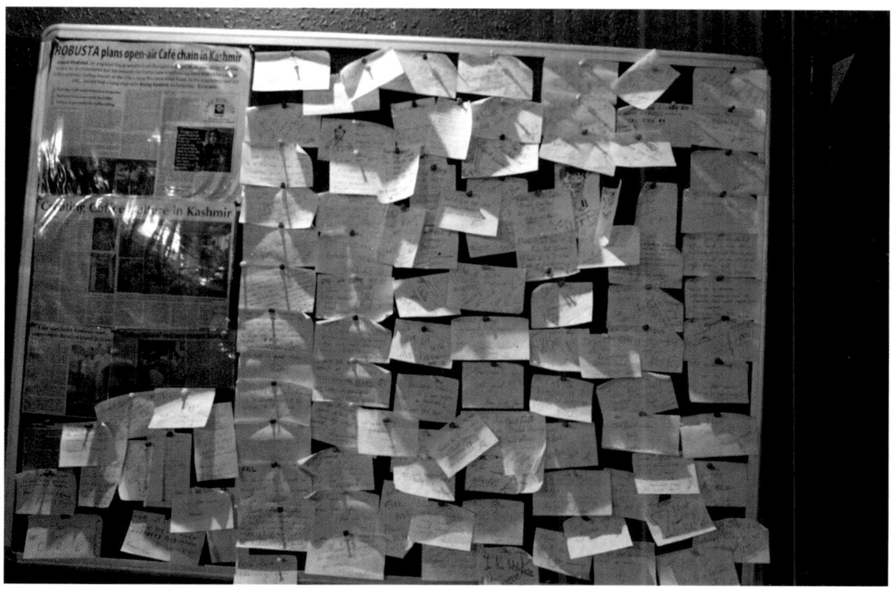

At a coffee shop, in uptown Lal Chowk in Srinagar, one find messages from romance to jihad, posted on its board

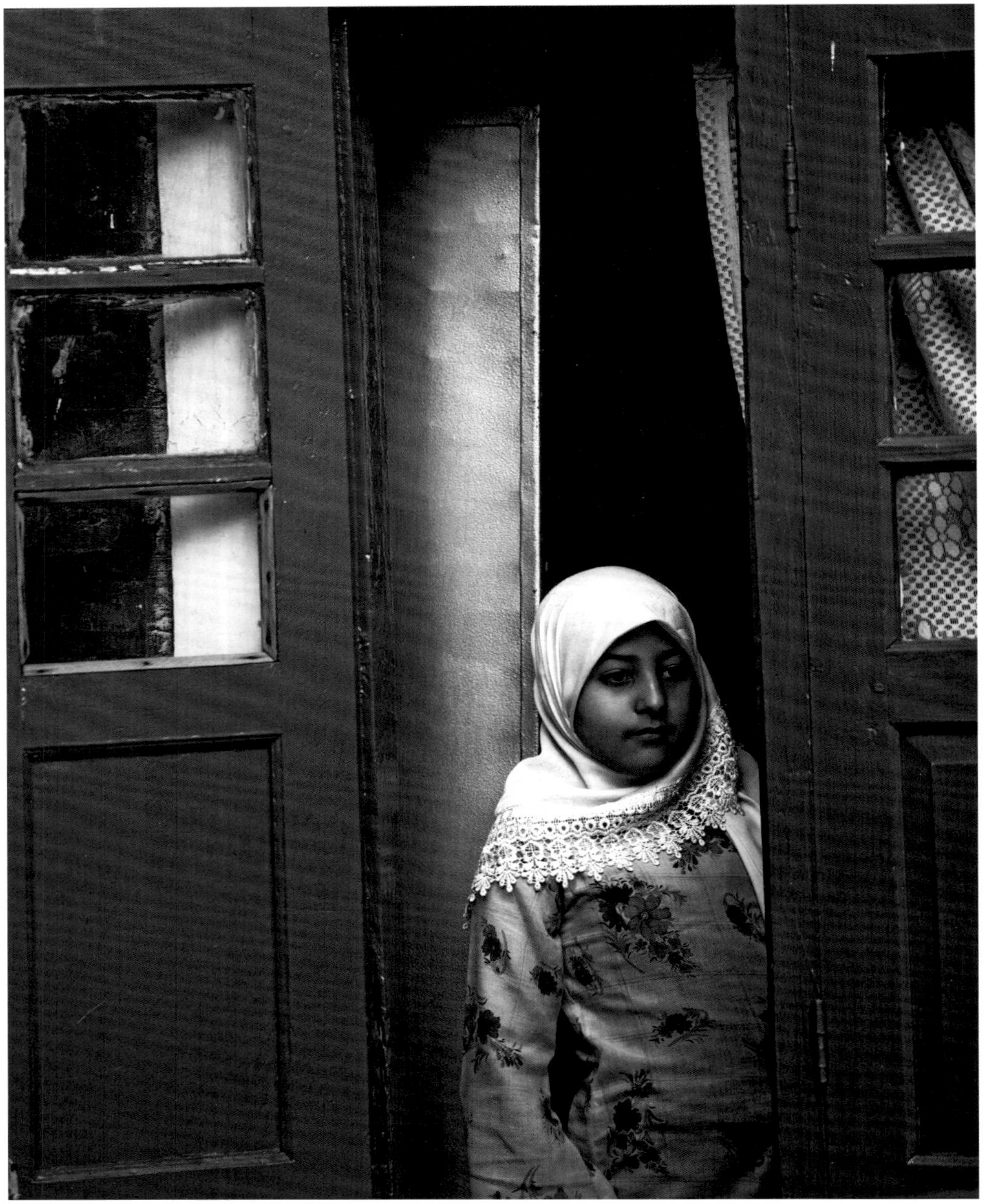

A girl looks out from a window at Maisuma. She was not born when her father disappeared. She still looks forward to his homecoming. There are thousands of Maisumas in the Valley

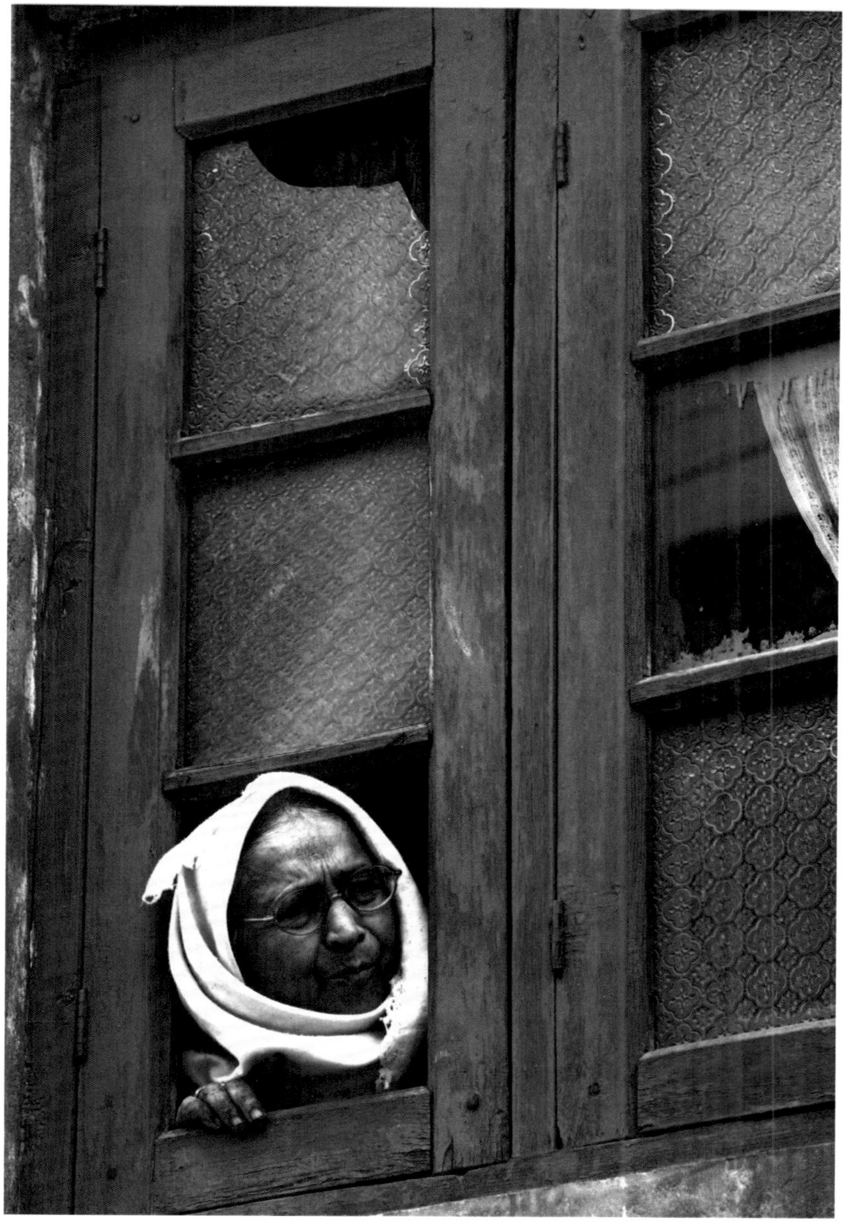

In Nowhatta an old woman looks from her broken window, waiting for her only son who had been missing since morning. A protest had been brewing on the streets below and she worries her son may have been involved and arrested by the police

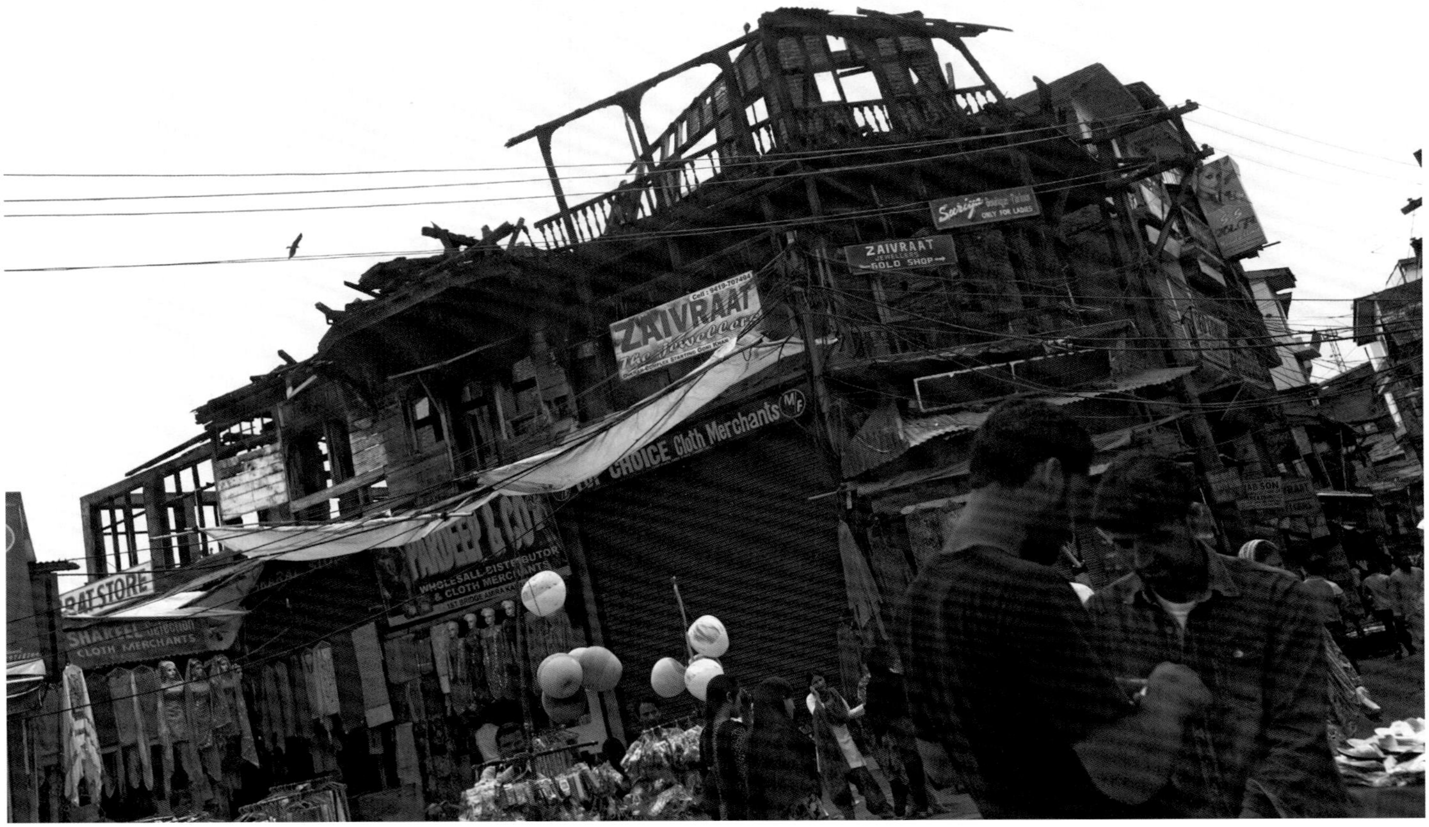

During the nineties, rising militancy and pro-Pakistan actions had seen many houses destroyed and bombed. Some are still visible

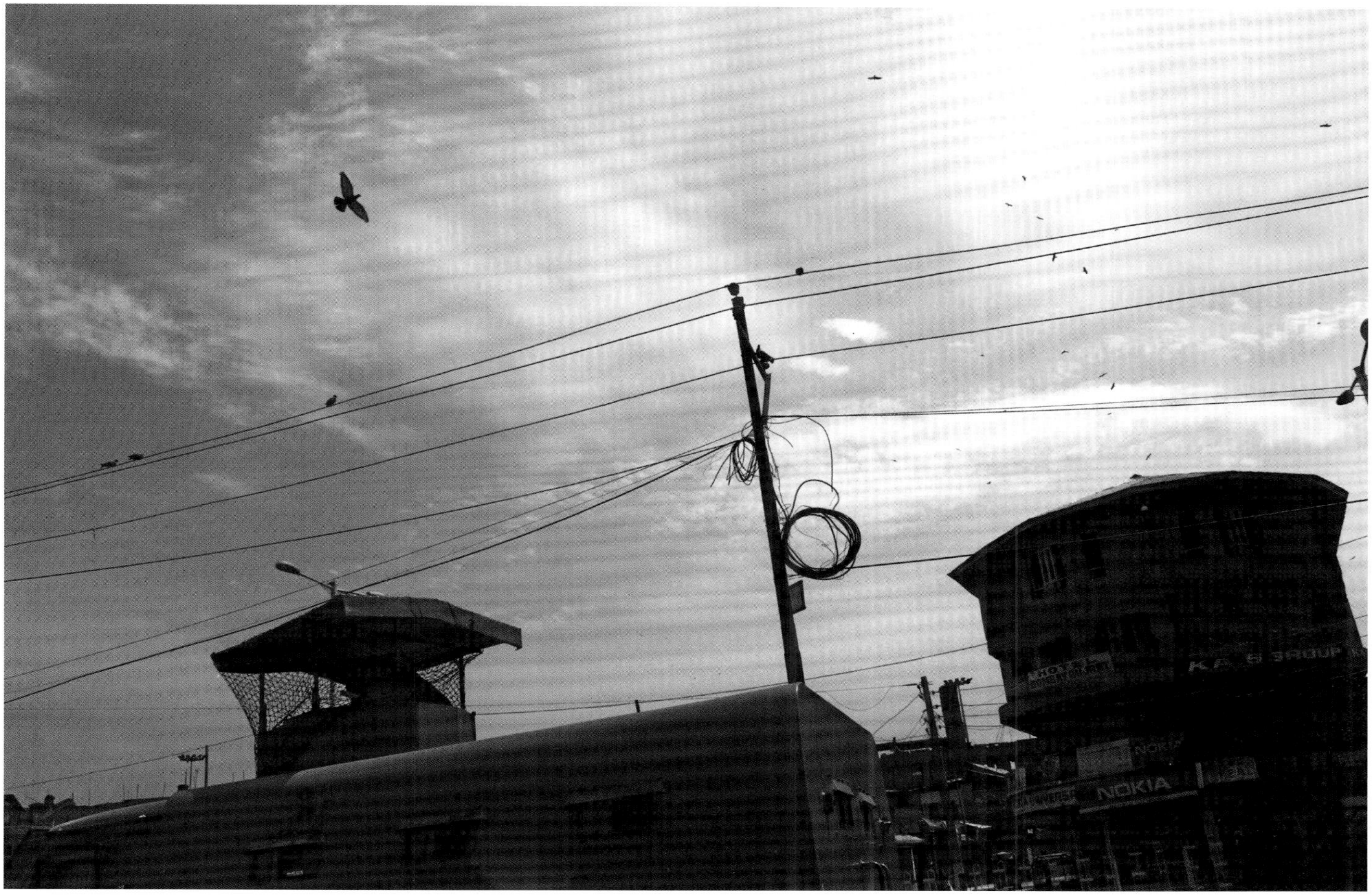

Central Reserve Police Force (CRPF), in riot-control vans, keeps a tight vigil on the alleys in Maisuma and downtown areas. A vulture flying high, looks for a prey

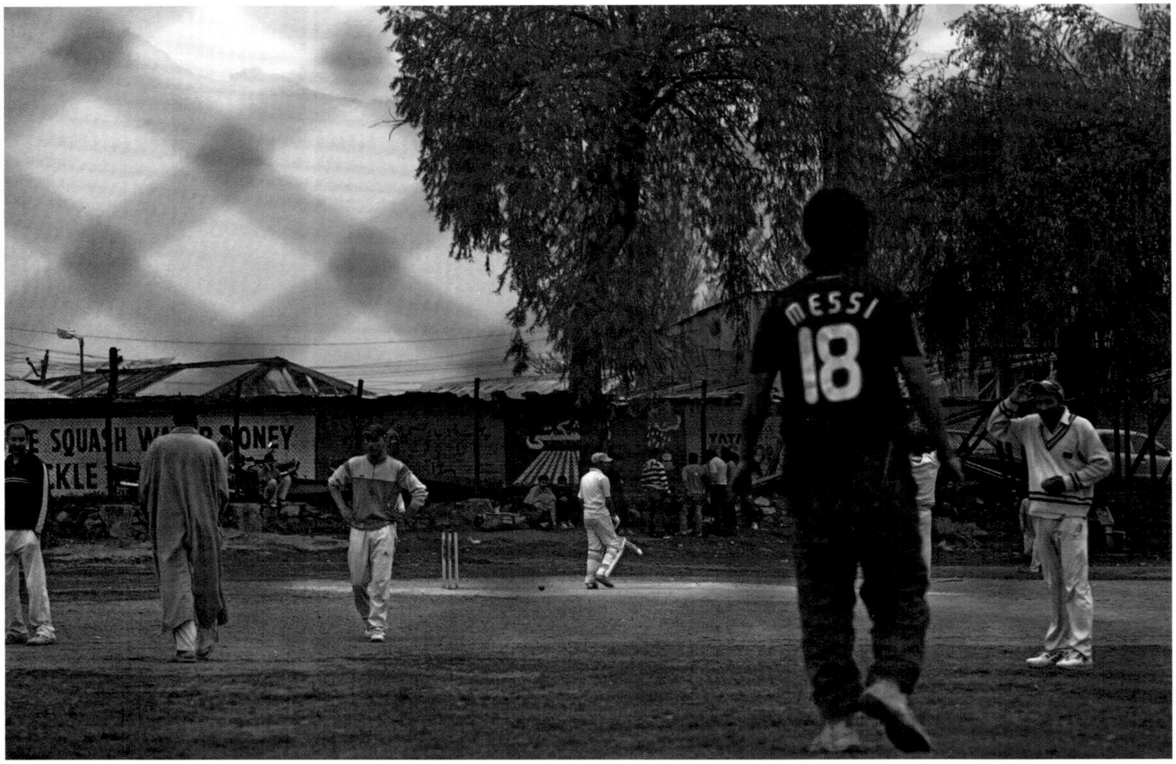

Argentine soccer player, Messi, has been a great inspiration to the newly developed football teams in the Valley. But cricket is still the favourite and is the game that has so far dictated the diplomacy between India and Pakistan

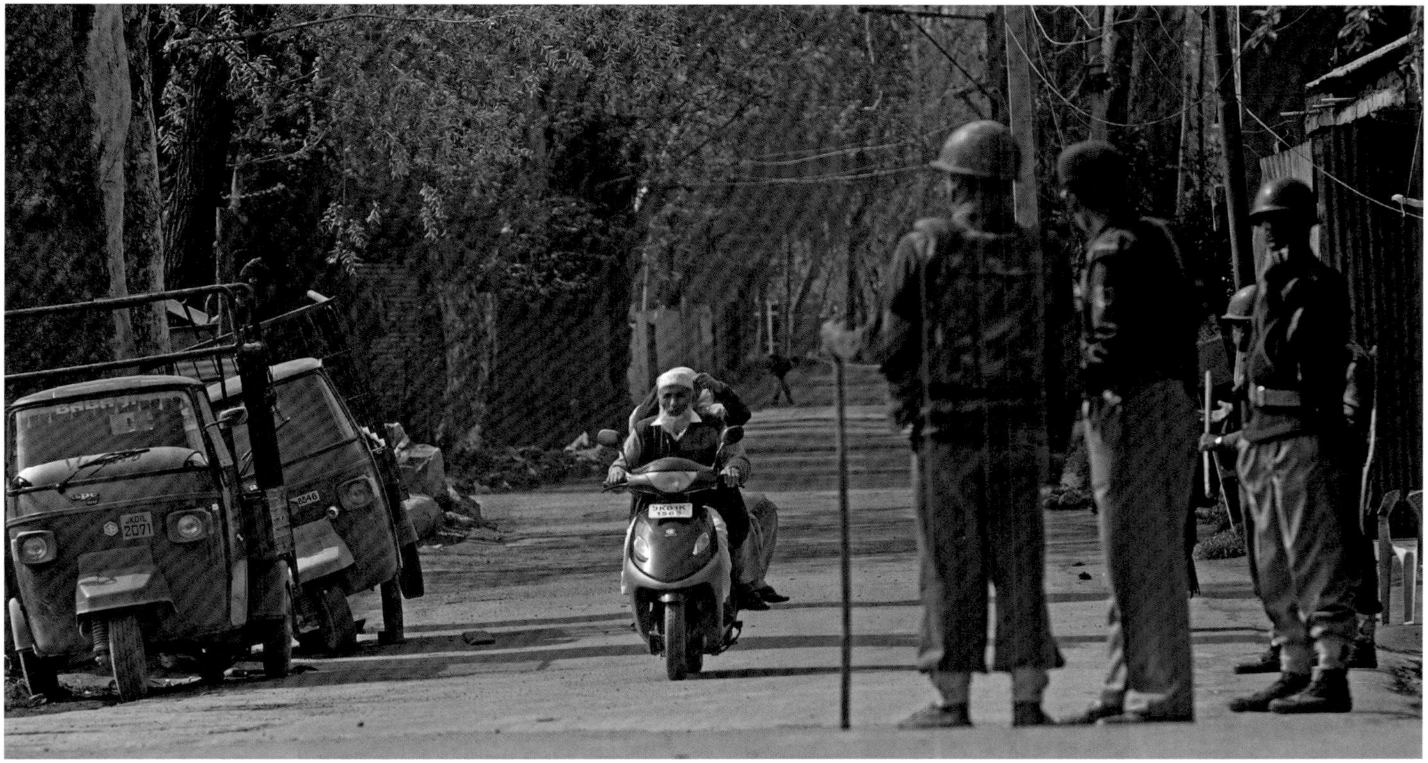

Indian security forces, which includes paramilitary forces, police and army, do not see eye to eye with the citizens due to the ongoing implementation of AFSPA and unabated military presence

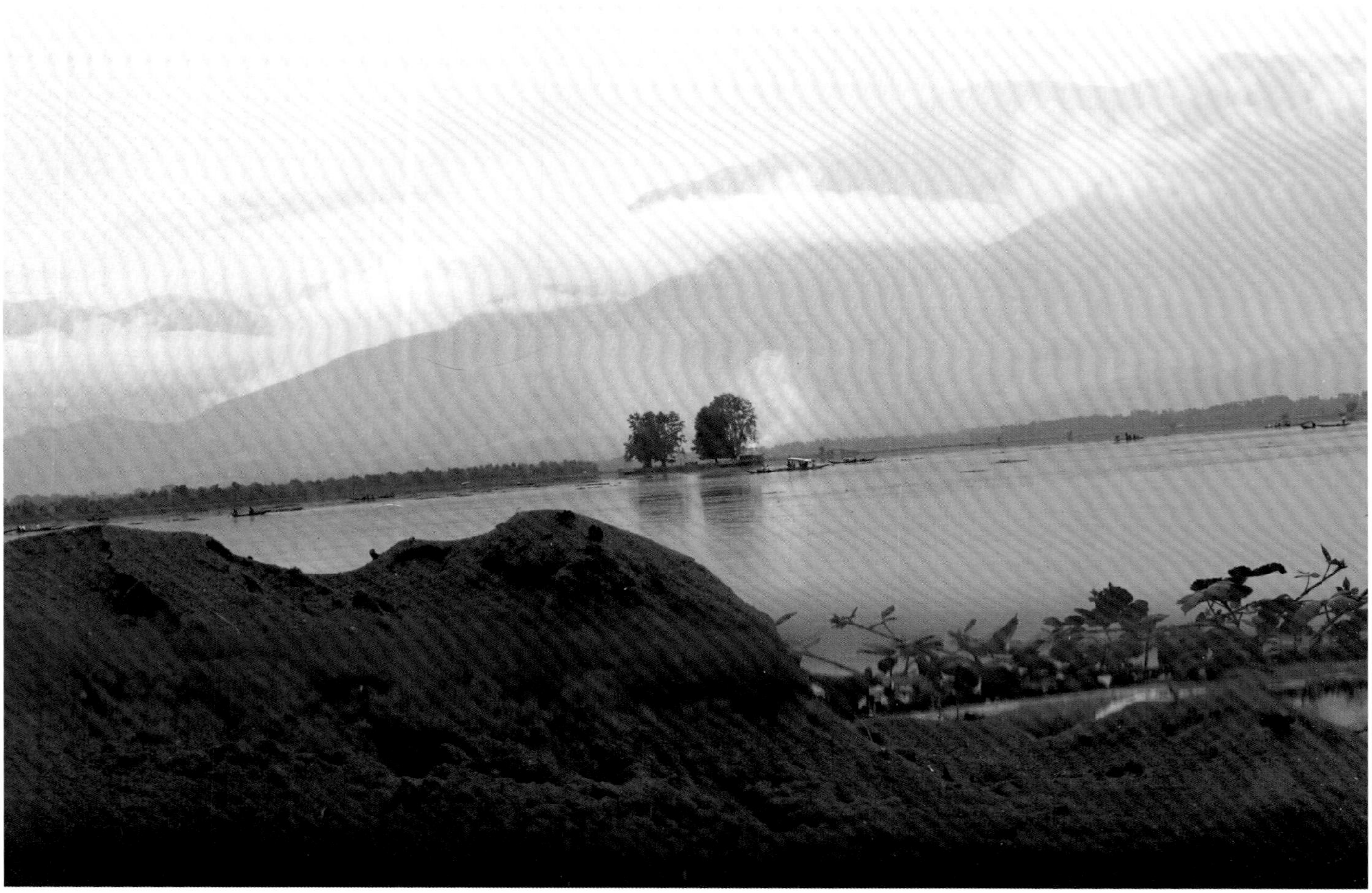

Dredging at the Dal Lake. Tourists who come to Srinagar have been polluting the Dal Lake with beer cans and plastic

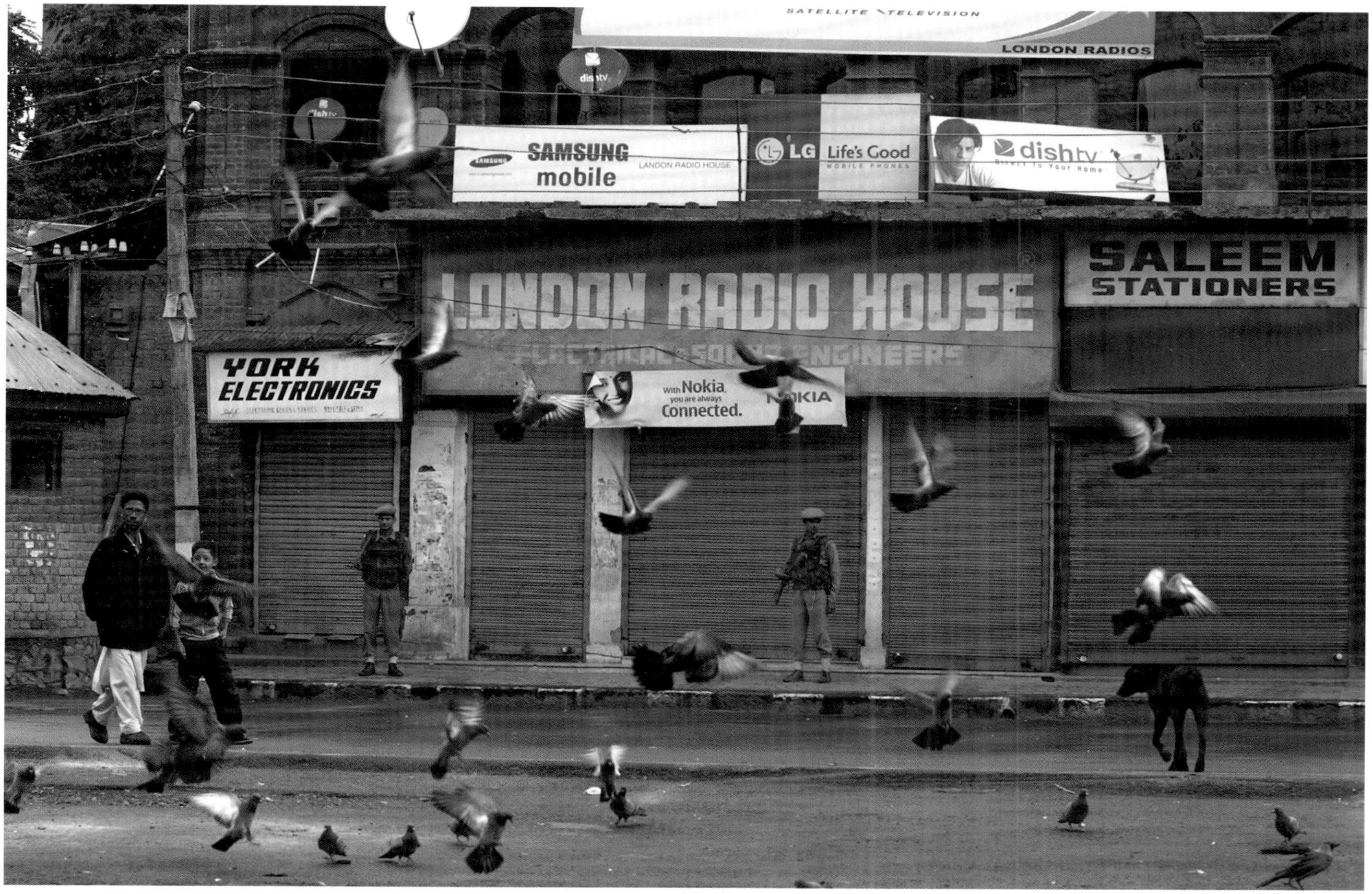

On a day of a strike, called by the hardliners of the Hurryiat party, the city square looks deserted. A boy along with his father negotiates the streets which had been cordoned off by the Indian security forces. The doves are an emblem of peace but the state has gone to the dogs

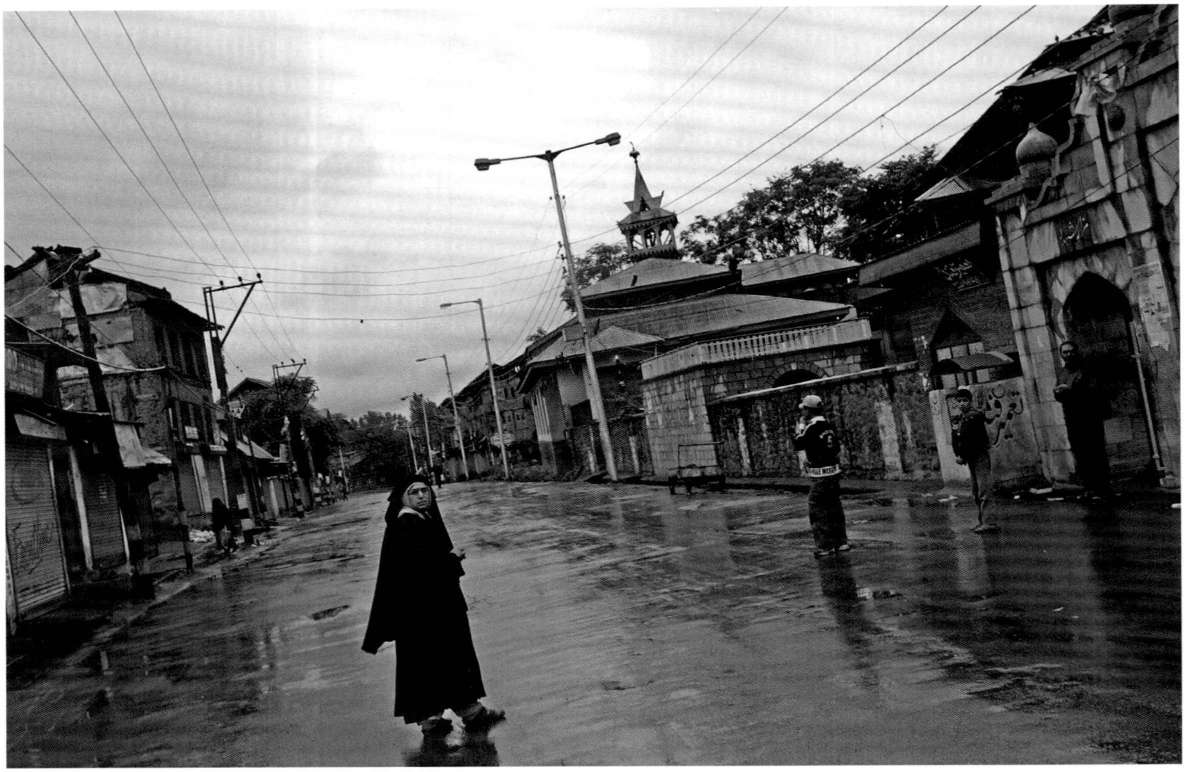

In downtown Srinagar protests have been called due to the killing of an innocent boy. The muezzin calls for a prayer with provocative speeches, enthusing the crowd to call for a riot

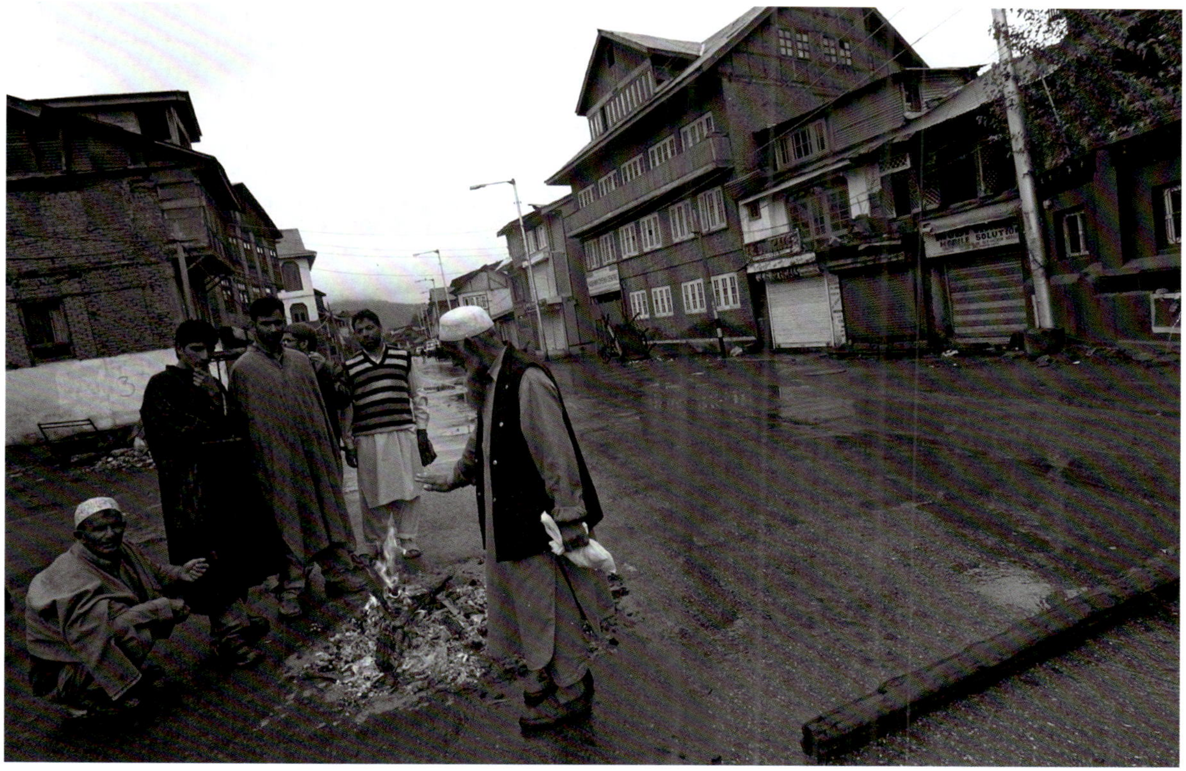

A roadblock to protest the death of an innocent civilian in a crossfire between the Indian security forces and militants. Civilians are a victim for no fault of theirs

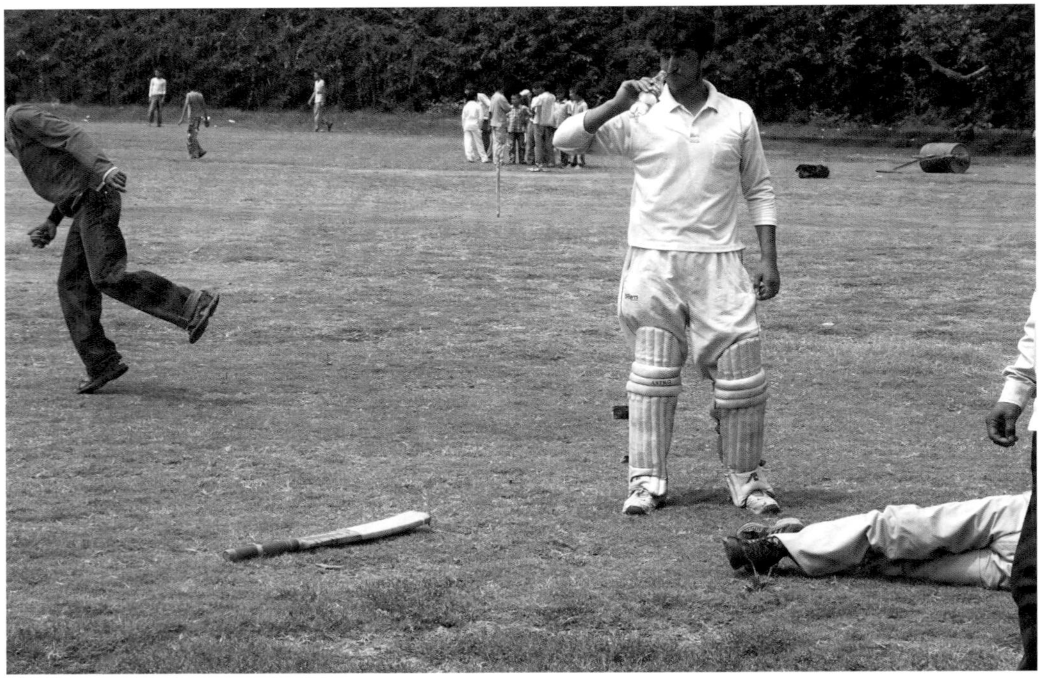

Practising cricket at the stadium. League matches take place and players are even selected for the Ranji Trophy team

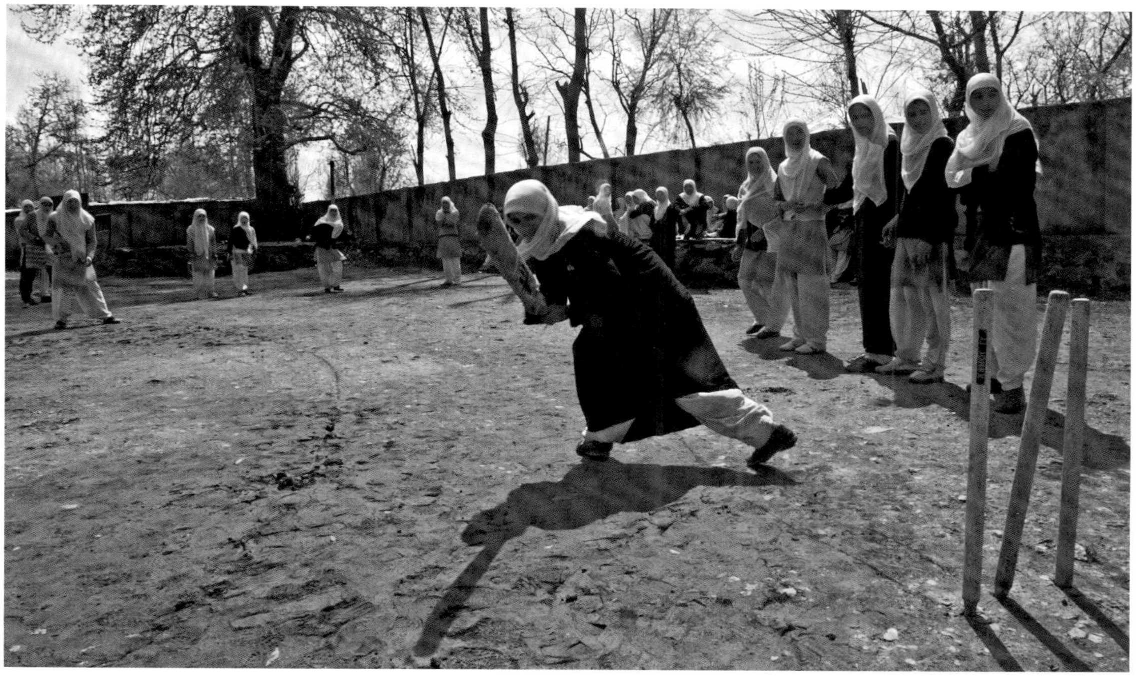

At a school in Sopore, girls wearing headscarves play cricket during recess. The conservative Sunni Muslim society does not allow them to be photographed

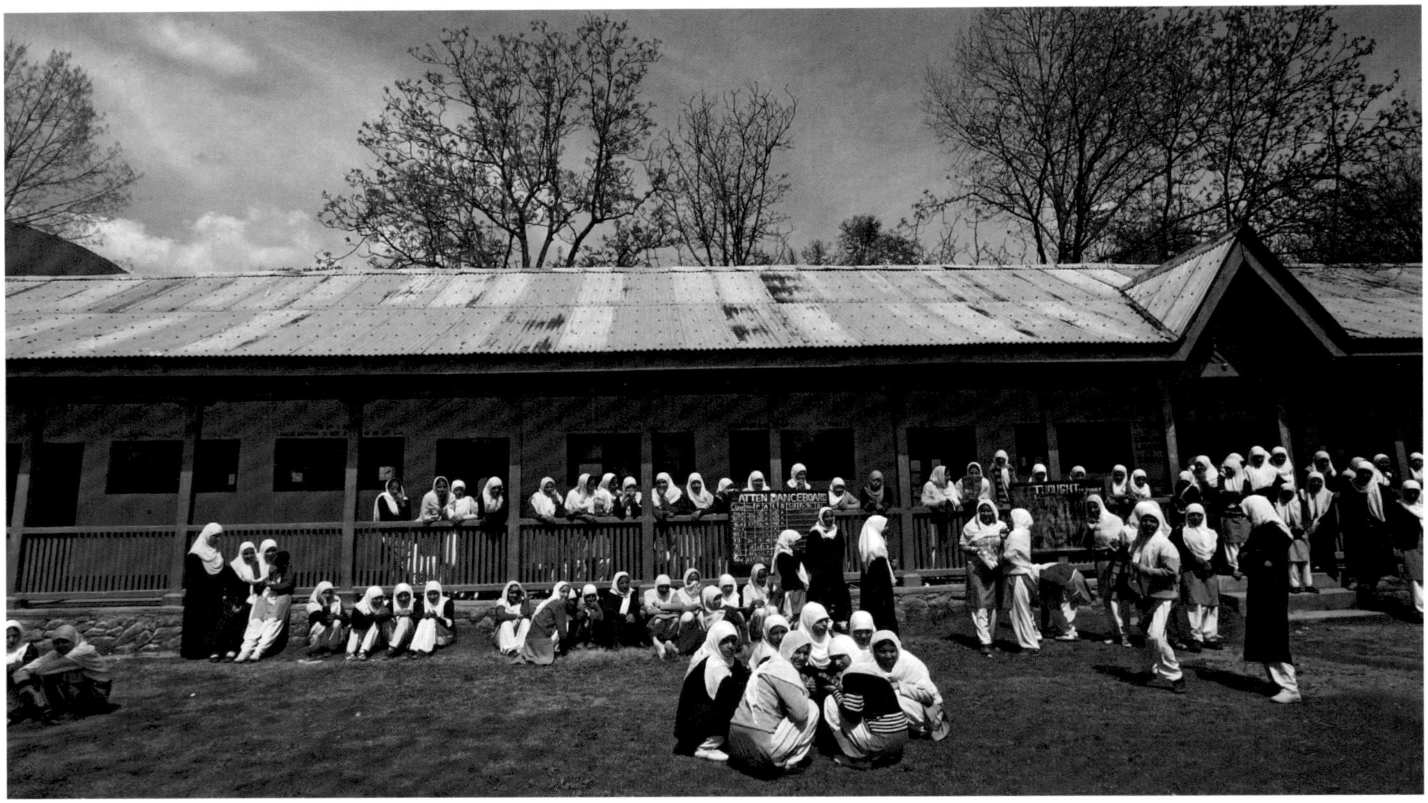

Girls during recess at a school in Bomai in Sopore. A RR camp that lay adjacent to it was moved in 2009, leaving them feeling much more relaxed

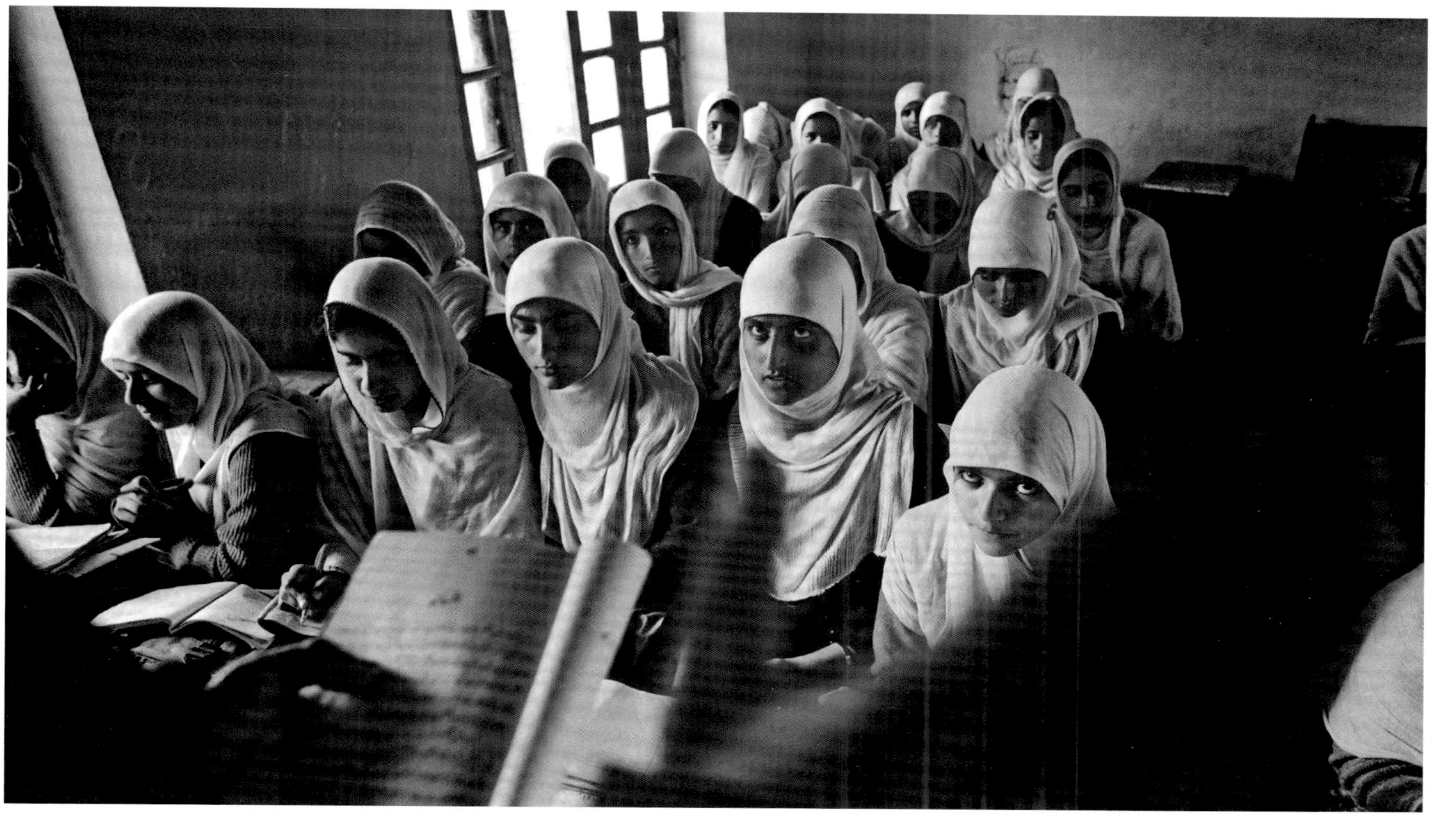

Girls in hijab learn Urdu at a school. The teachers are mostly men

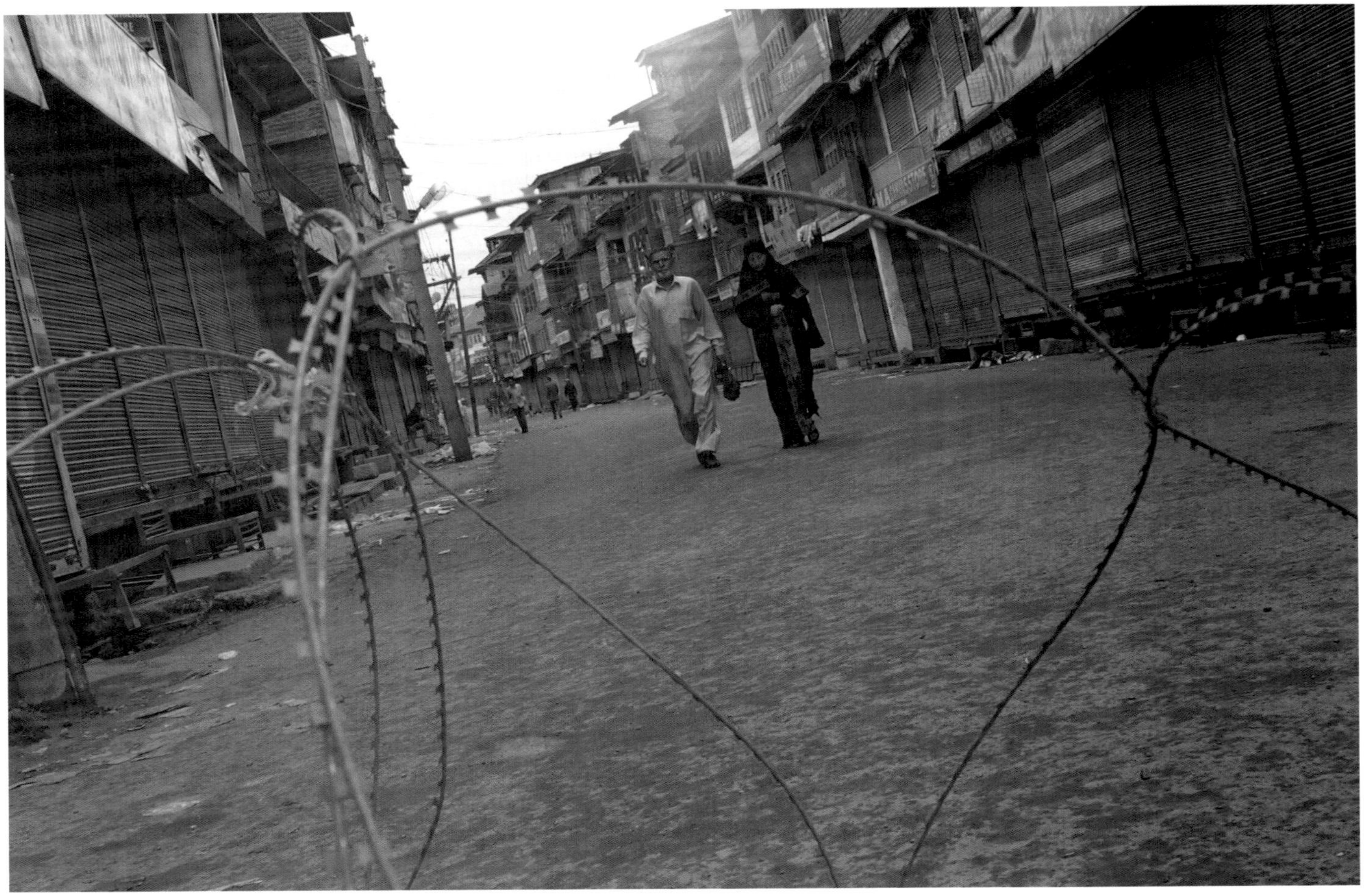

A daughter and her father leave for the hospital despite a curfew. Barbed wire is used to restrict people's movement and individuals have to carry a curfew pass along with special certification that has been provided by the J&K government, an annoying obstacle in day-to-day life

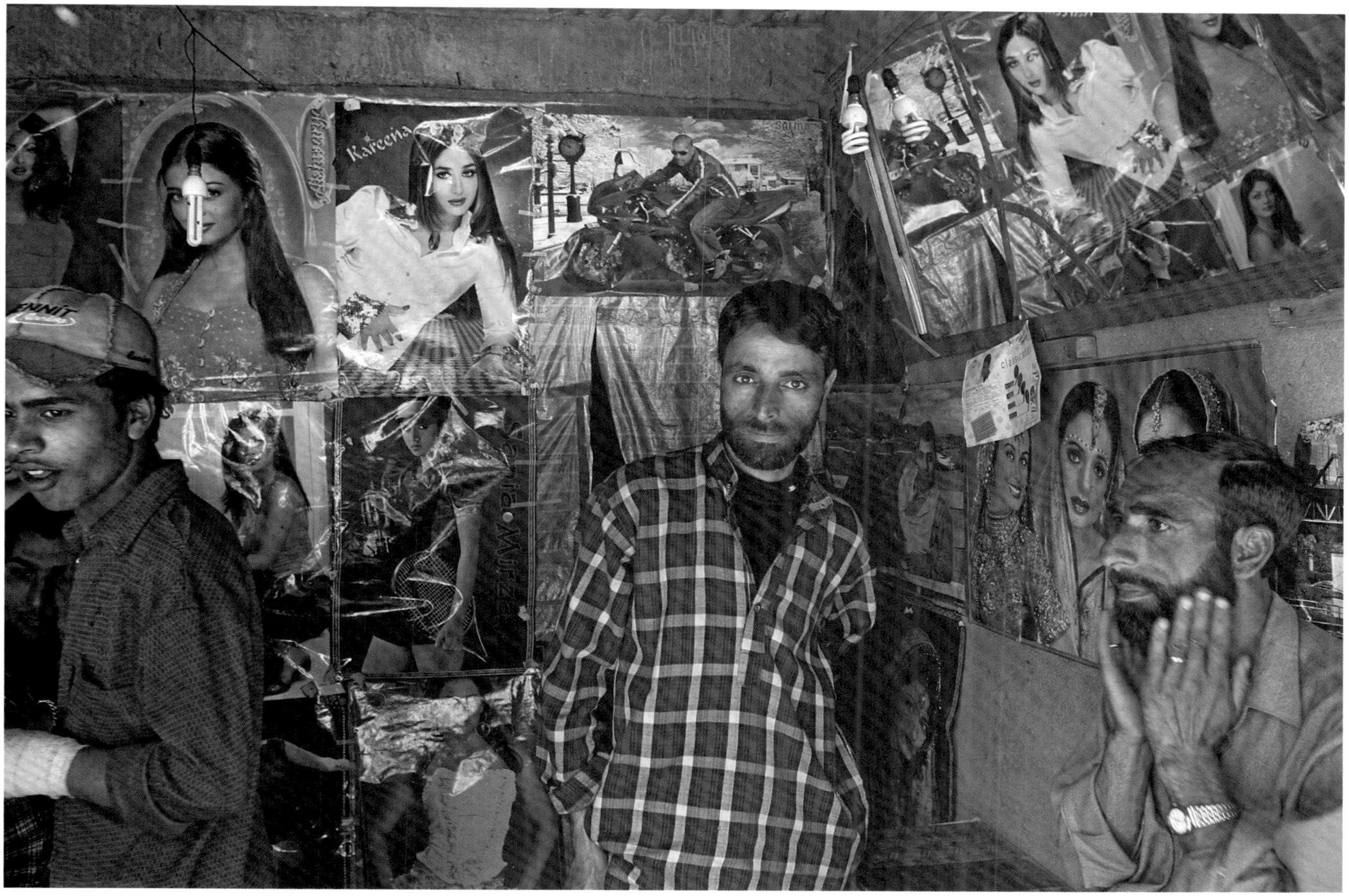

Some Kashmiris may nurture staunch differences with the Indian government but Bollywood still rules their heart. At a roadside saloon posters of Bollywood stars adorn the walls

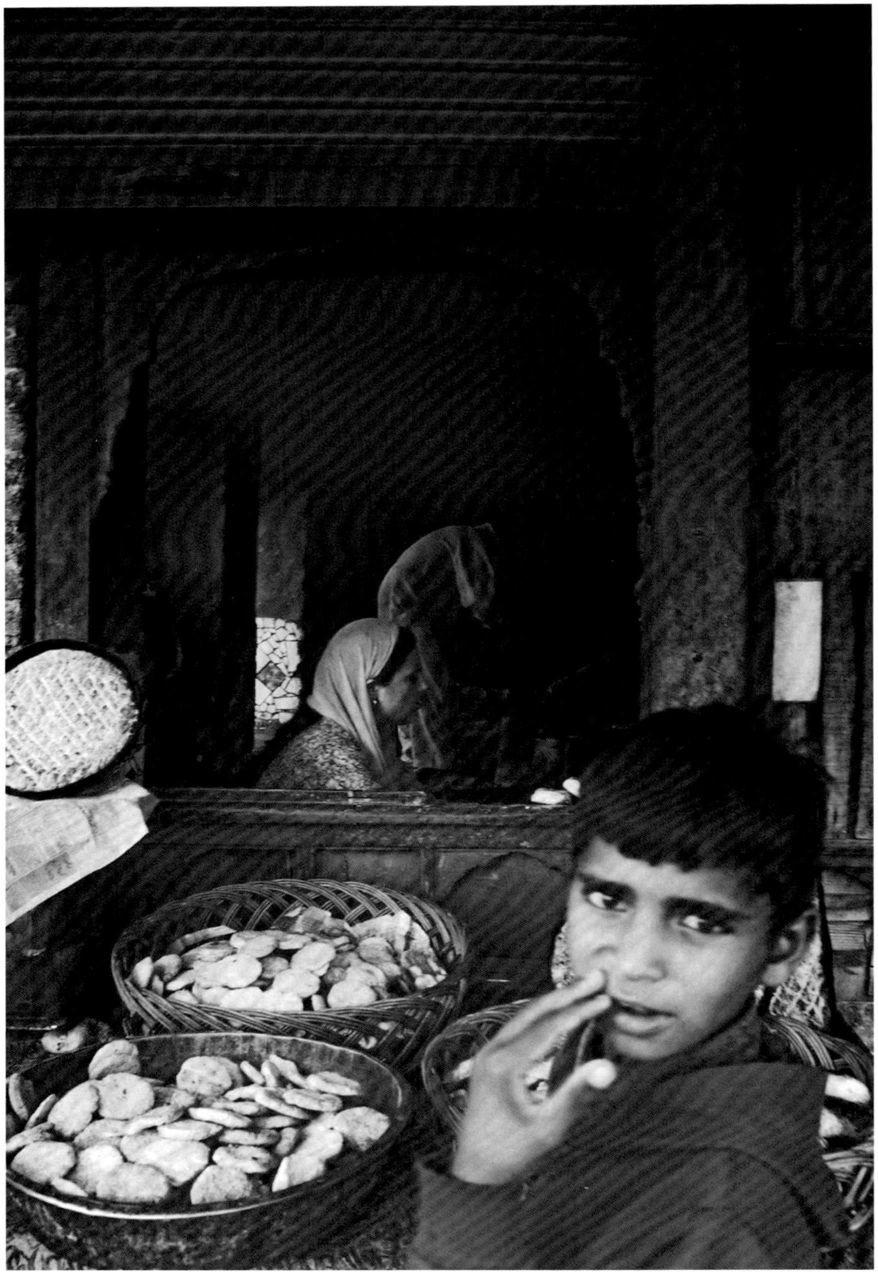

A bread shop in Hazratbal, near Srinagar

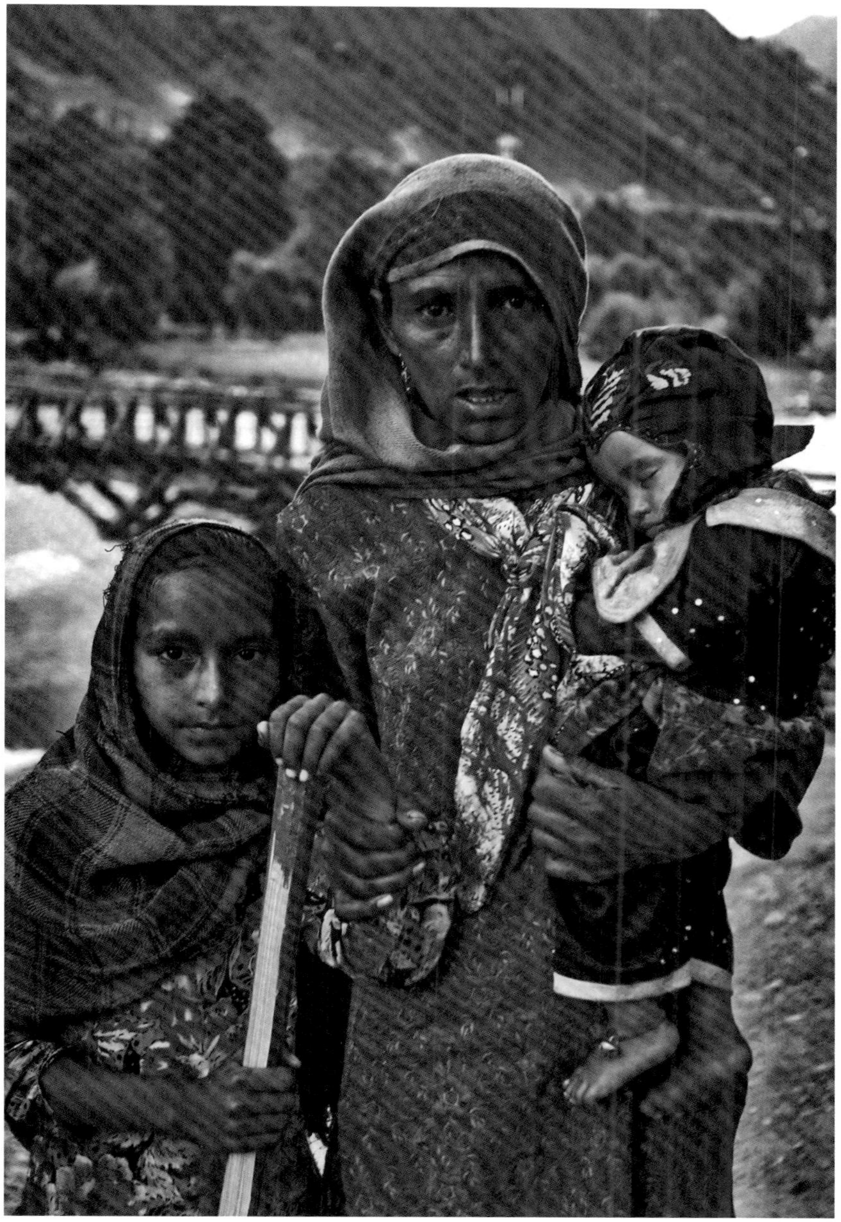

A Gujjar woman with her children. Nomads, they move from one place to another depending on weather conditions. These people were the first ones to share information on the intruders at Drass, in 1999

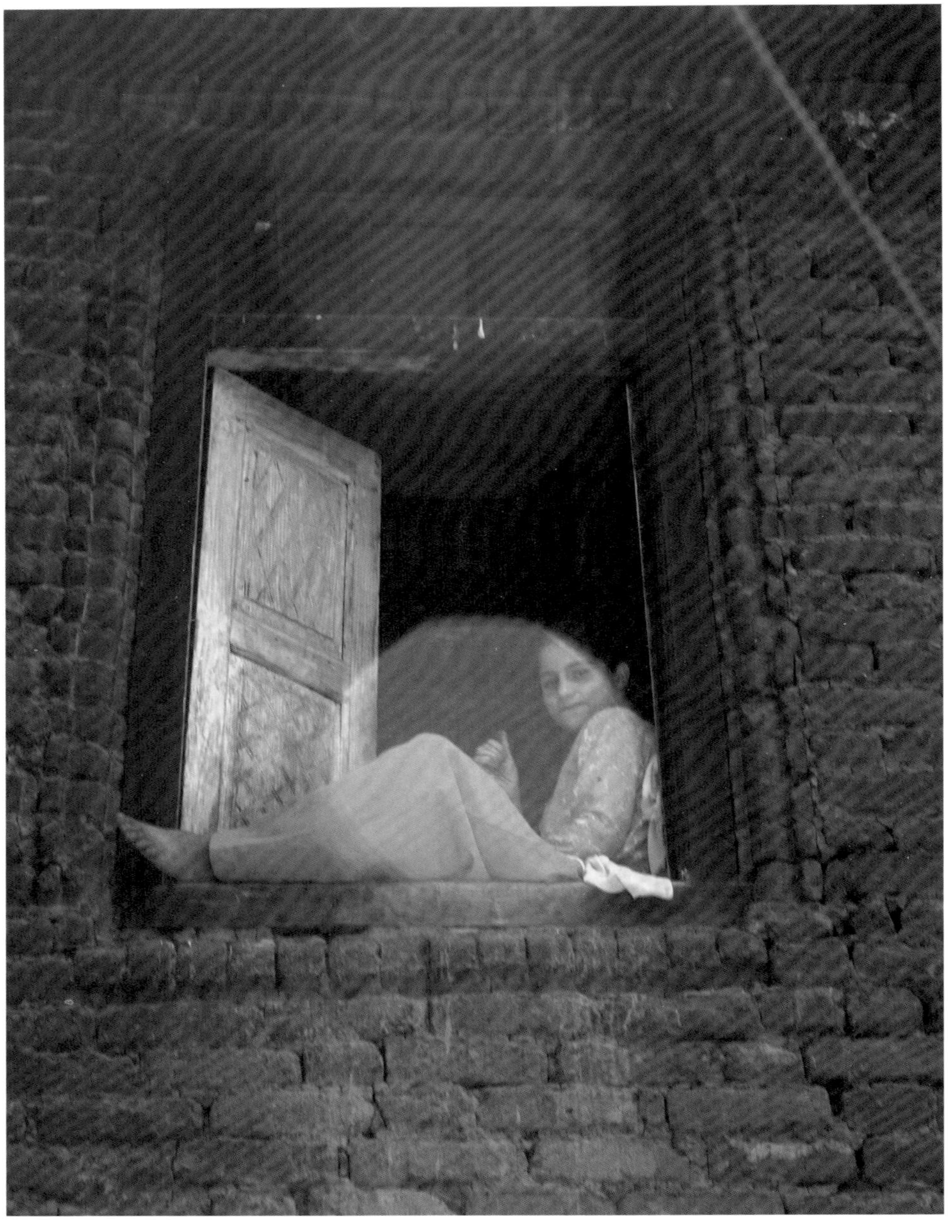

A young girl sits at the edge of a window in Sopore, in north Kashmir, which has been a hotbed of militancy. Many houses have broken windows due to shelling and crossfire, but people donot repair them fearing it may happen again

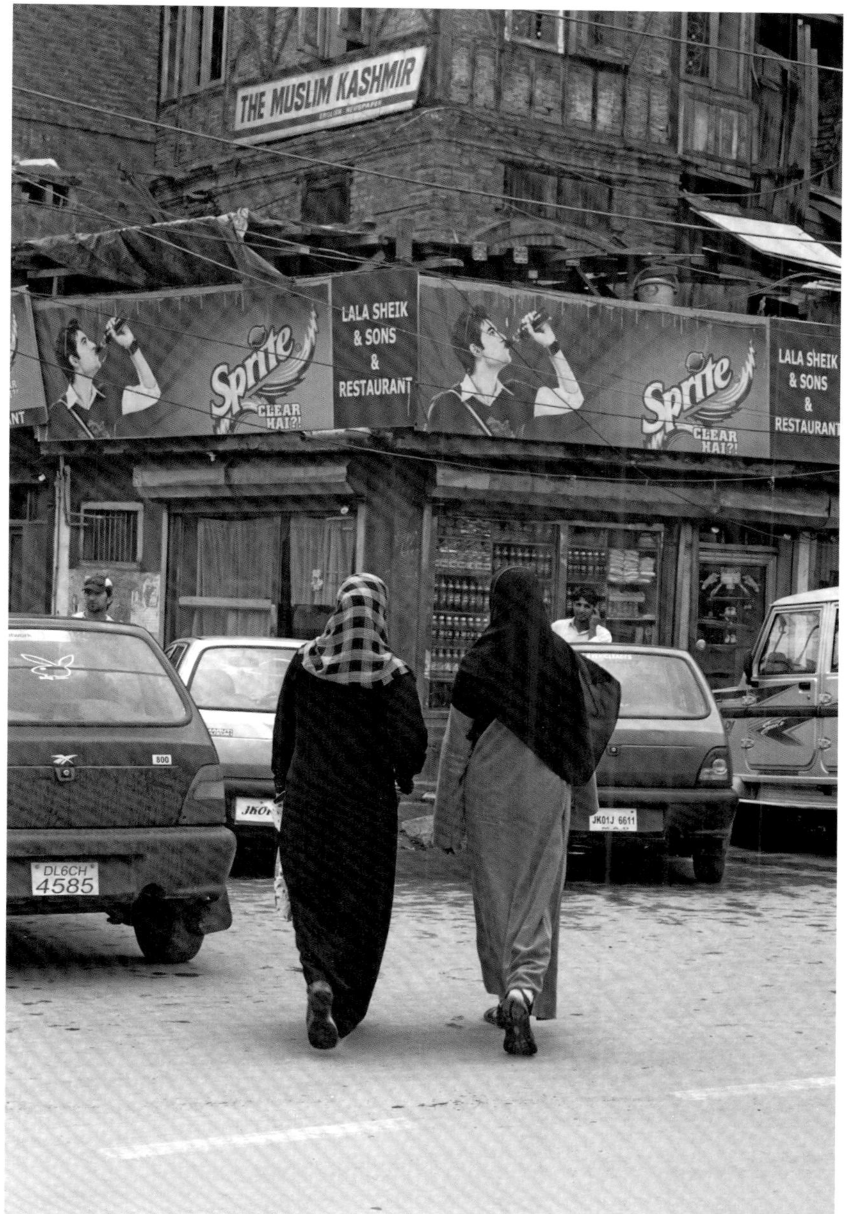

Kashmiri women in their attire. Headscarf is a must. They are sometimes made of silk

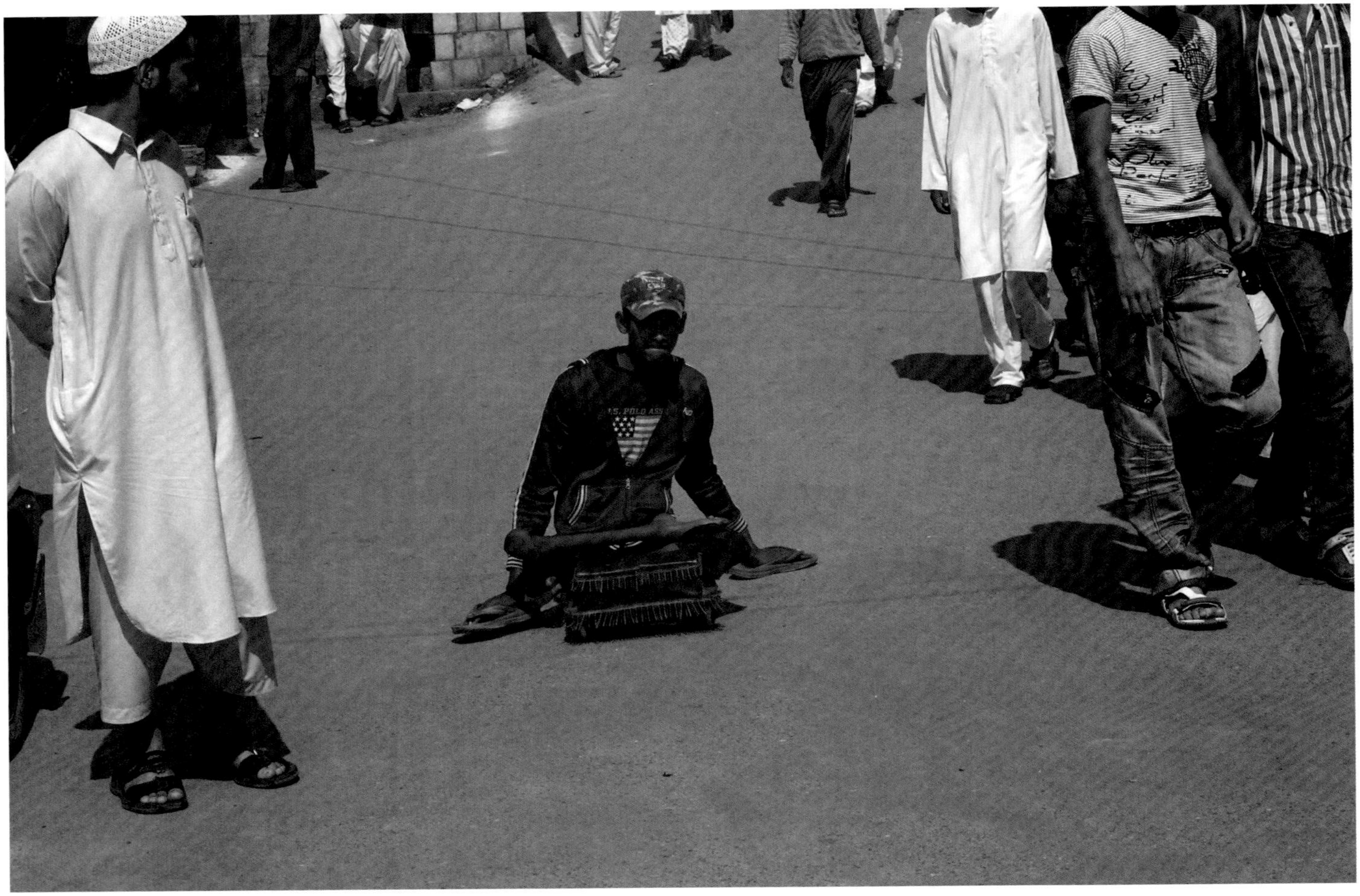

A beggar is a rare scene in Kashmir. Here is one wearing a T-shirt with an US flag drawn on it

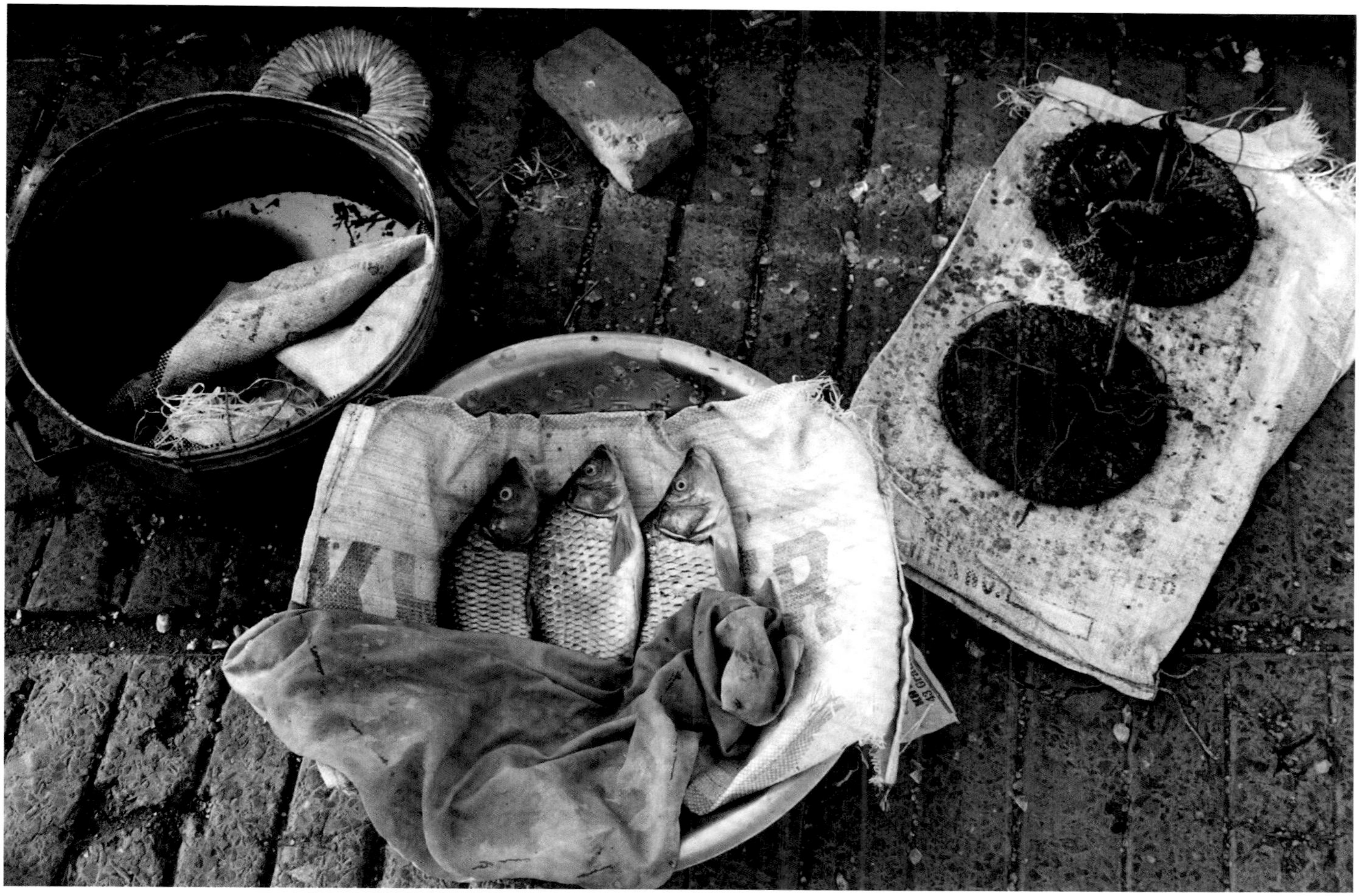

Trout being sold at the roadside market near Amira Kadal. They are quite expensive when served at restaurants.

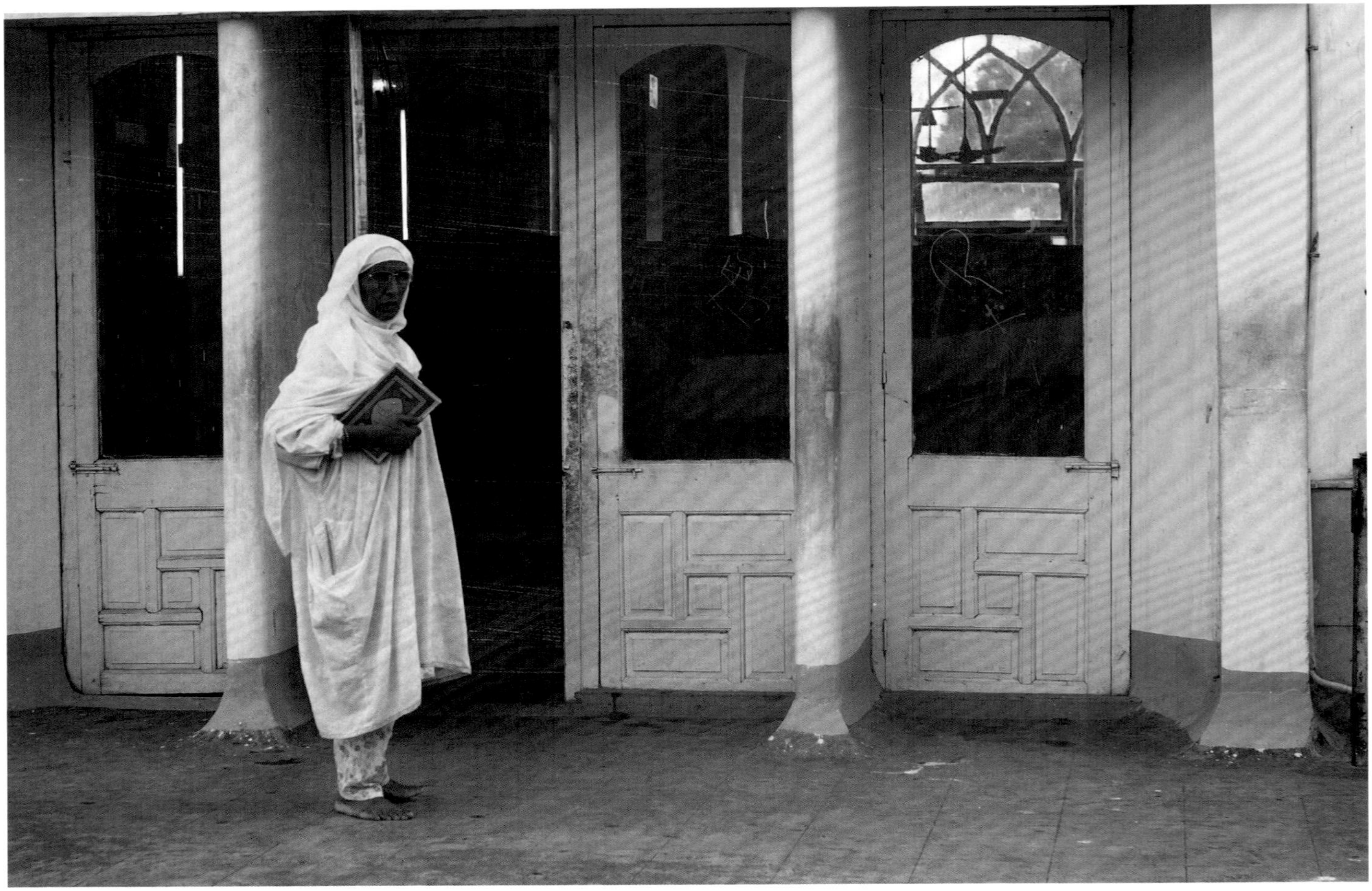

The entrance to the Koran reading room for women at Hazratbal. Men are not allowed here, not even photographers

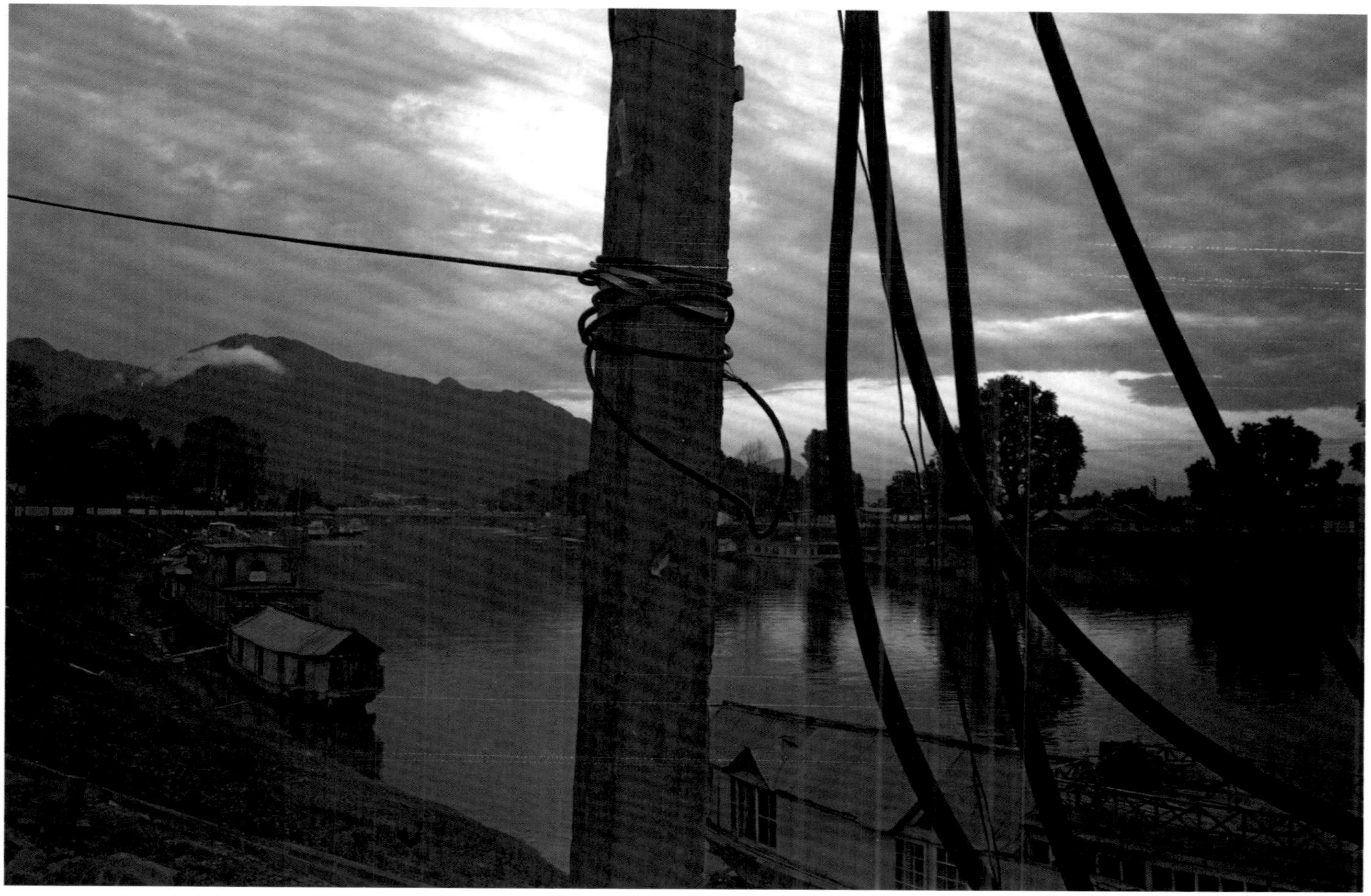

Houseboats lined up along the Jhelum are usually homes of poor Kashmiris who eke out a living from these waters

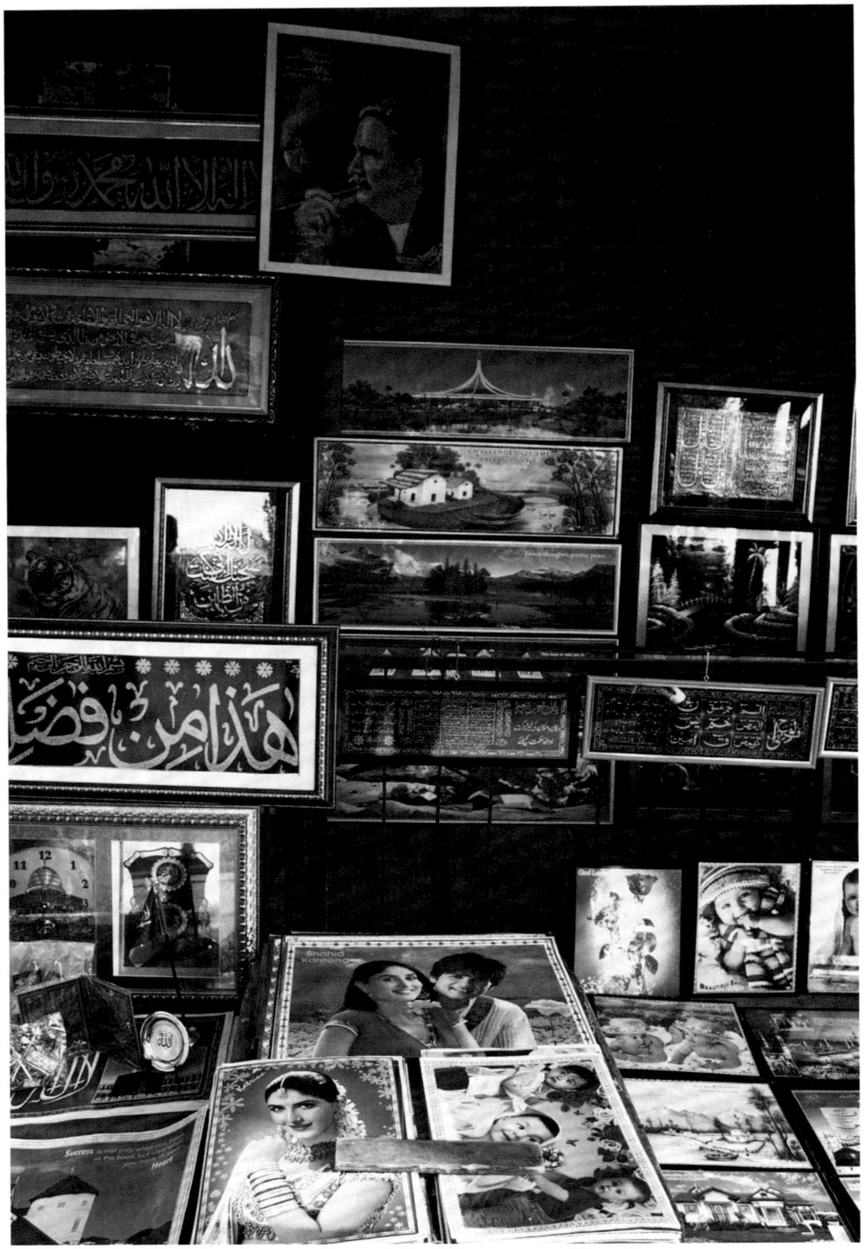

A roadside shop hawking pictures of a picturesque Kashmir alongside pro-Kashmiri-freedom poet, Iqbal.

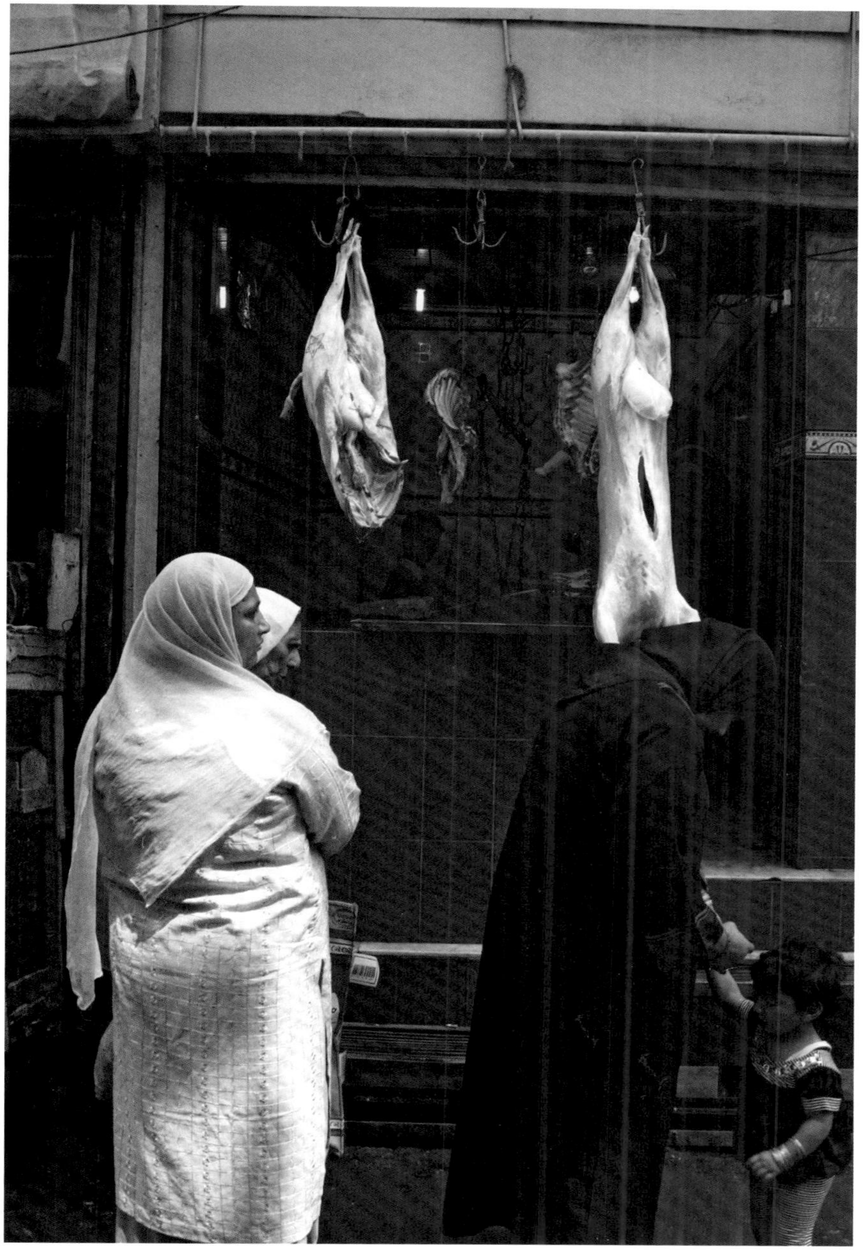

Meatshop in Dal Market. Lamb is an essential part of a Kashmiri meal. Dishes like tabak maaz, kebabs and rogan josh are enjoyed by both Muslims and Hindus living in Kashmir

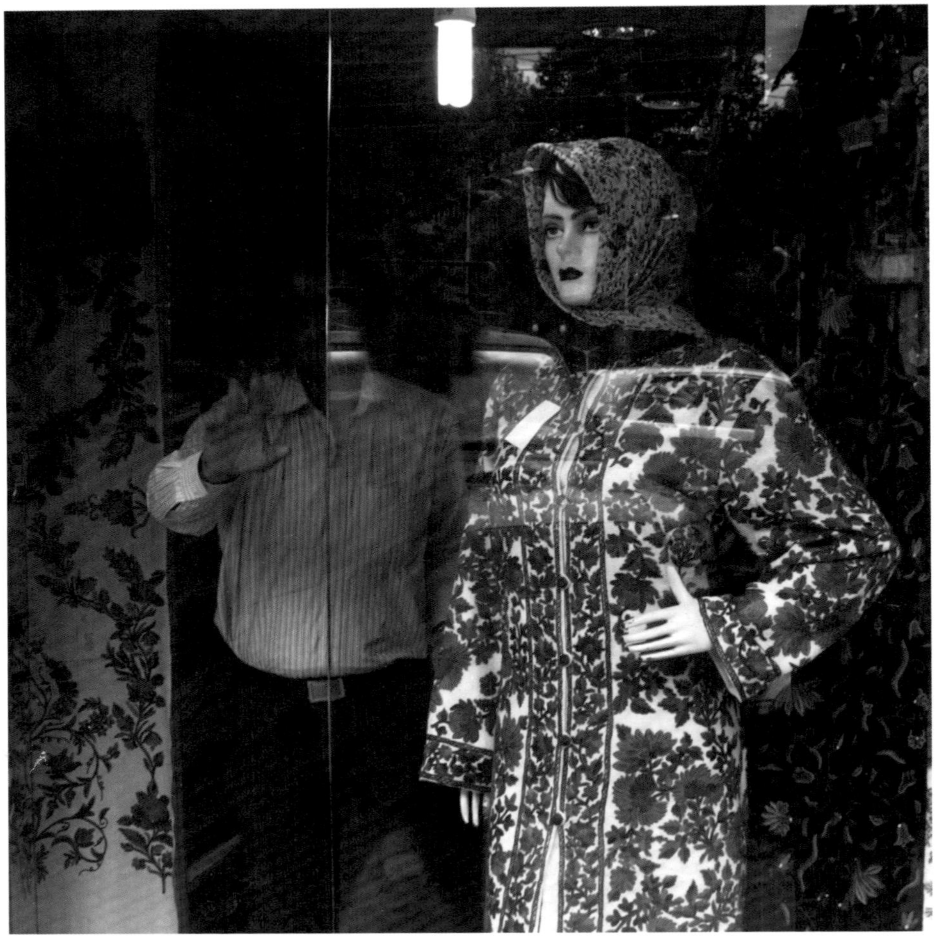

A shop selling a Kashmiri-style dress. Shop owner does not want to be photographed

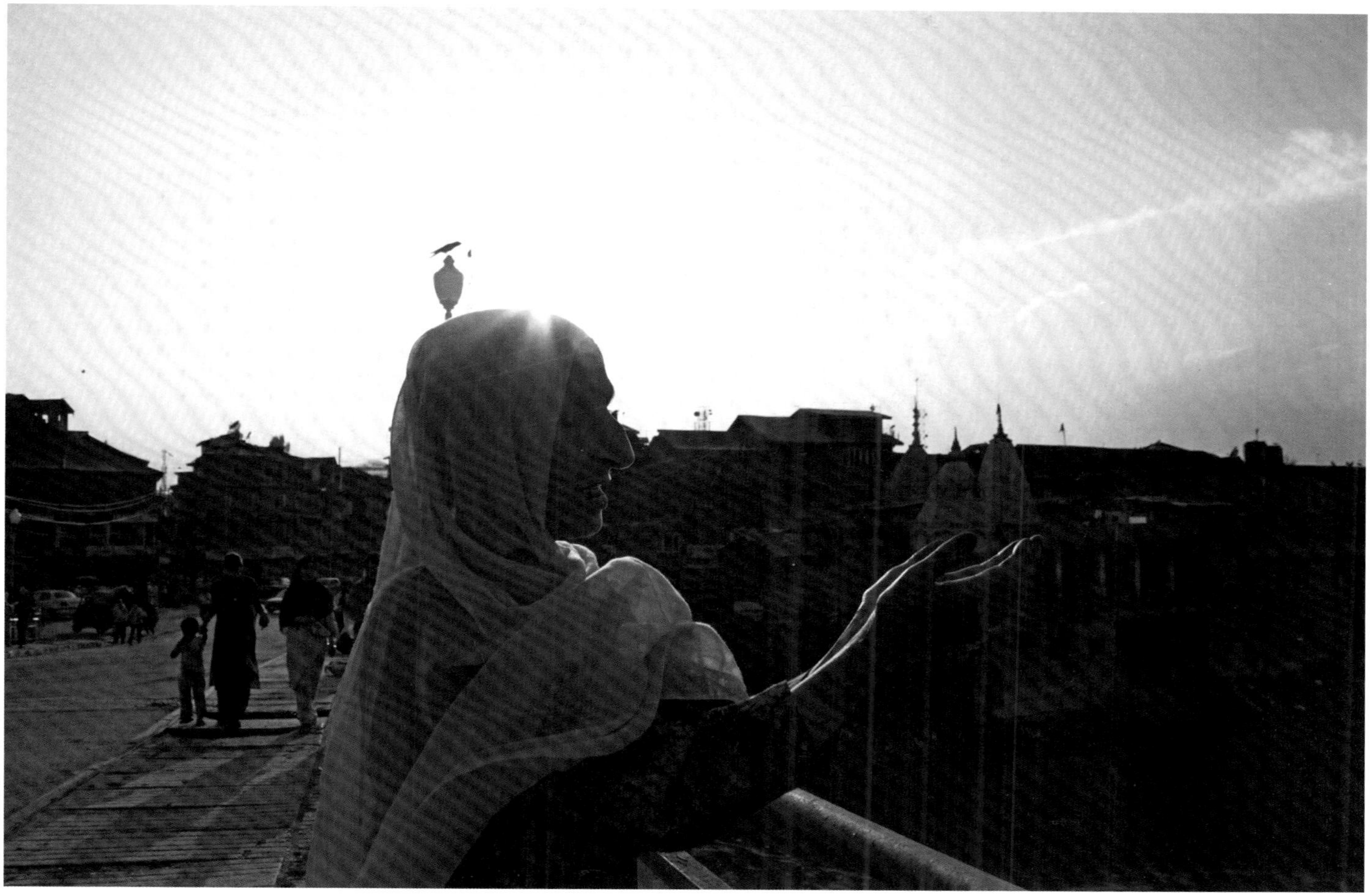

A muslim lady prays, with the sun setting sun along the river Jhelum

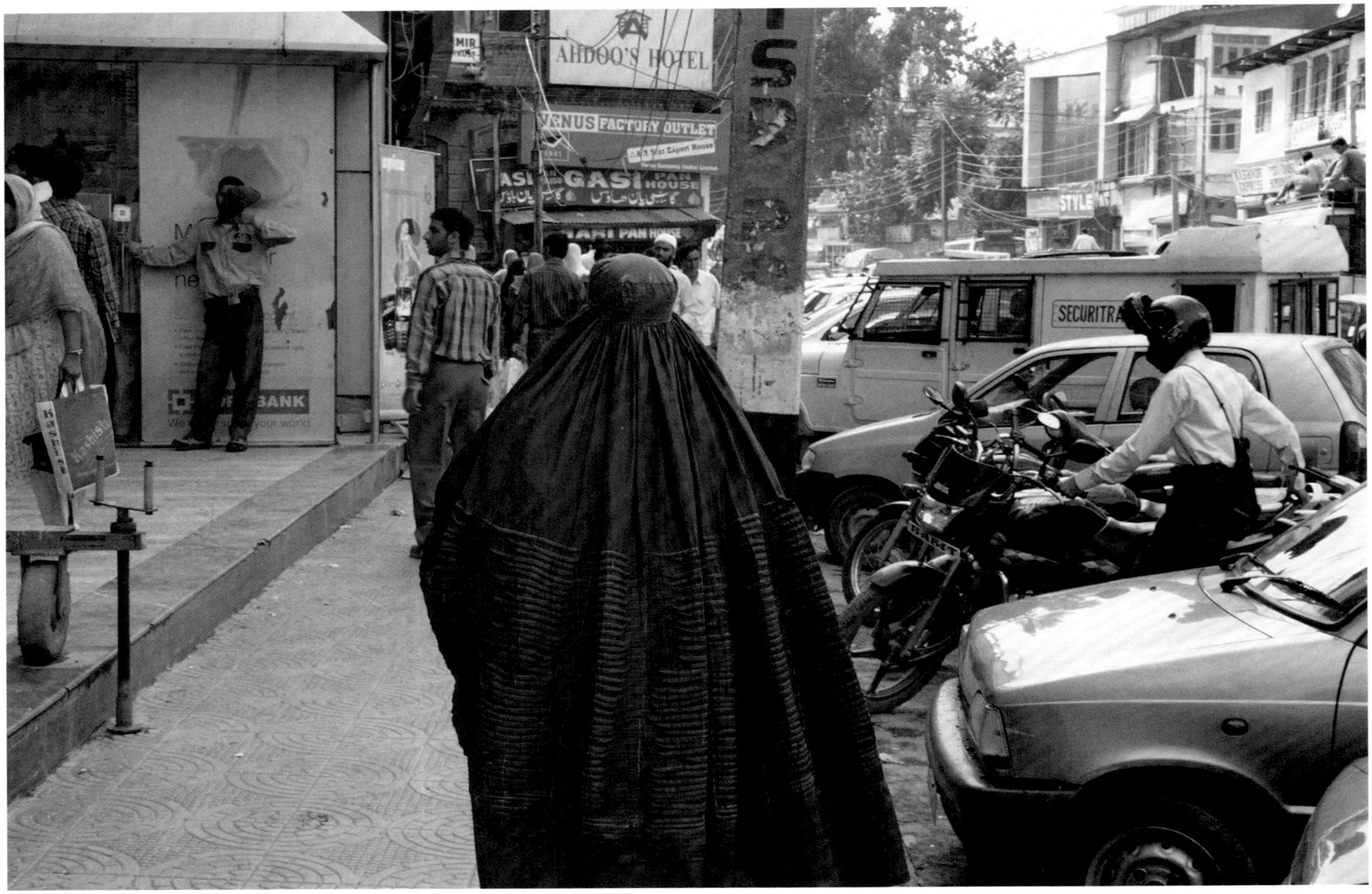

A woman in her traditional burqua, which is rare in these parts

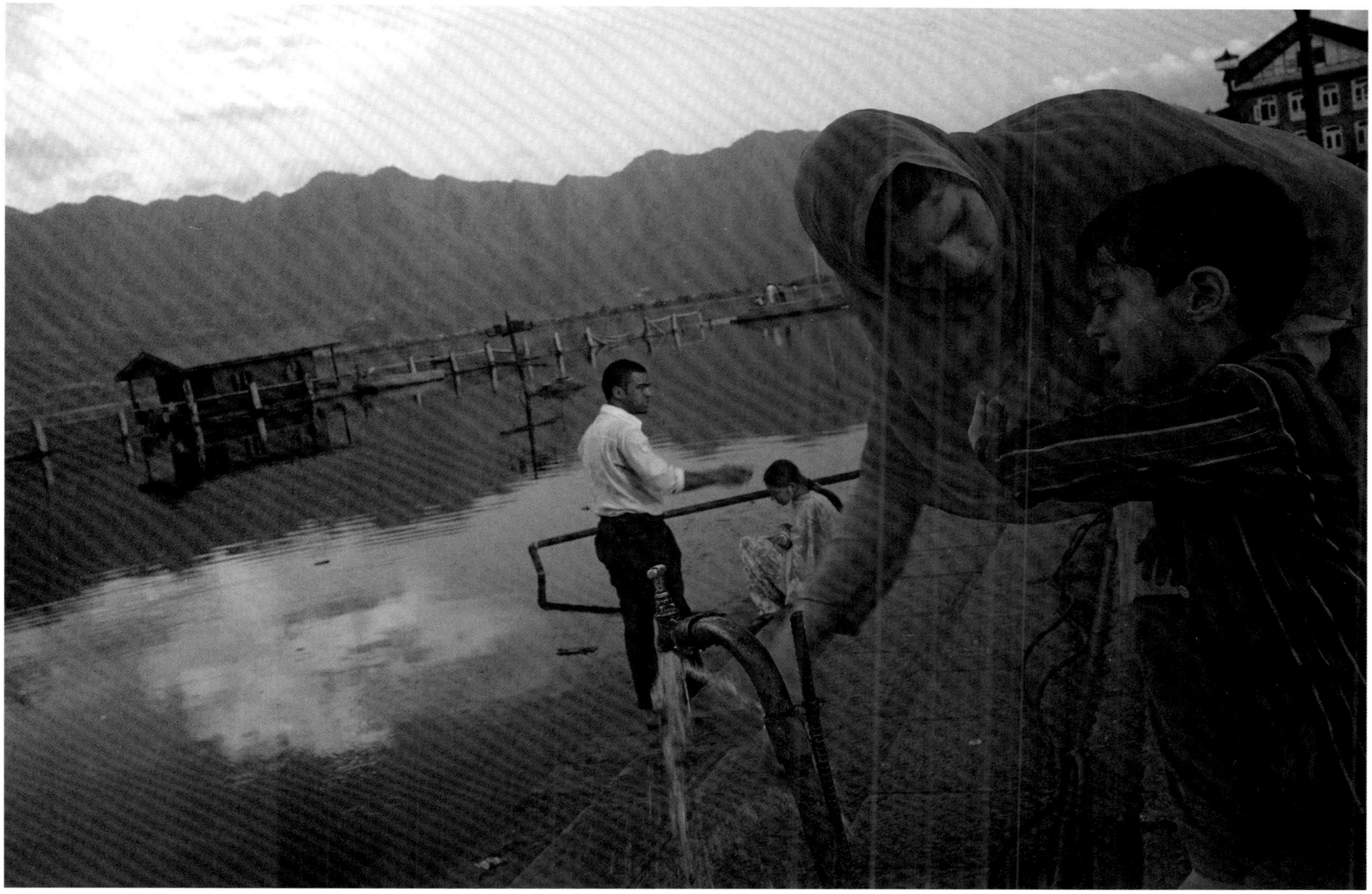

Along the Nagin Lake

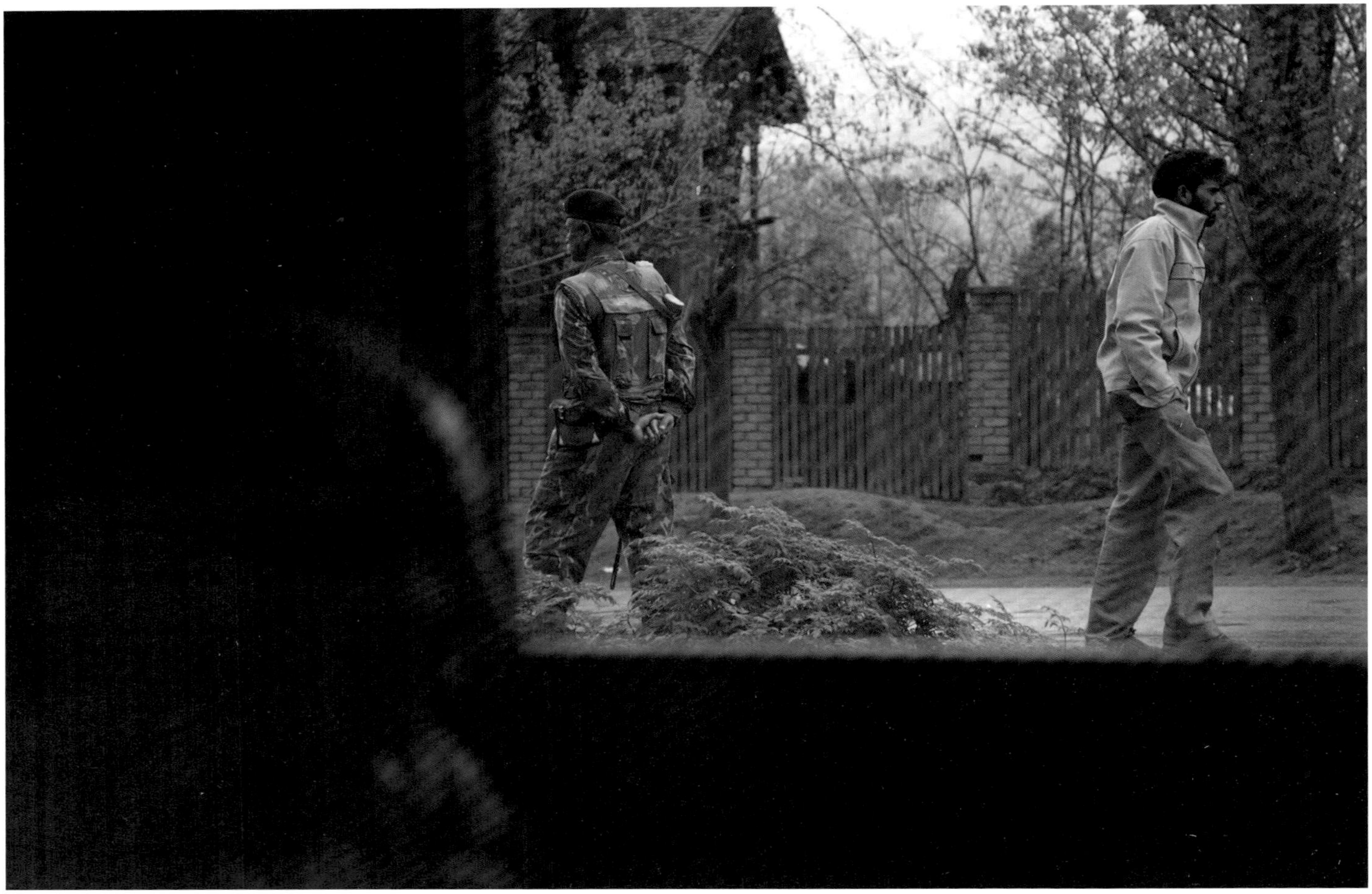

A paramilitary personnel keeps a tight vigil from his bunker in downtown Srinagar. They are on constant alert against sneak attacks

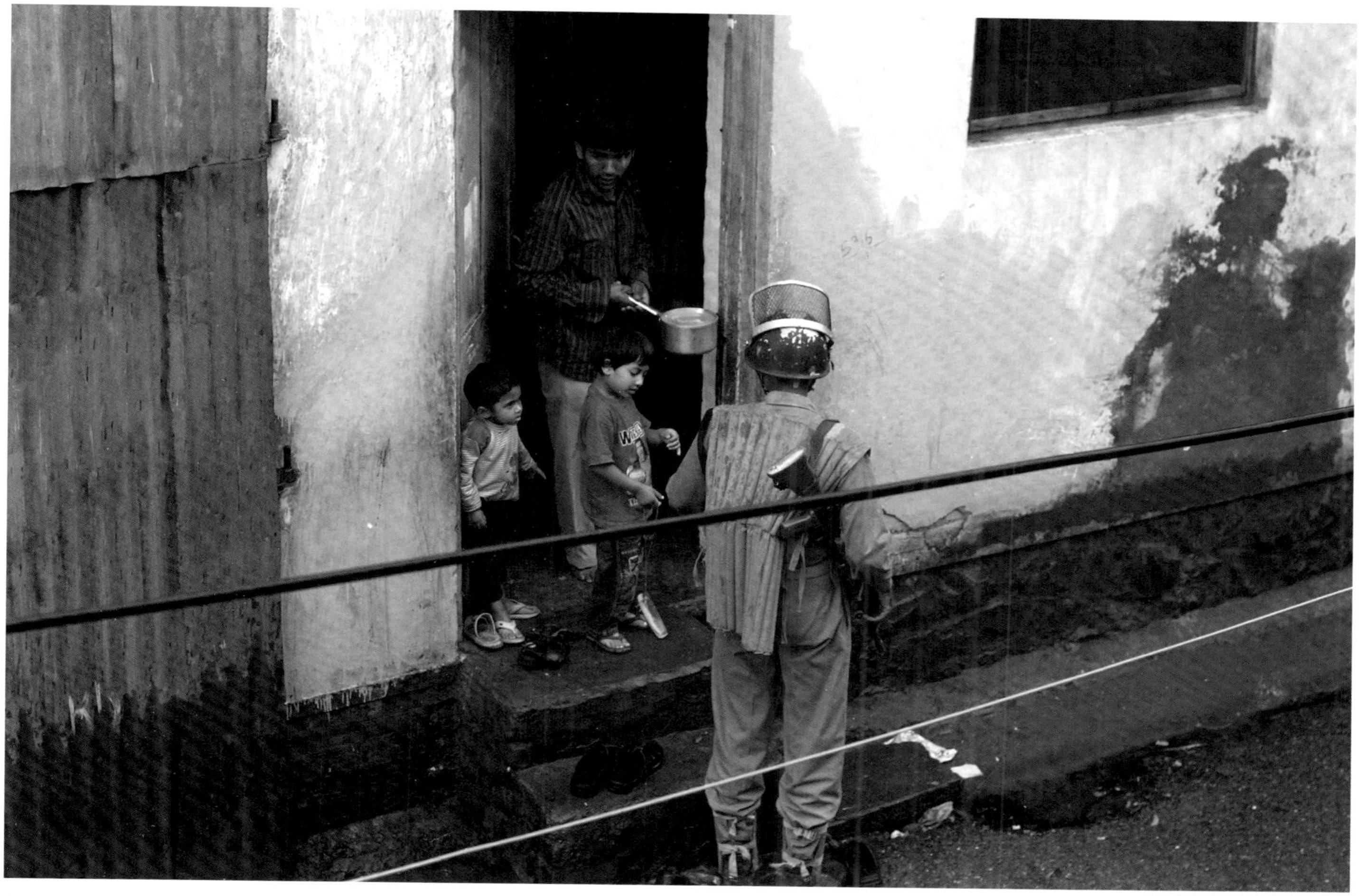

A security man stops to drink water at a local house, and to gather information

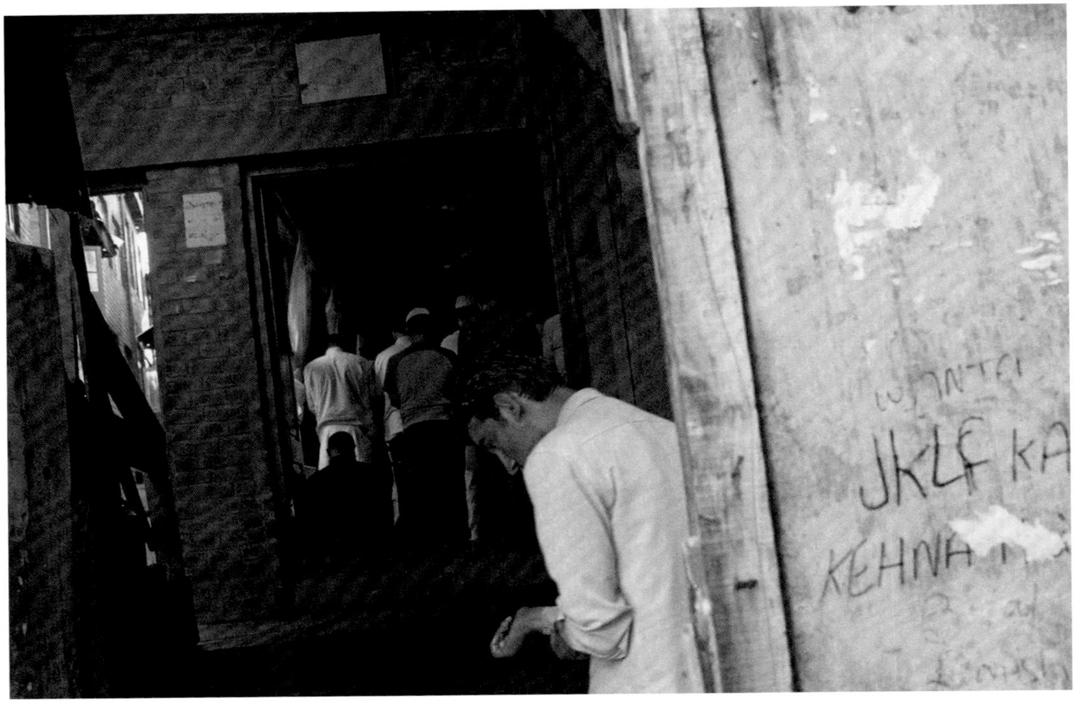

JKLF slogans on the walls of a newly built mosque, at the Press Enclave in Srinagar

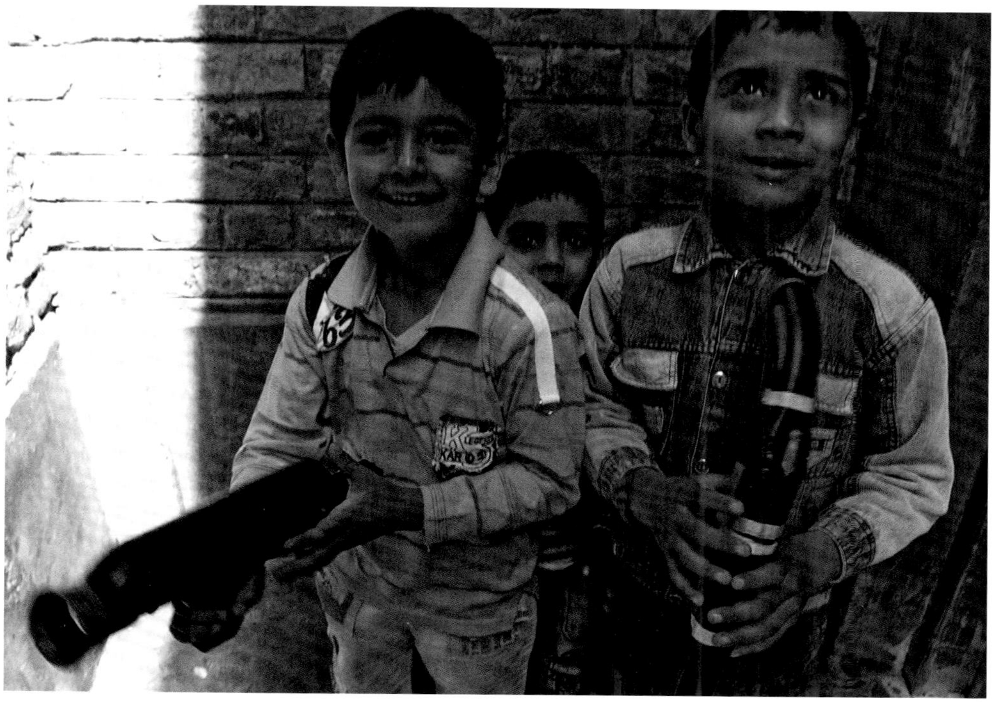

Children like these at Maisuma, a stronghold of JKLF, have grown up seeing guns. Toy gurs are common play items they use while shouting pro-Kashmiri freedom slogans

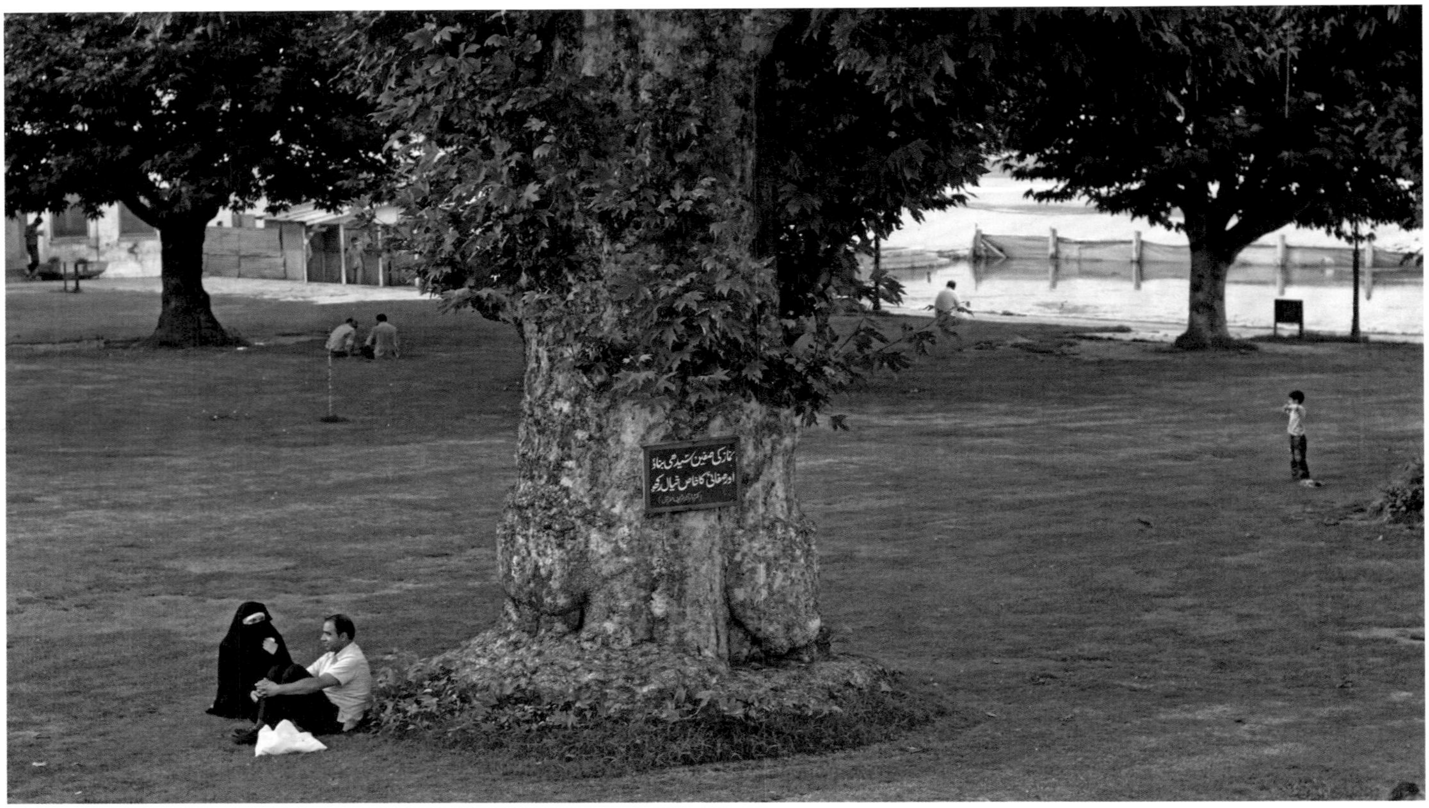

A couple enjoying the evening at Hazratbal

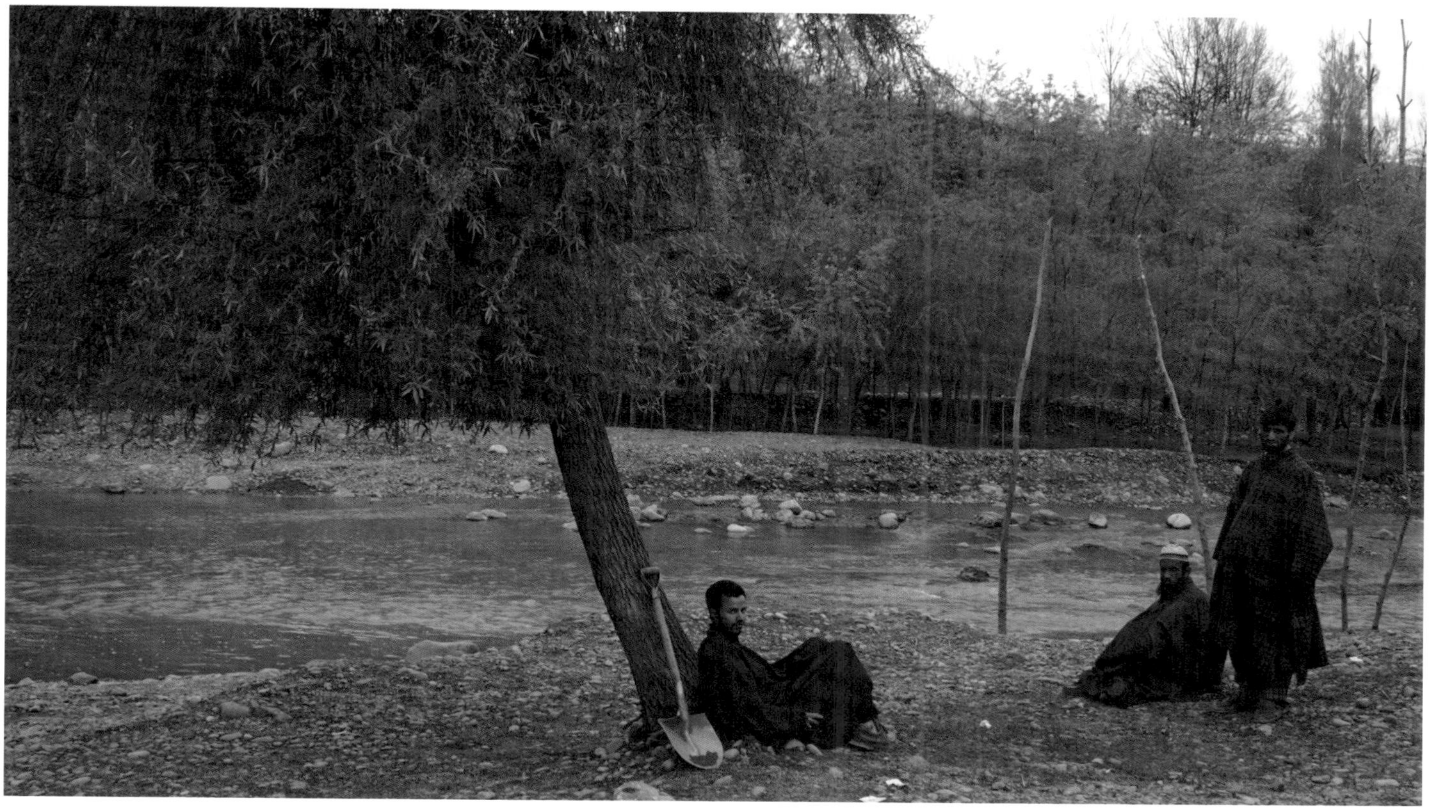

Labourers caught resting on a chilly autumn afternoon, along the road to Pahalgam

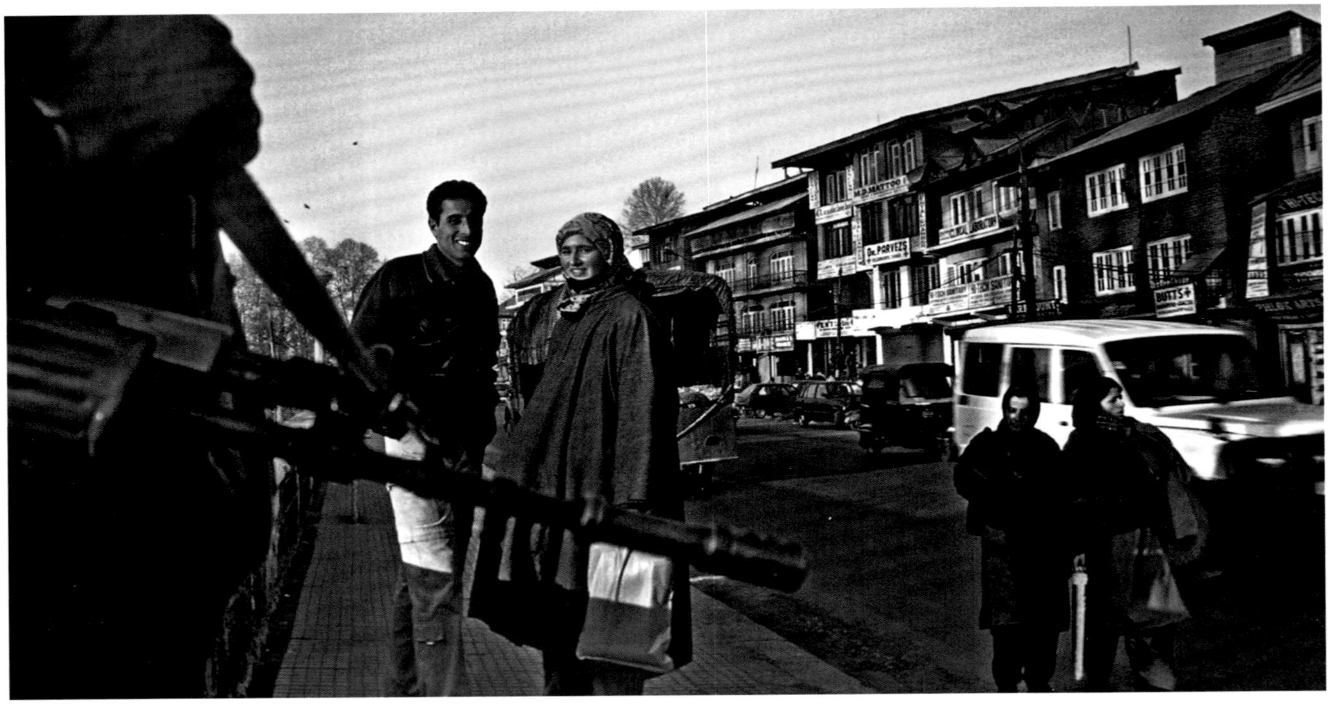

Couples enjoy a cool winter evening, while the BSF constable guards with full attention. The Boulevard, which starts with the congested Dal Gate, is a maximum security area

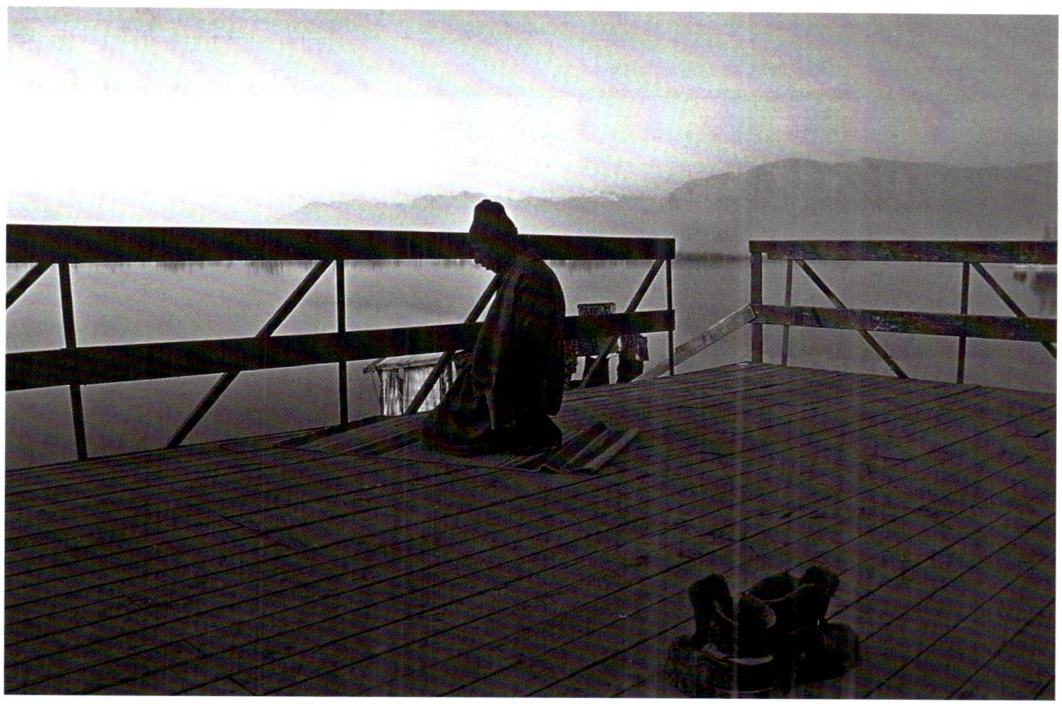

An old shikara owner takes a break for his namaaz. He is facing the holy city of Mecca, beyond the Dal Lake and Zawarwan hills

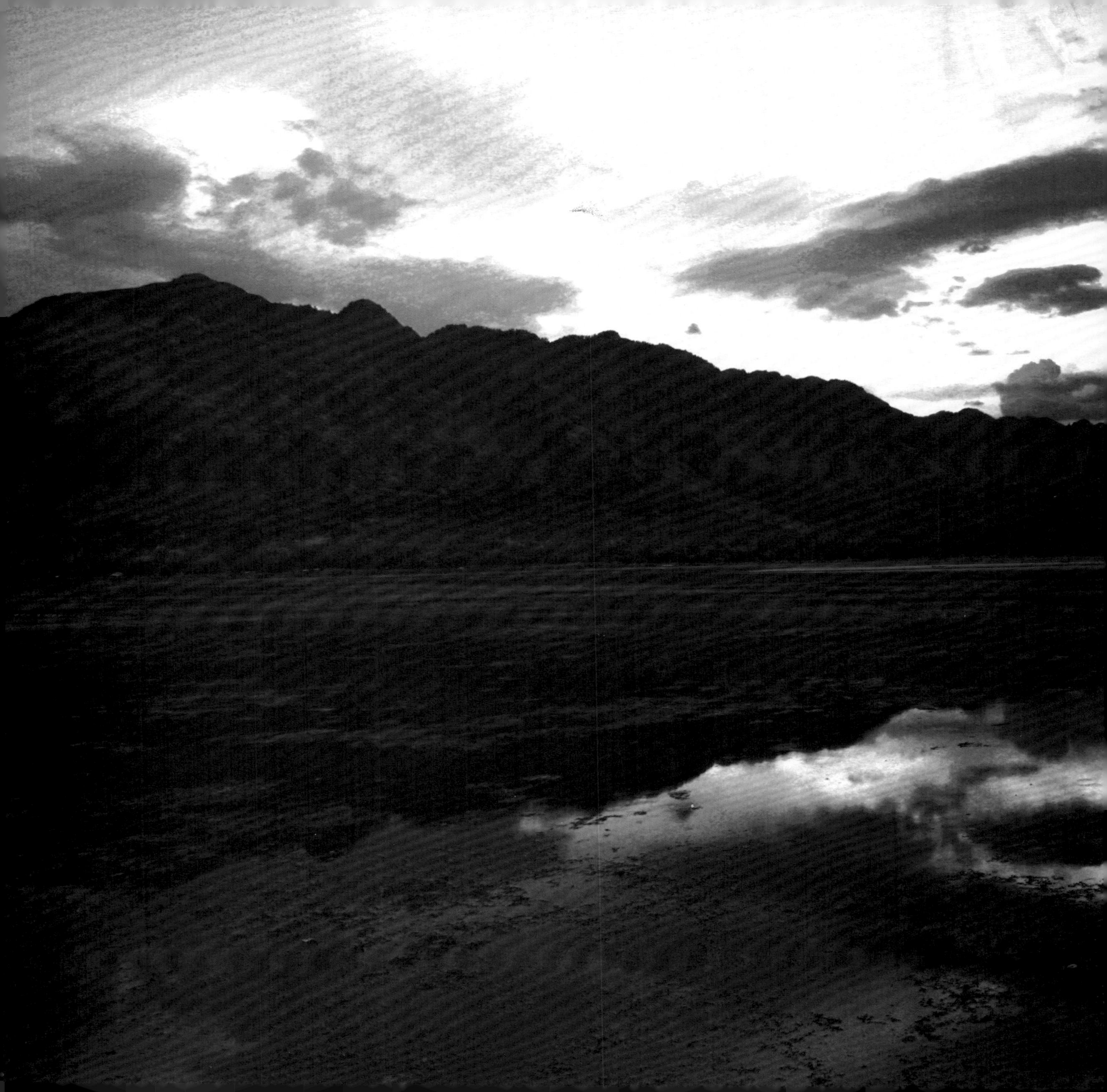

LANDSCAPE

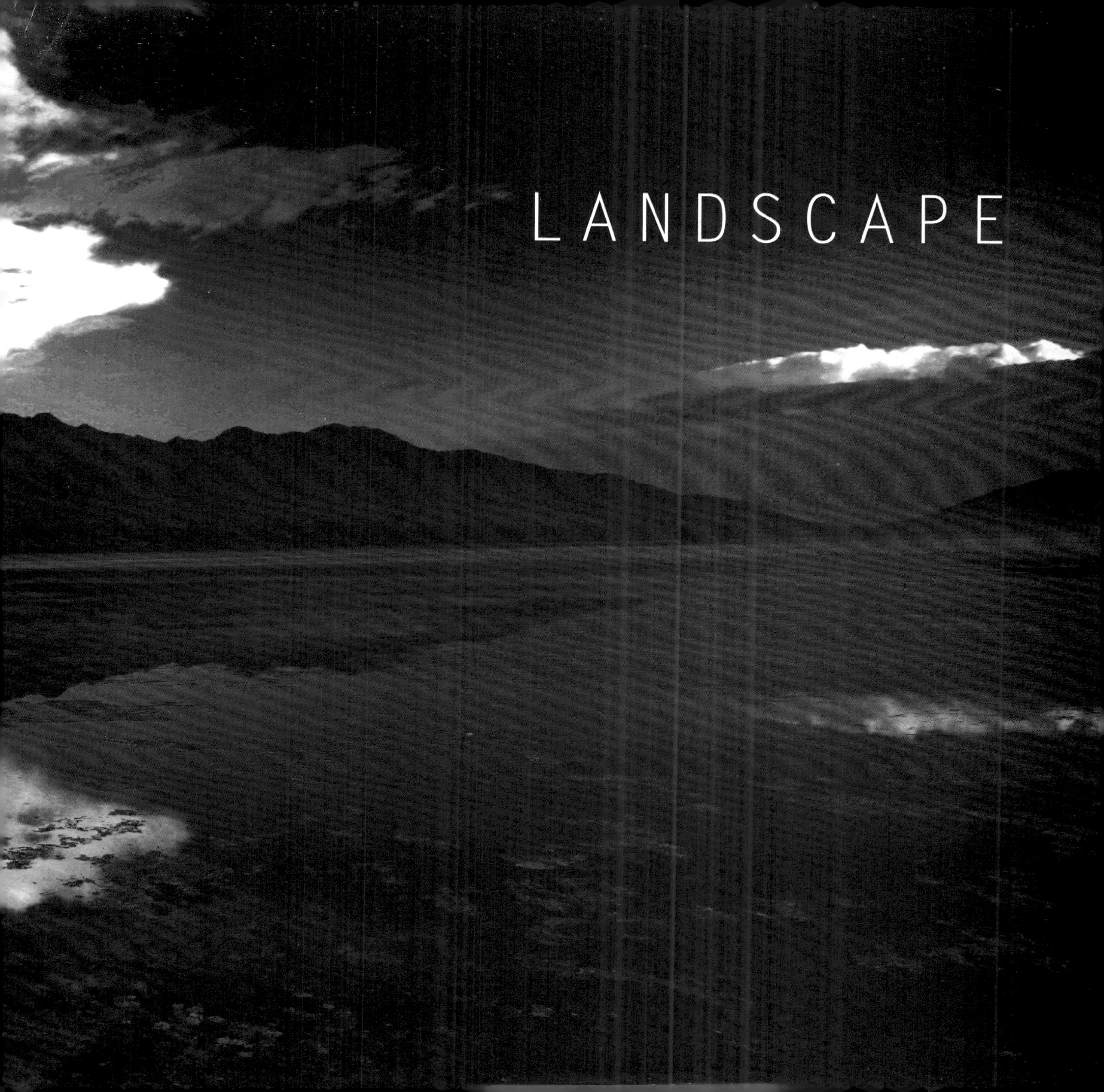

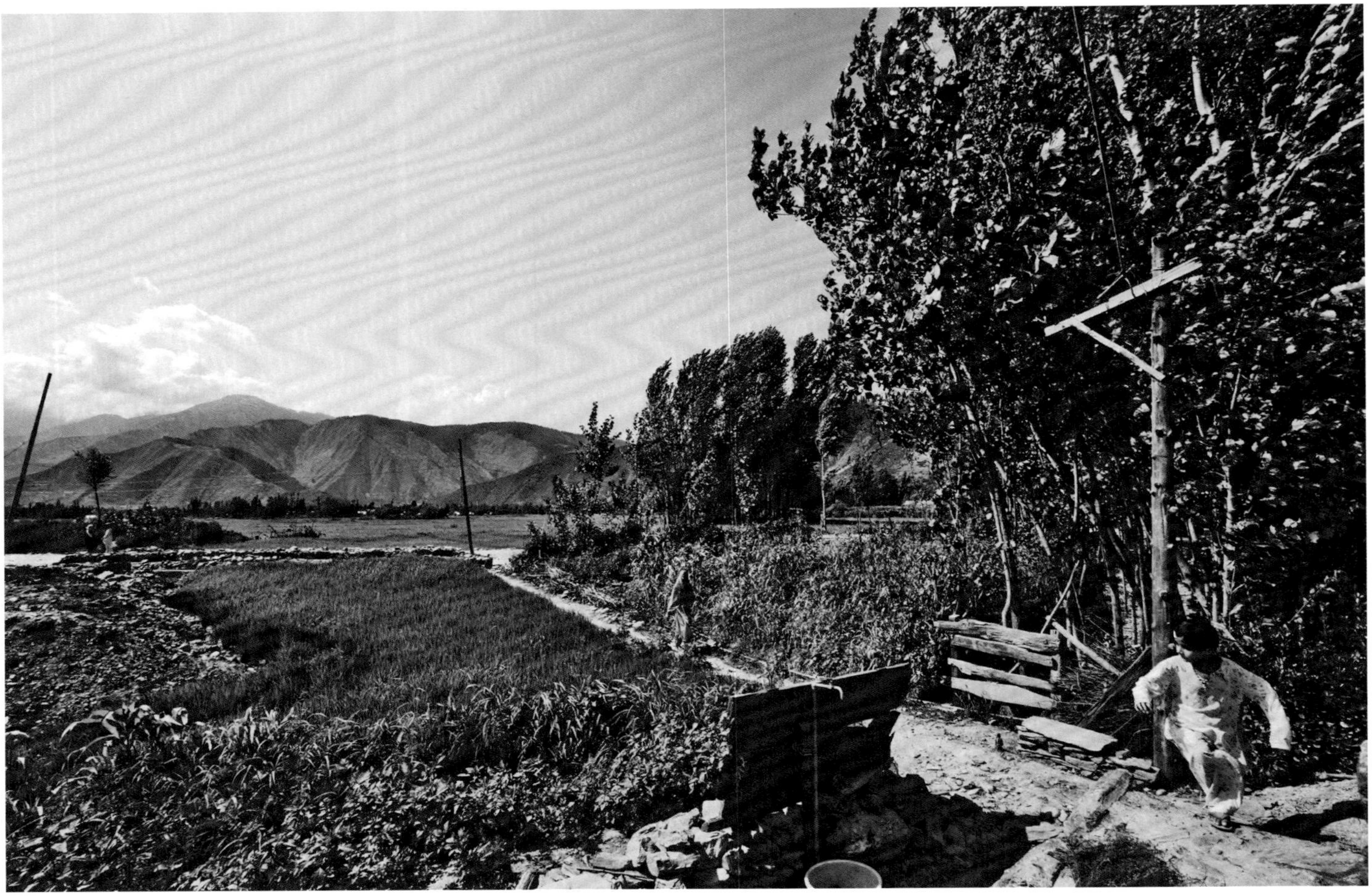

Baramulla located on the banks of the Jhelum has been known as the Gateway of Kashmir Valley. This is one of the regions that harvested the legendary Basmati rice for the first time in autumn 2008, which is considered a minor revolution in the agrarian history of the Kashmir Valley

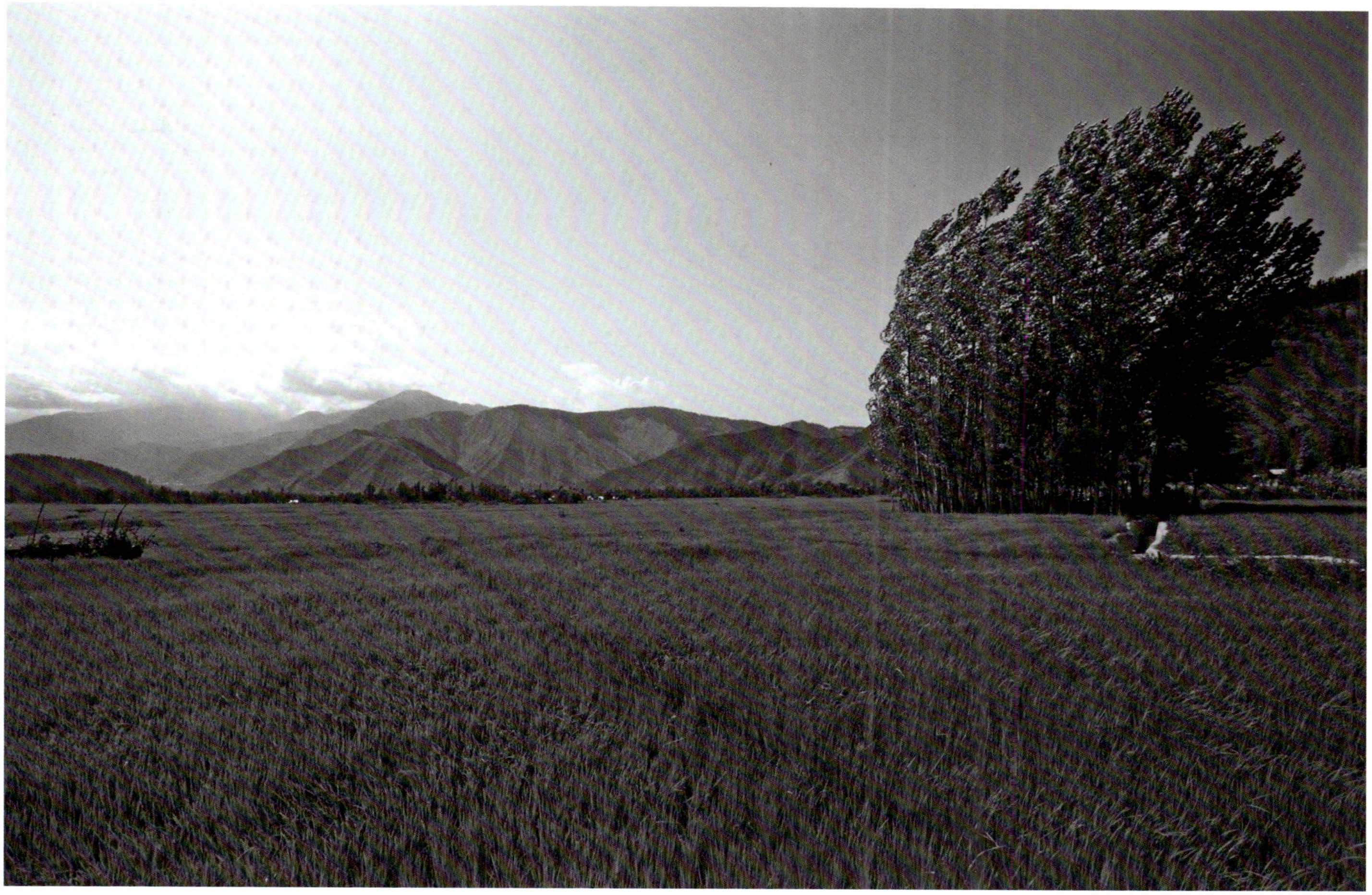

Kashmir is indeed a paradise of a kind. There is beauty everywhere one looks around. Militancy and insurgency may have created a black spot but the Kashmir Valley is still gorgeous and vibrant

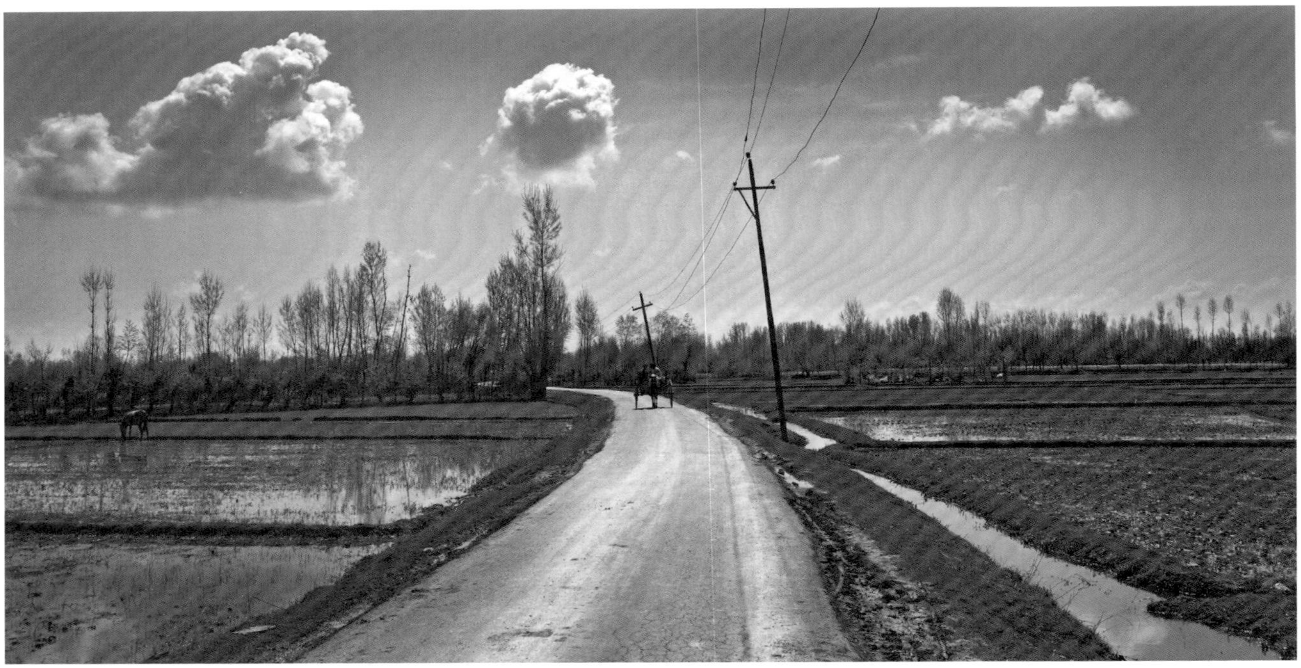

Sopore is indeed beautiful. Its undulated landscape covered in a veil of mist, its serpentine roads and cloudy skies, make it look ethereal

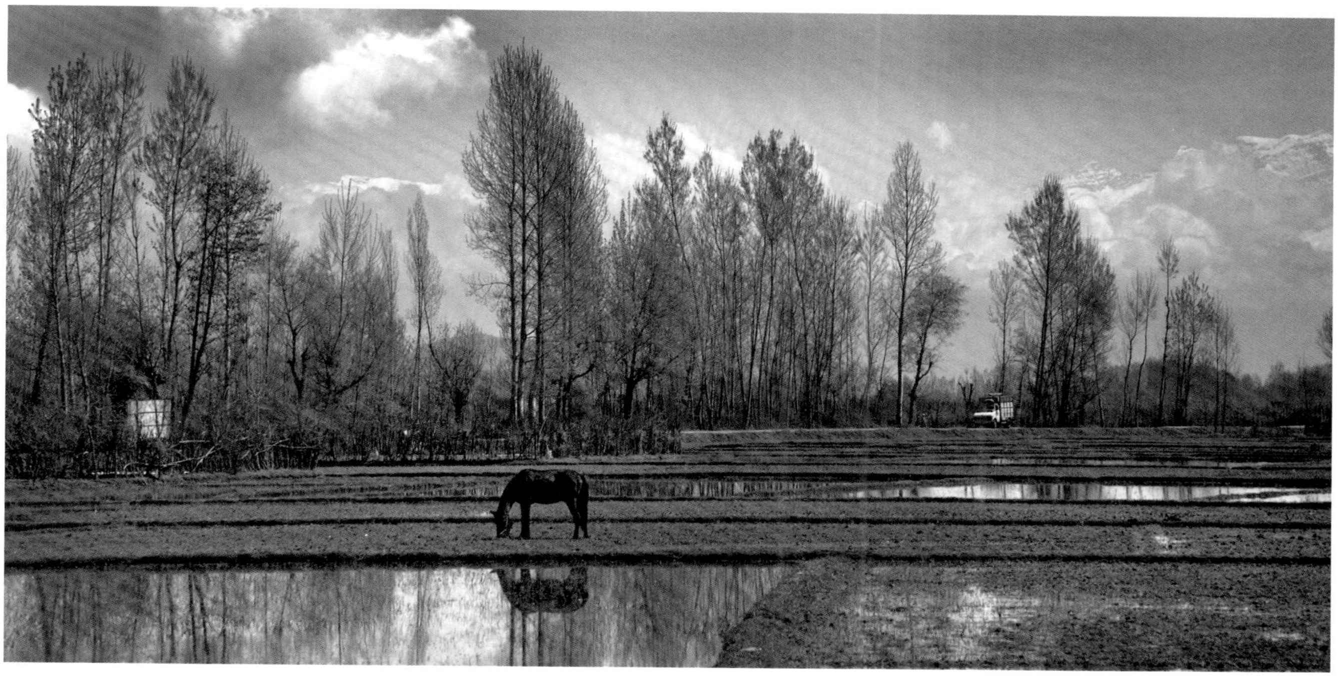

A horse grazes between the poplars in Sopore

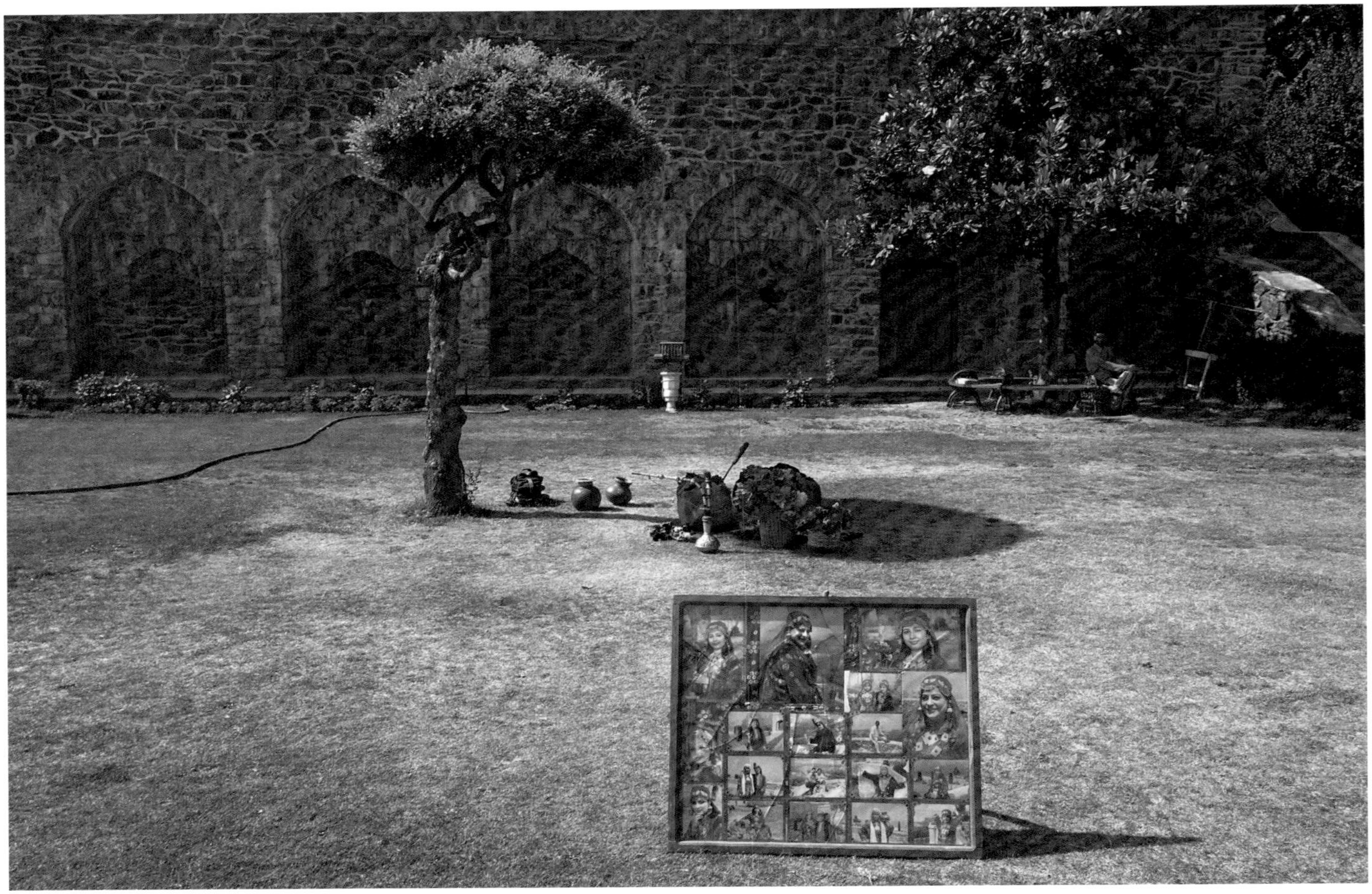

Photographers wait for customers at Chasmashahi Garden, one of the Mughal gardens. Due to rising militancy and sporadic riots, visits to these gardens reduced for some time

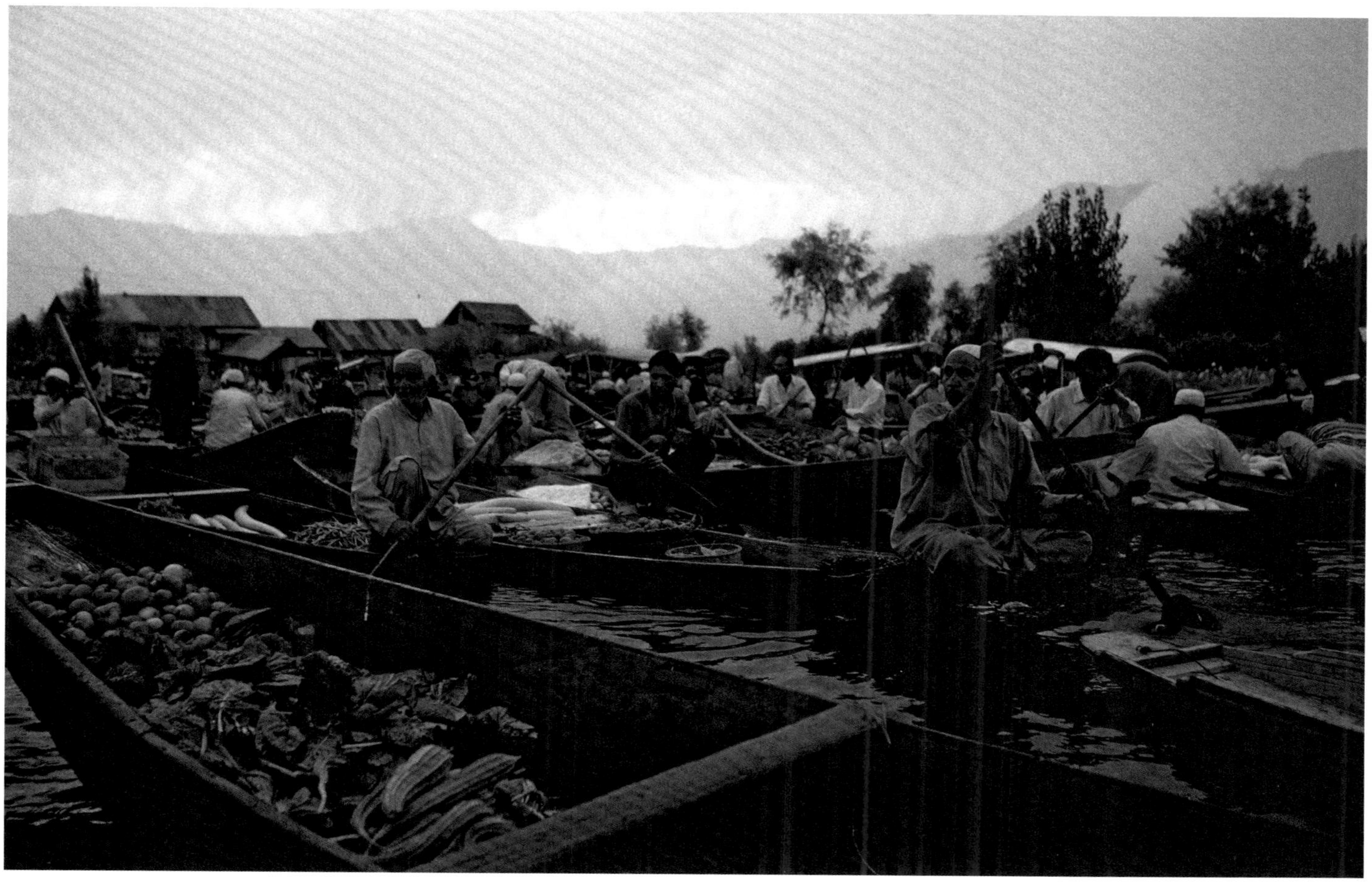

An early morning vegetable market at Dal Lake. This floating market not only sells vegetables but also meat and other items, catering to the needs of the large number of people living on the Dal in houseboats

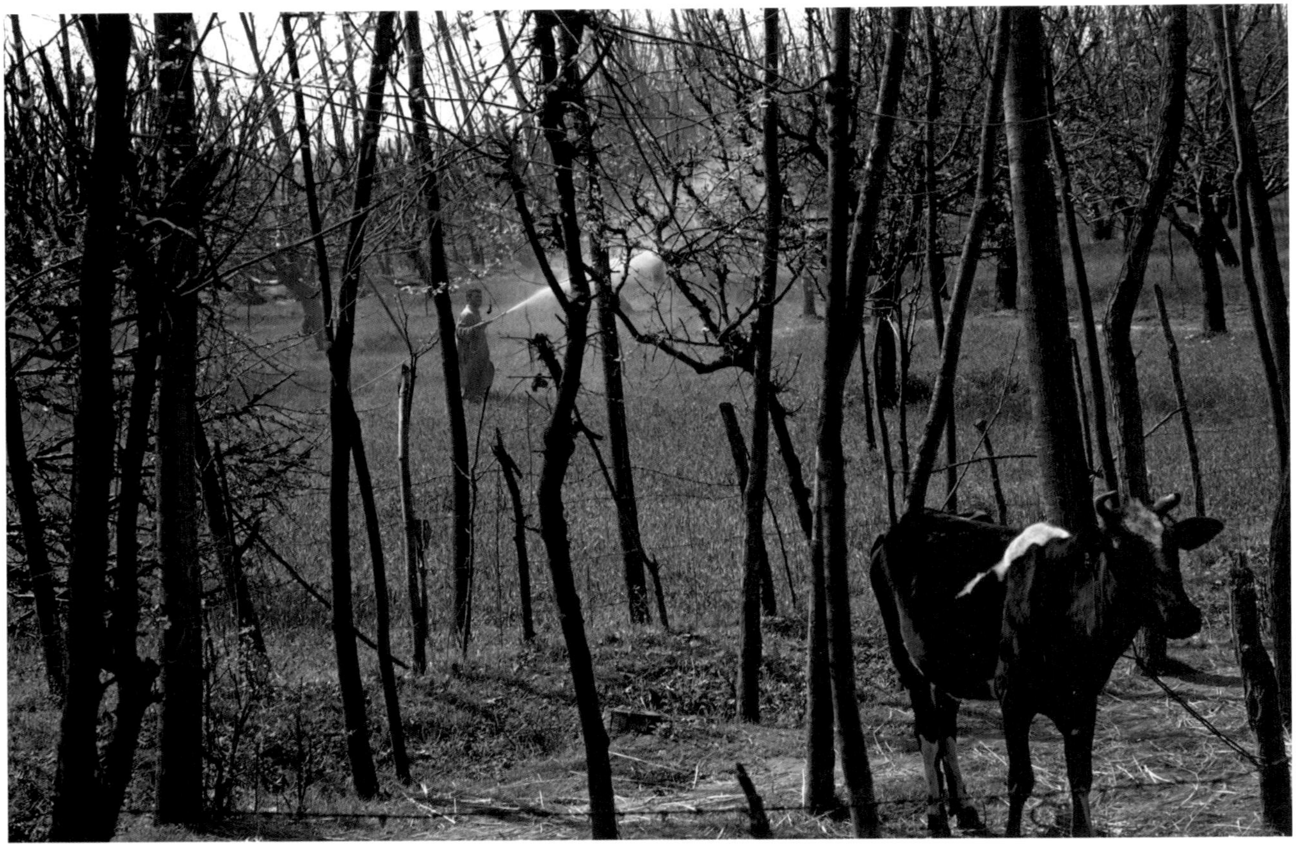

Cattle grazing among the poplar trees in the hinterland

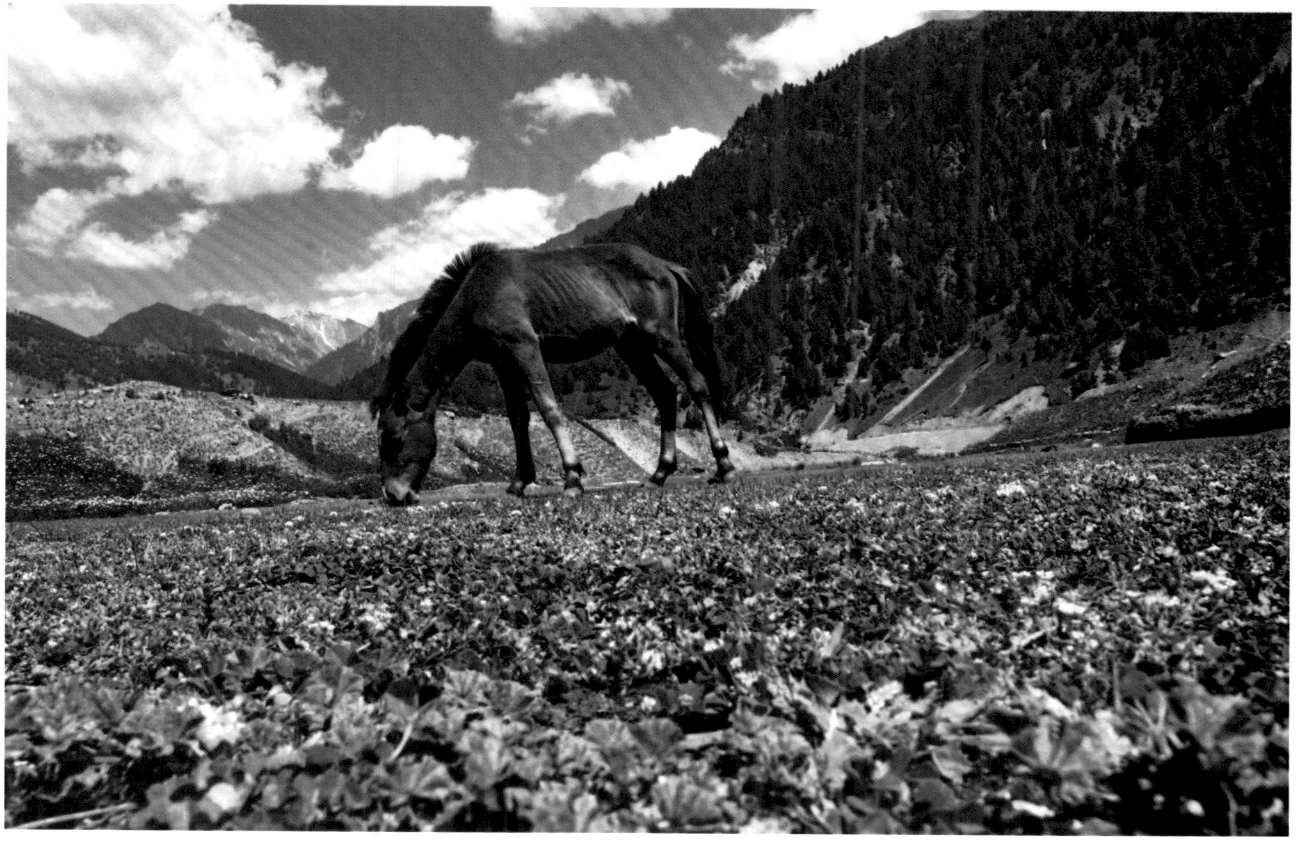

A horse grazing in the meadows in Sonamarg famous for the glacier which attracts lots of tourists

Mustard fields bordering the villages along the LOC

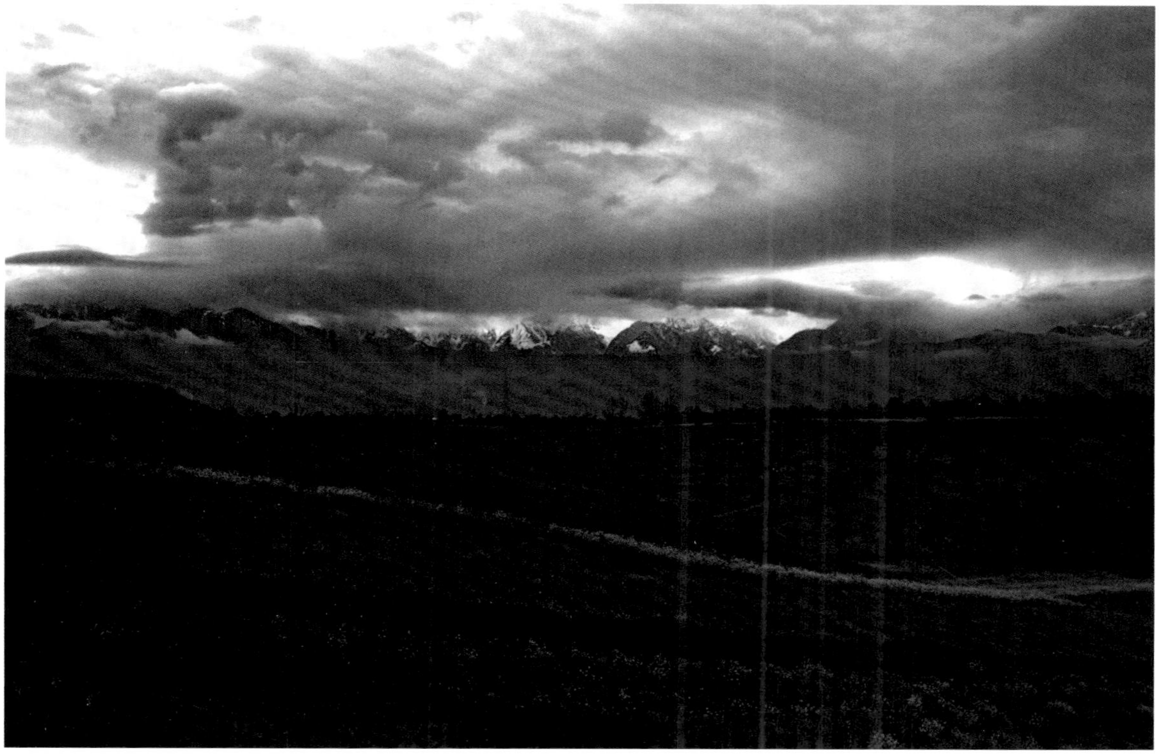

The green meadows and the hills at Ananatnag

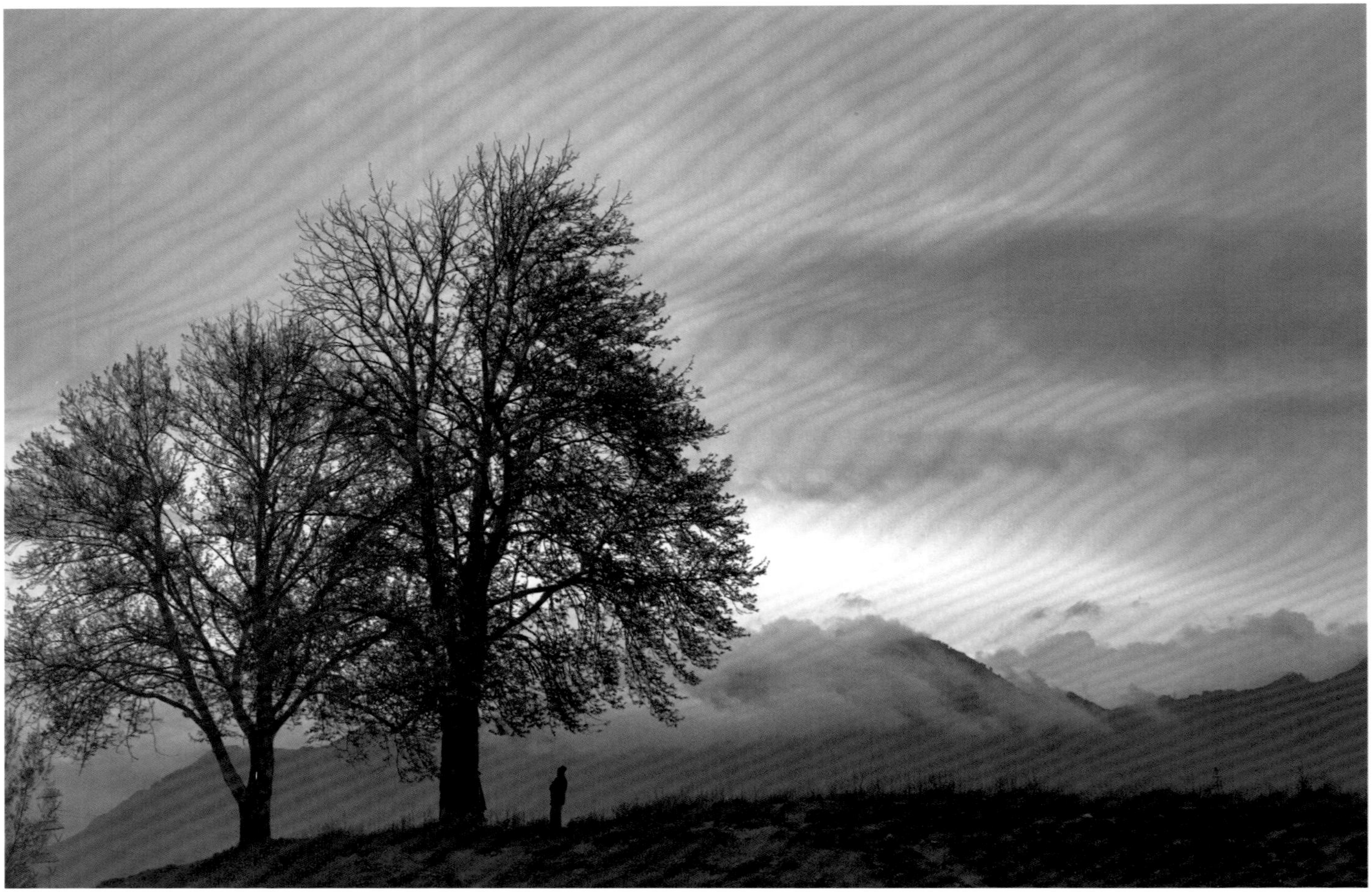

Pahalgam, famous for River Liedder; the tall chinars add to the romance

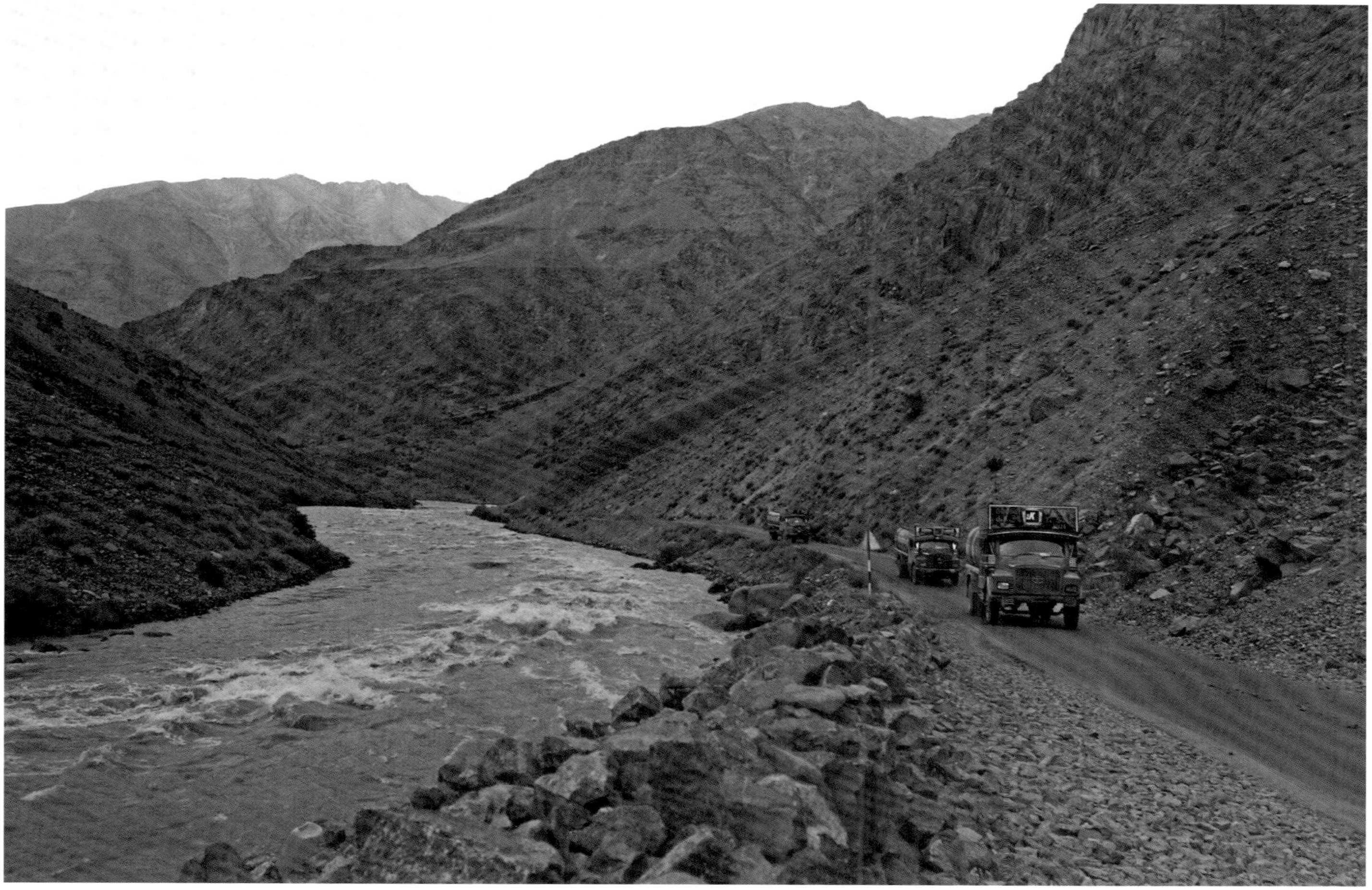

Goods move from Srinagar and other parts of India to Ladakh region through the arterial road National Highway 1A, which forms the backbone of Kashmir. Pakistan coverts these areas for strategic advantage

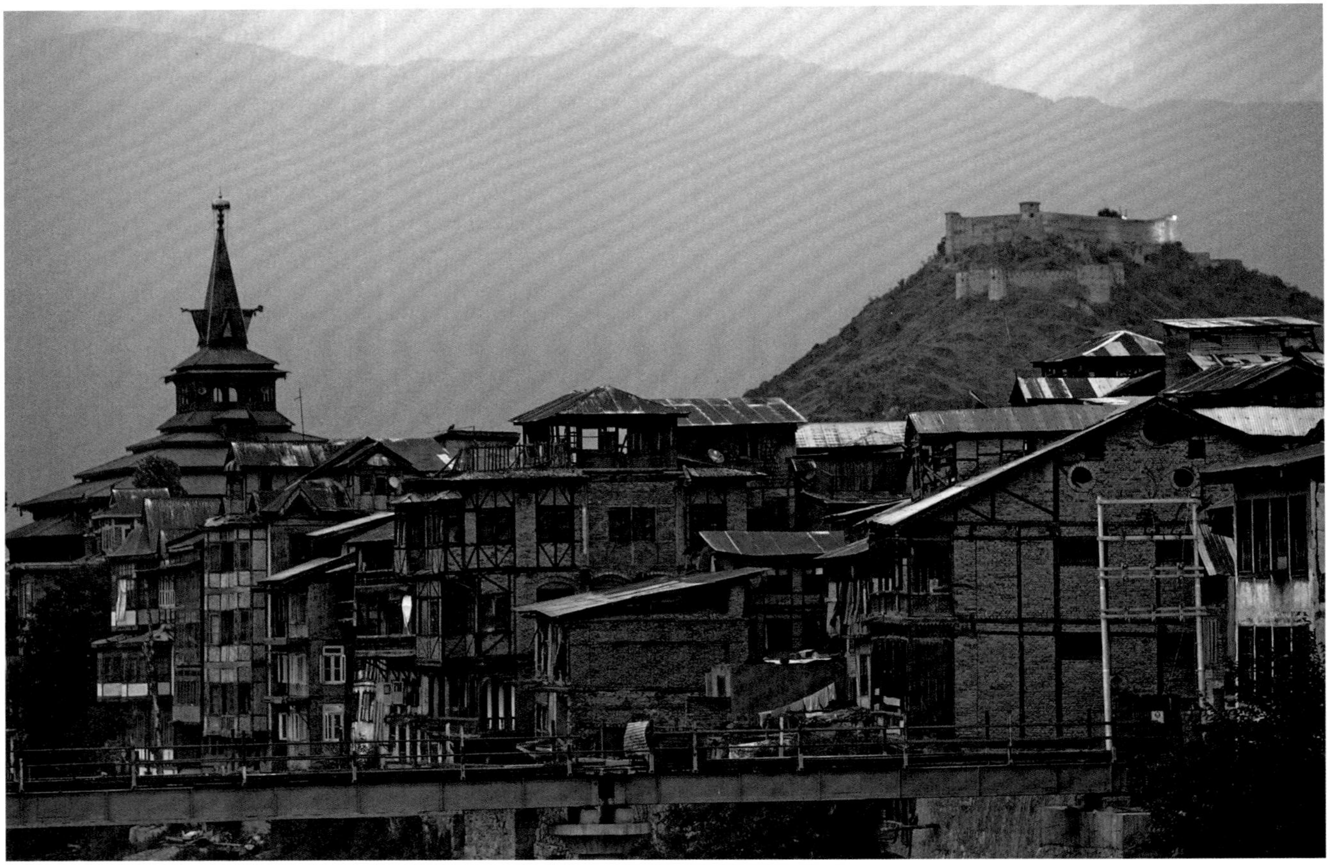

Hari Parvat, as seen from Amira Kadal in Srinagar

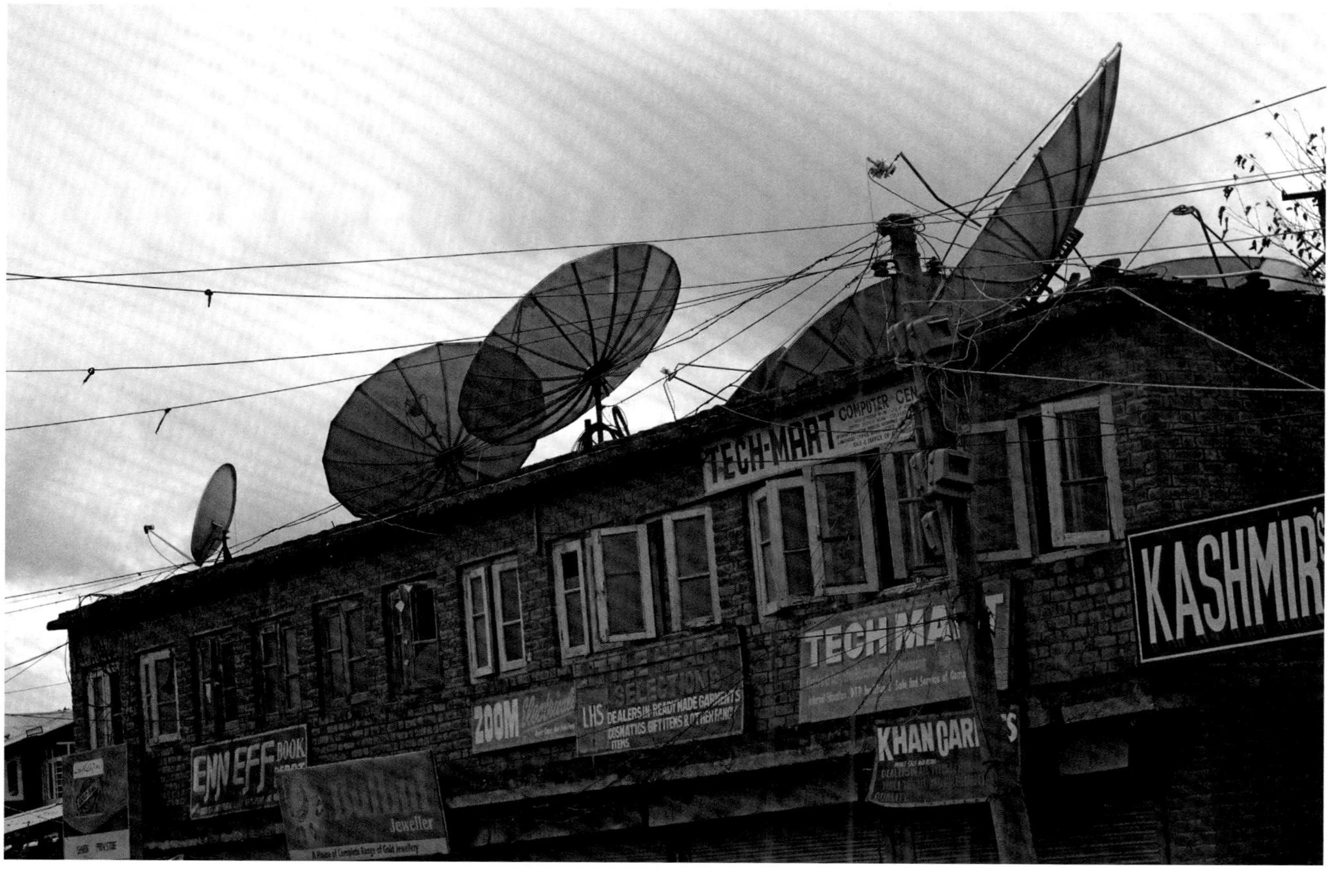

Cable television operators carrying on business out of old buildings, in Srinagar

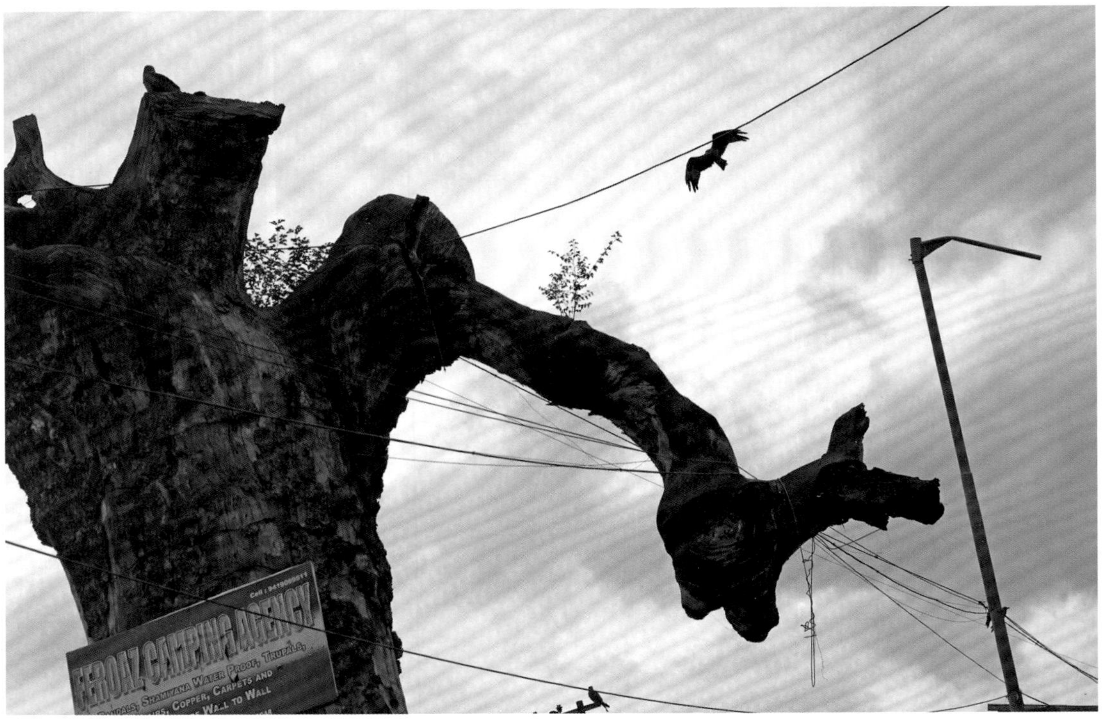

In Kashmir in the winters the trees shed their leaves, but dead trees are not common in Kashmir

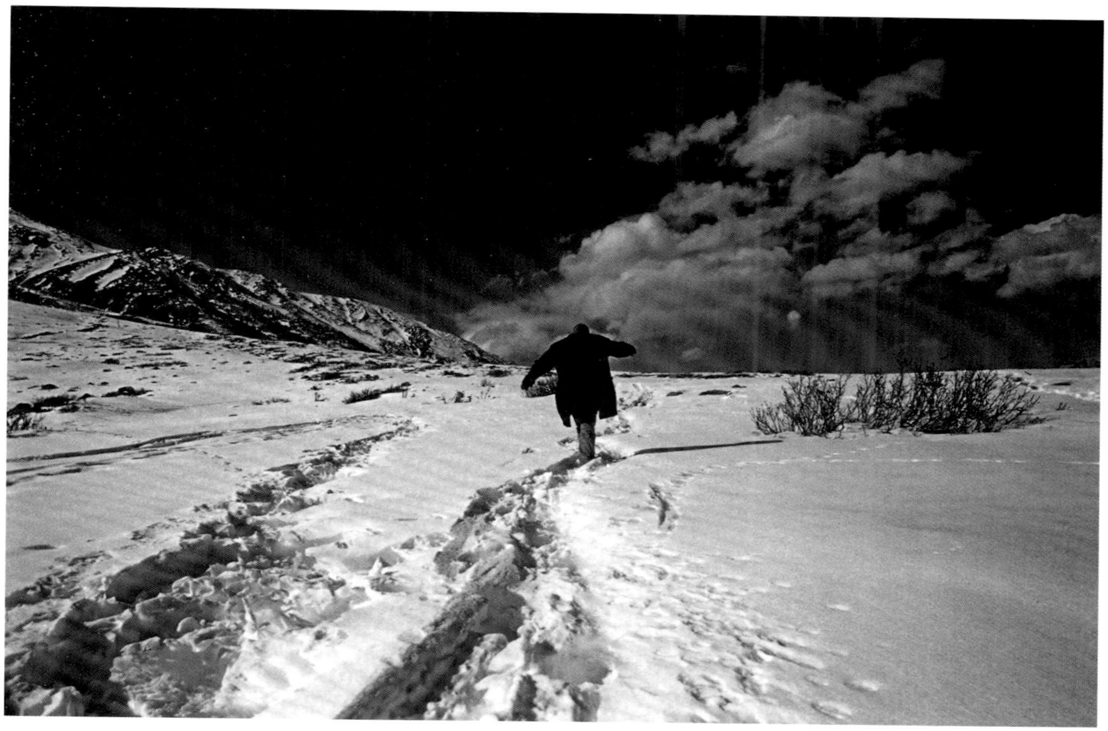

Gulmarg, Khilonmarg, Tangmarg and many parts of Srinagar receive heavy snowfall in the w nters. A local tries to negotiate the snow-clad meadows in Gulmarg

Sunrise over Jhelum

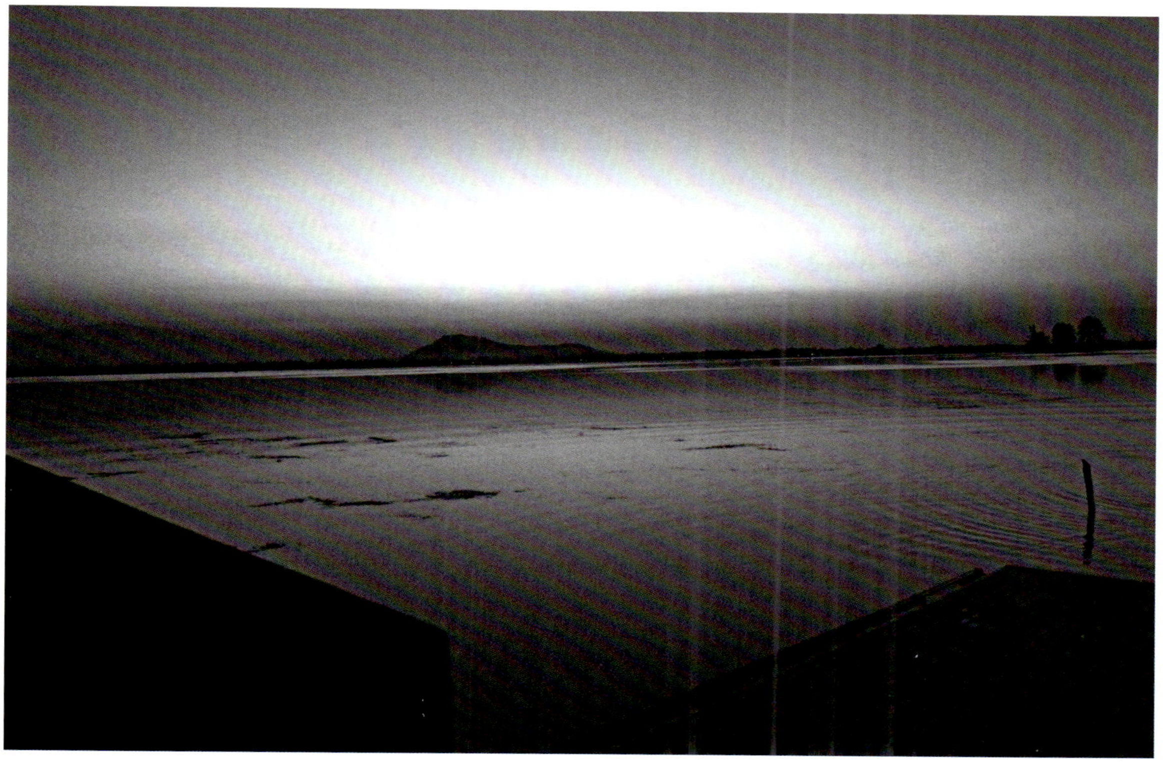

Sunset at Dal Lake

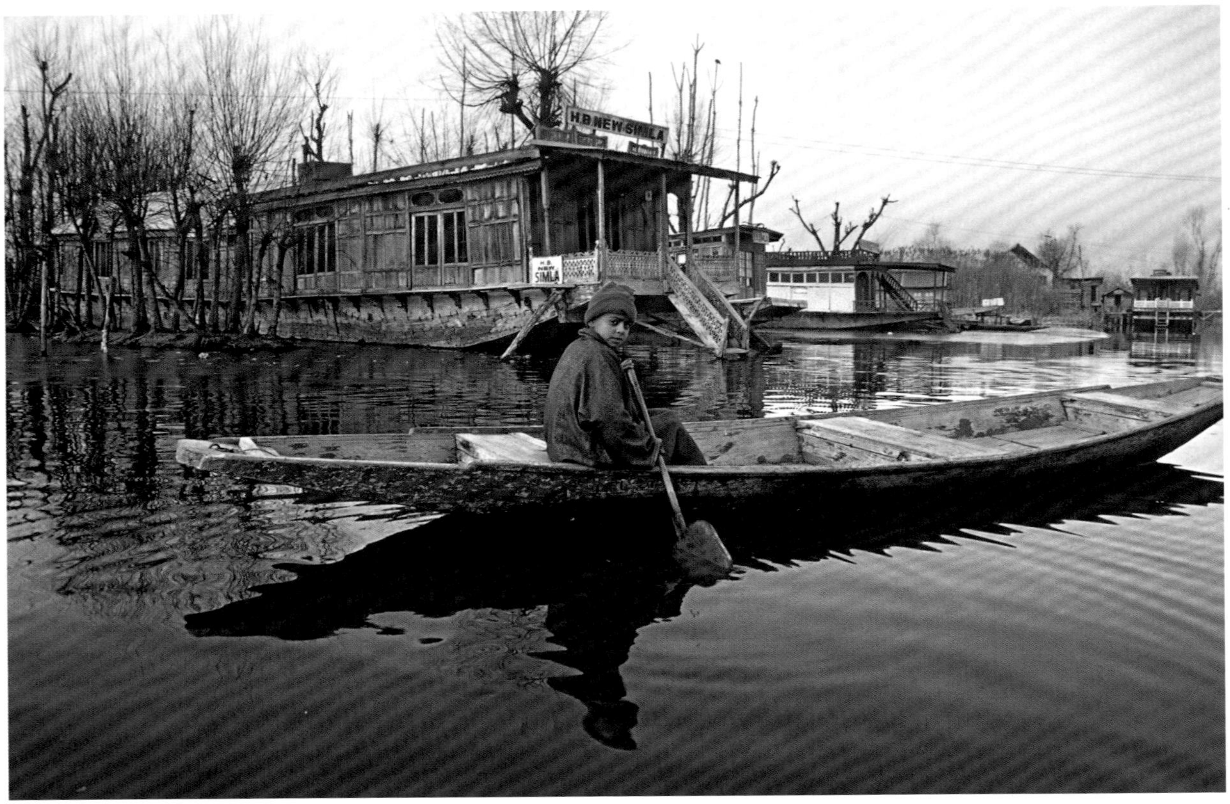

A young boy rows a shikara, wearing a pheran (local over-garment) on a chilly winter morning. For the houseboat dwellers their only conveyance on the Dal Lake are the shikaras

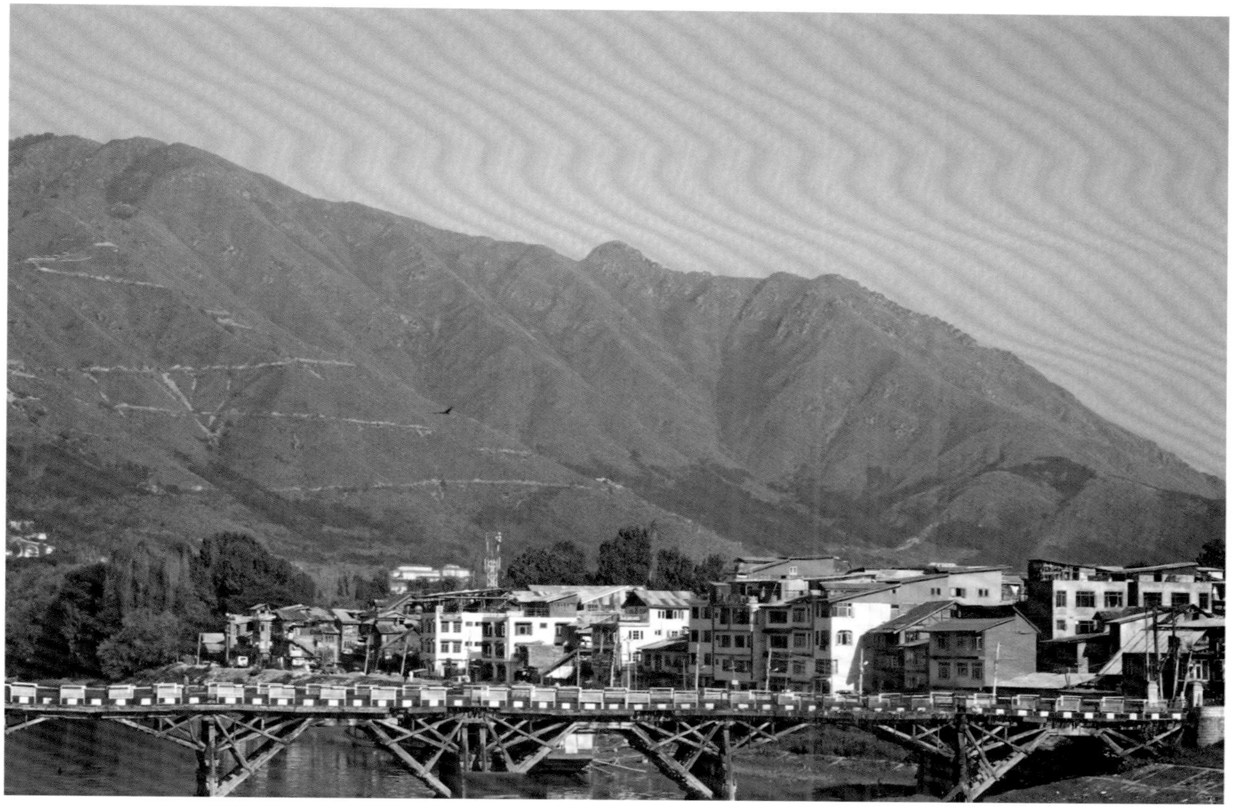

The old wooden foot bridge over the Jhelum

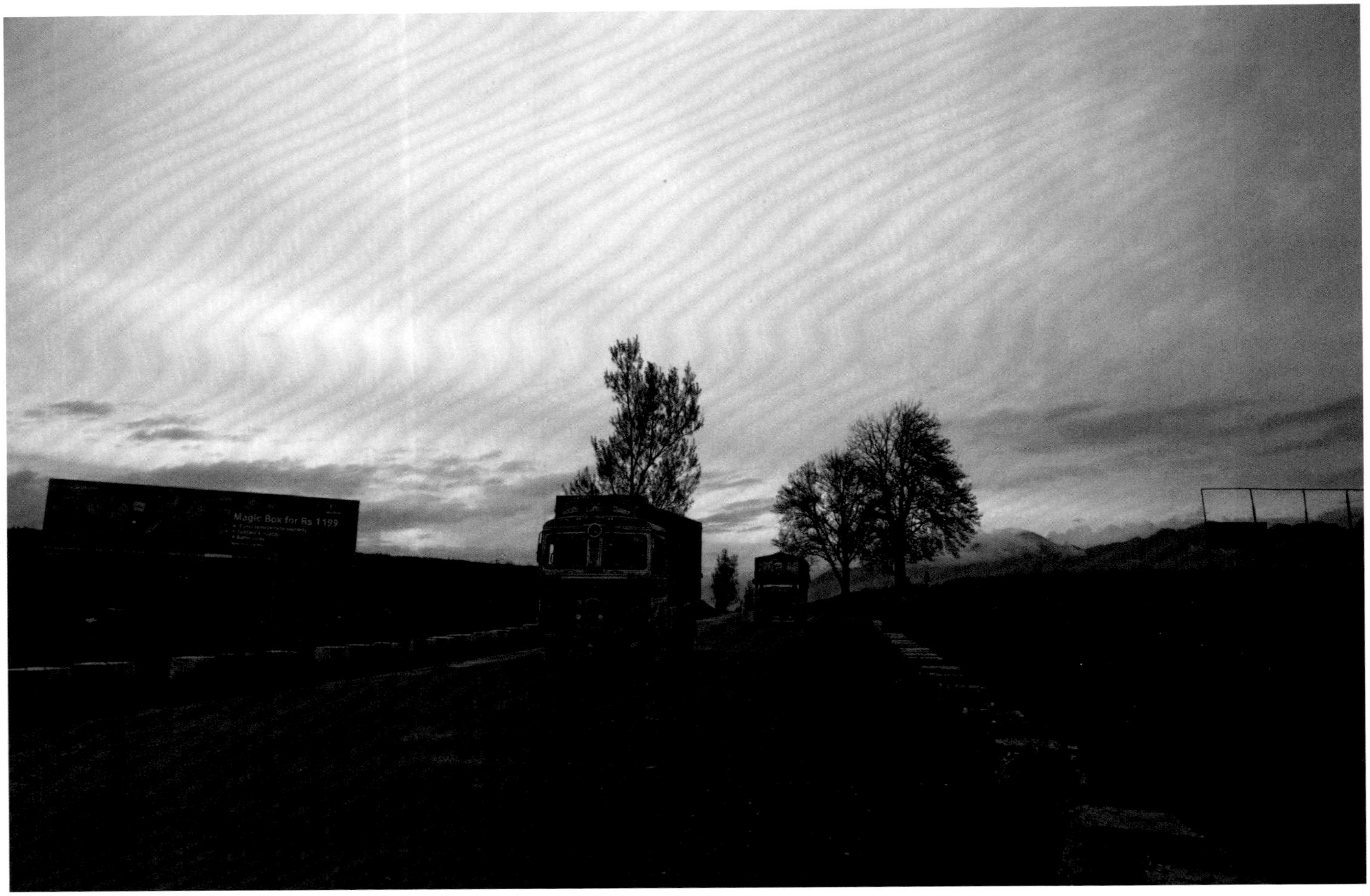

Trucks carry food and essential items to Kashmir through the National Highway 1A, after crossing the Banihal tunnel or Jawahar Tunnel, the gateway to the Valley

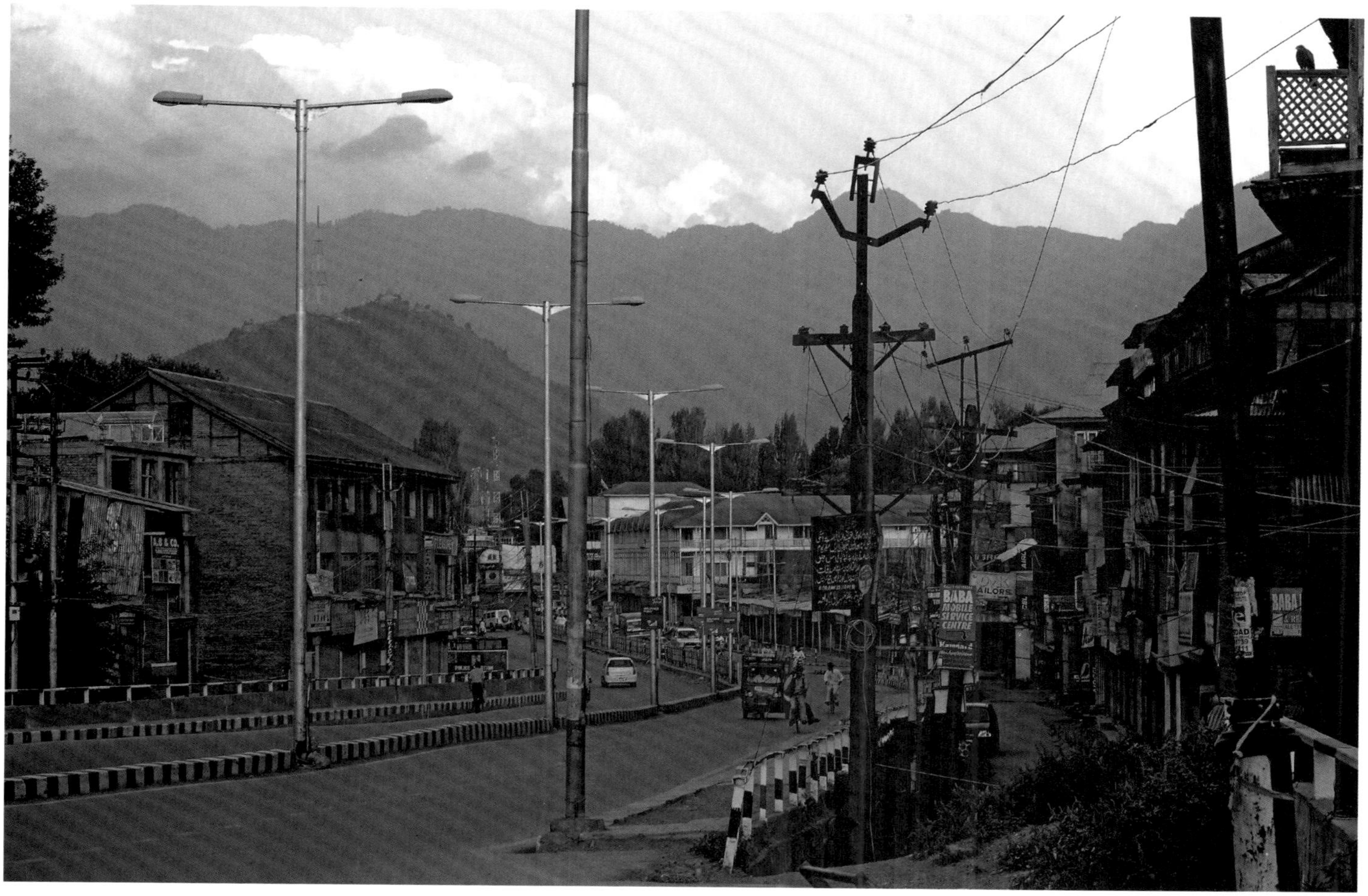

Uptown Srinagar waking up to a seemingly calm and quiet day with no protests in sight

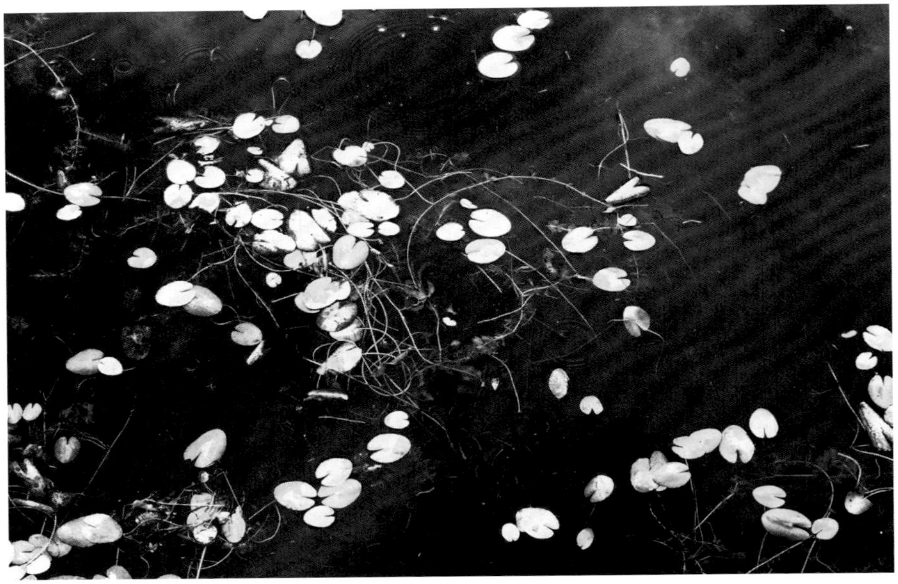

Lotus shoots

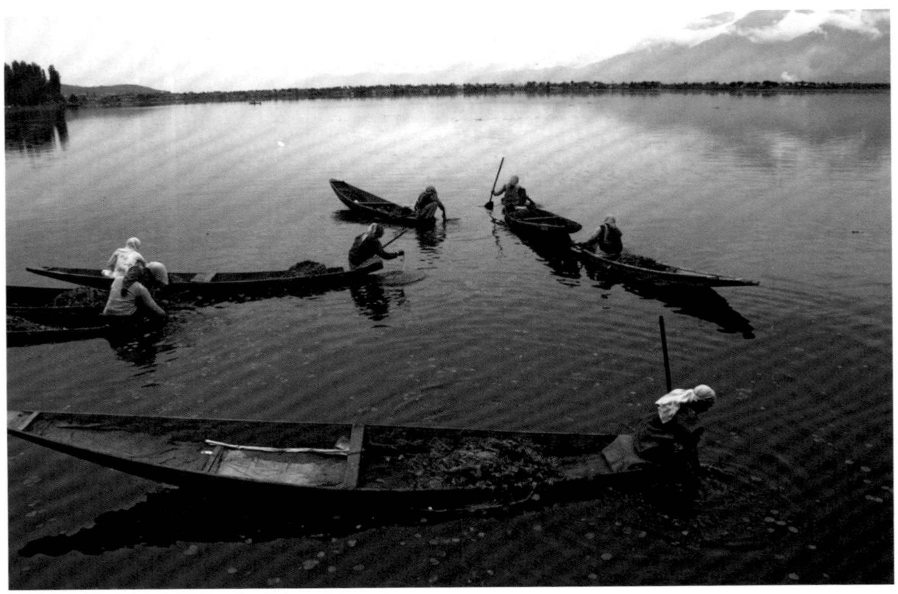

Kashmiri women collecting lotus shoots and stems, popularly known as 'nadru', from the Dal Lake

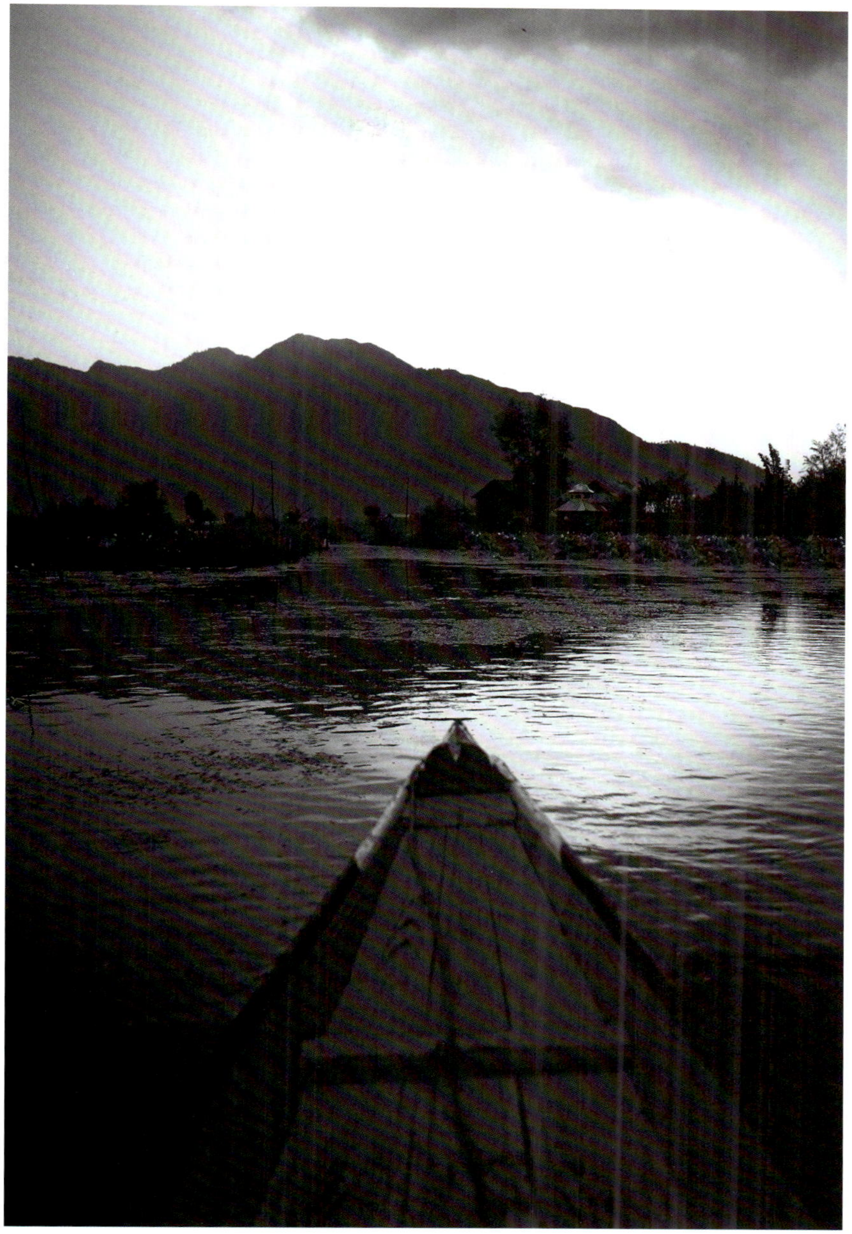

Early morning at Dal Lake along the Zabarwan hills

PEOPLE

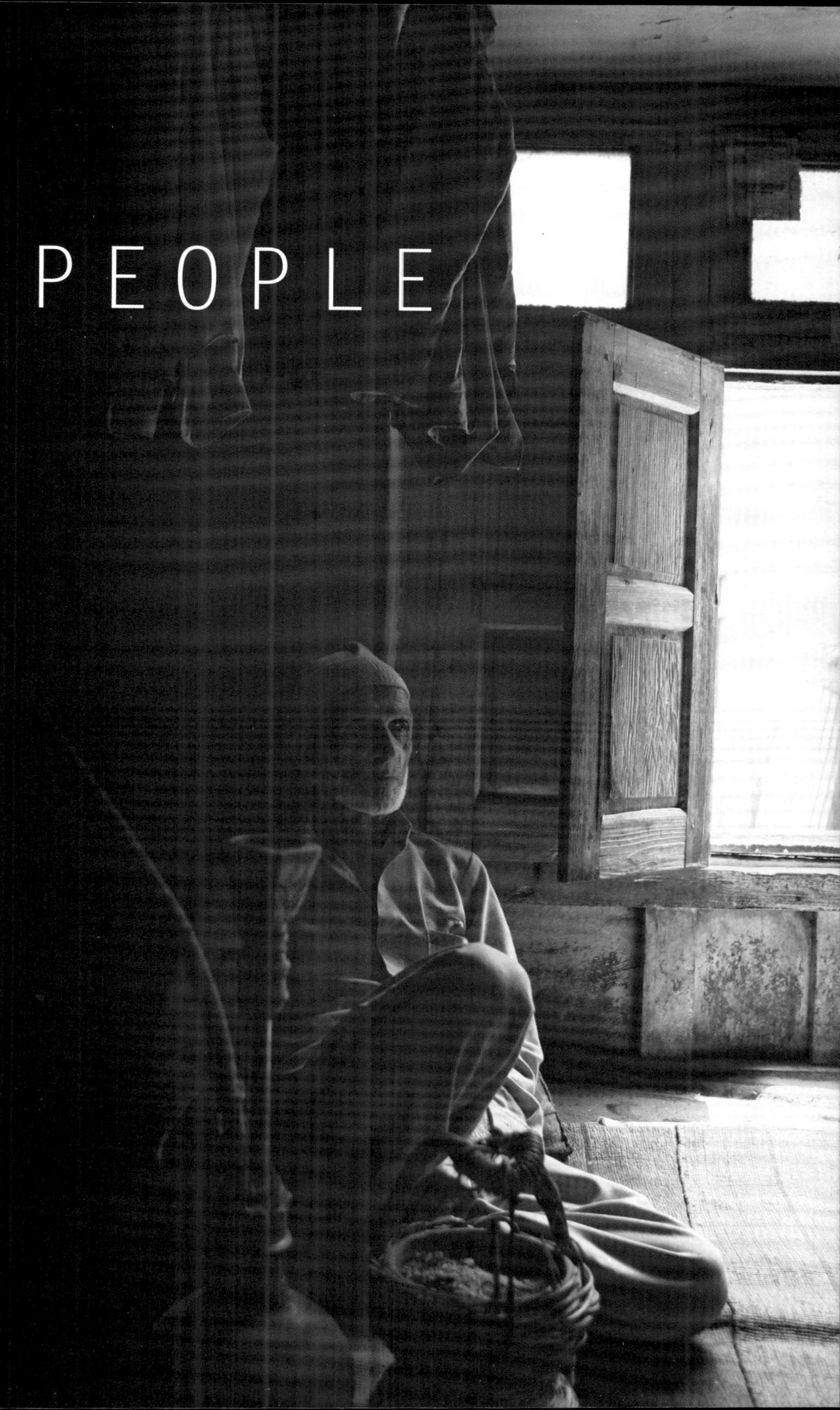

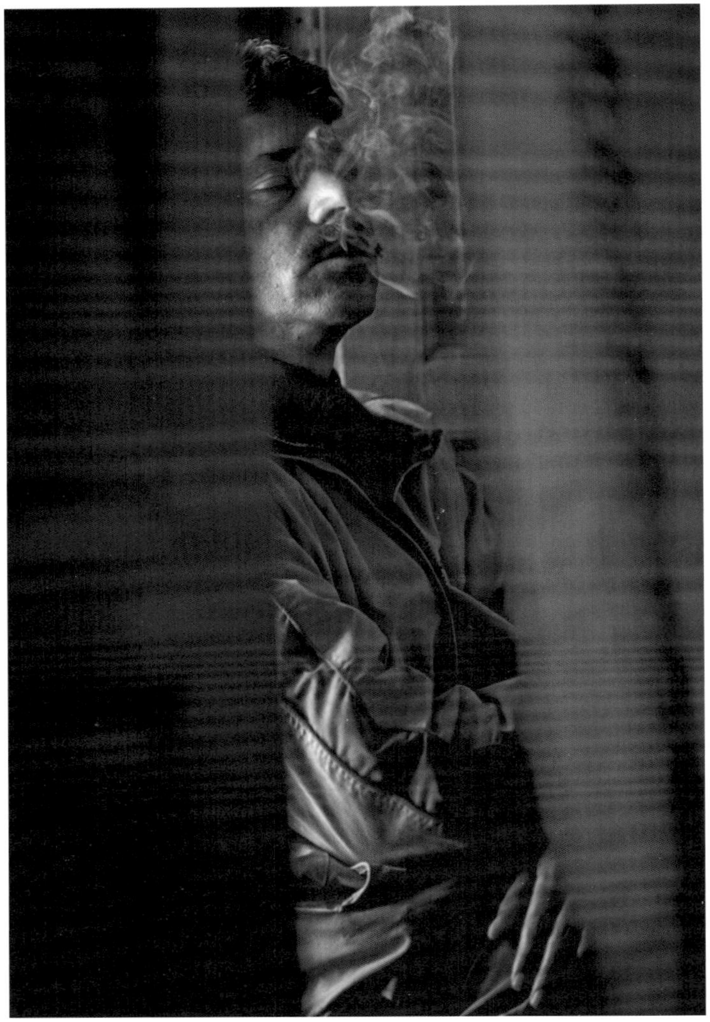

Tantre, a young businessman from Bomai, suffers from hyperglycaemia, hypertension and anxiety. His brother was gunned down by the Indian Army on suspicion of being a militant. He has not got over the loss

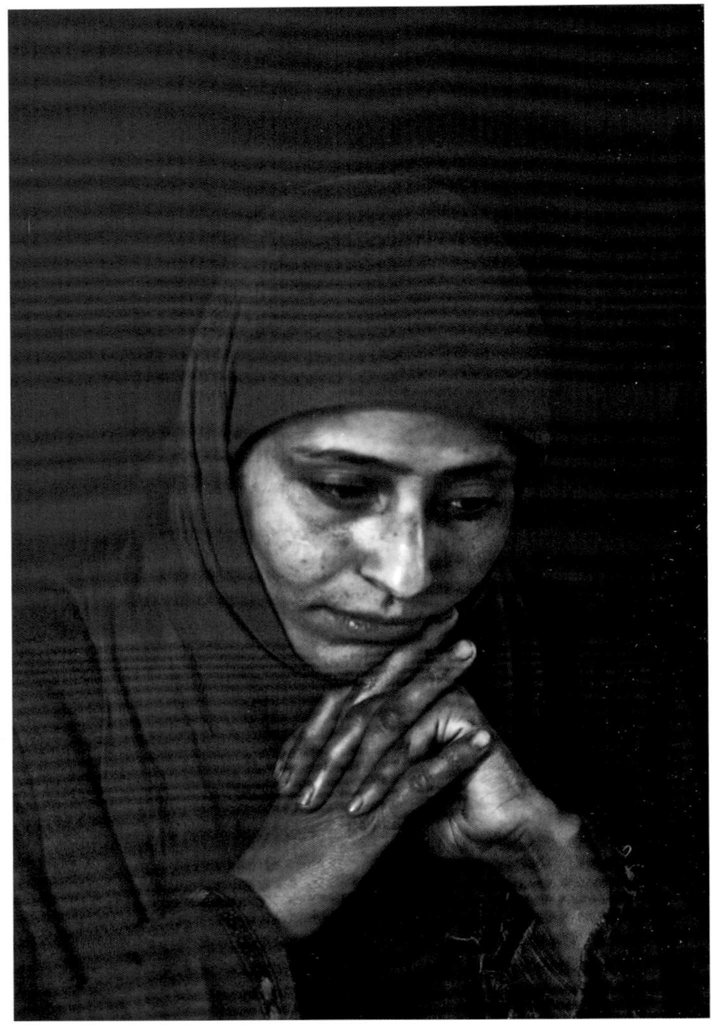

One of Tantrey's sisters, still in mourning

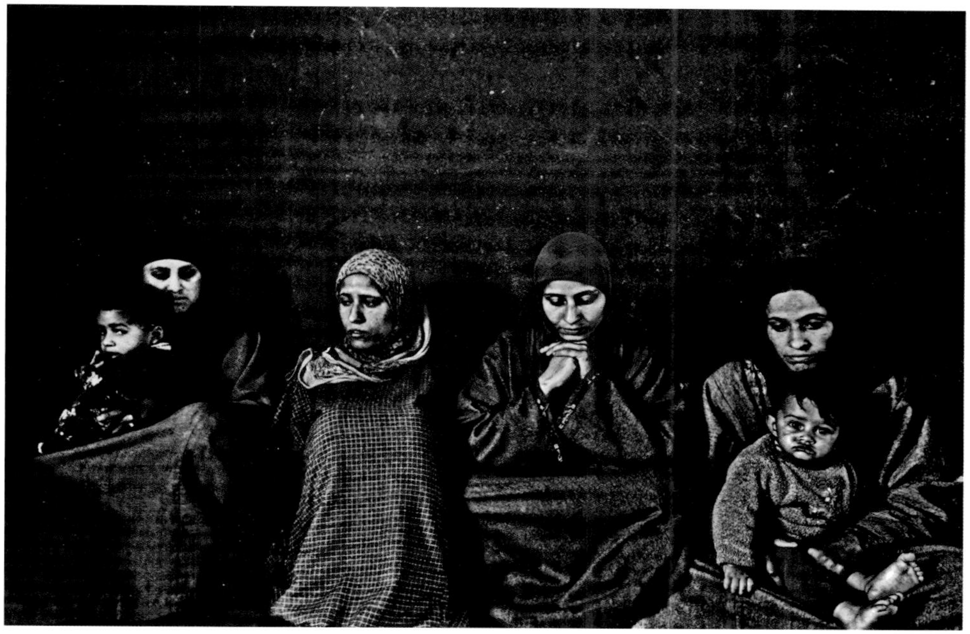

Smell of death lingers in the air as Tantrey's family mourns the death of a beloved at their home in Sopore. This is a hub of militancy with stray encounters between the terrorists and the security forces claiming many an innocent life

PAGE 101: This man, Md, was nine when the Pakistani raiders attacked the Valley in the autumn of 1947. He remembers gun shots, shouts and the sleepless nights and days. The raiders looted and plundered and the village watched silently. No army from the Maharaja or the Indian government came to save them. But today he lives amidst other atrocities

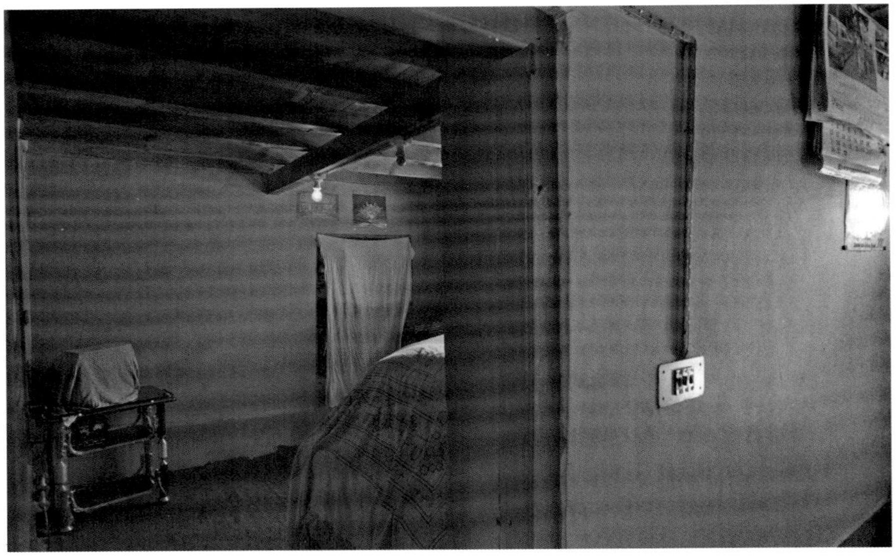

The room of deceased Md Amin Tantrey (aged 17). In 2009, Tantrey was caught in a crossfire, based on a wrong information provided to the security forces. He and his friend Javed Ahmad were killed by the soldiers of 22nd Rashtrya Rifles deployed there

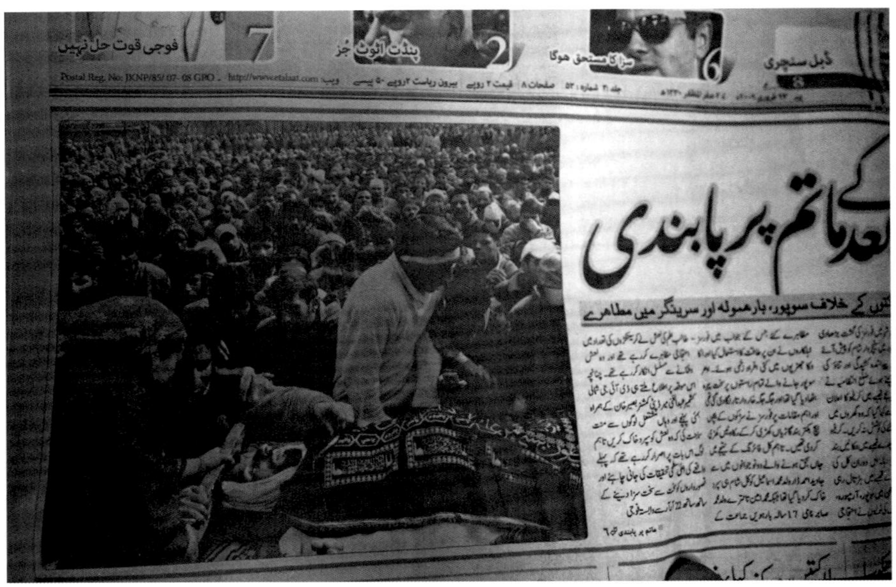

Md Amiin Tantrey's funeral procession story in the local paper

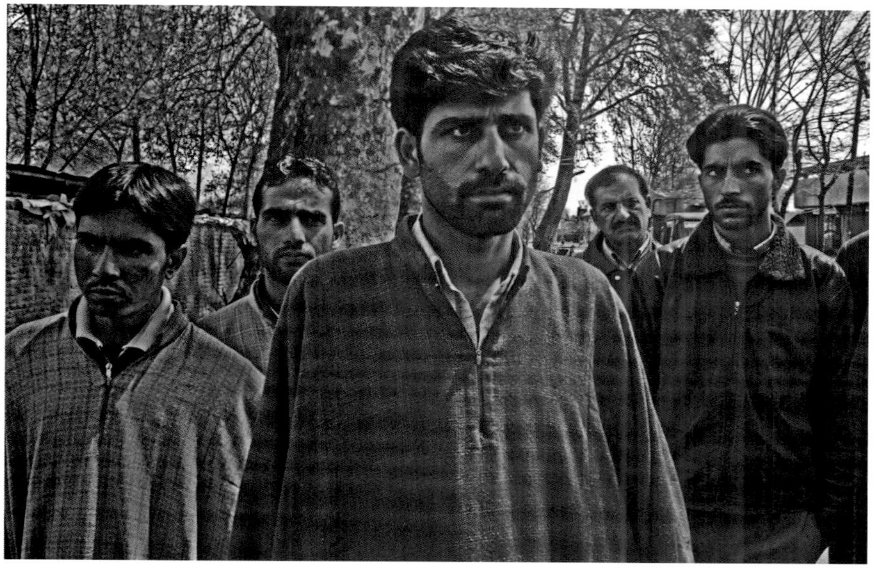

Angry faces after an encounter between the terrorists and the Rashtrya Rifles in Bomai in the summer of 2009, before the general elections in India

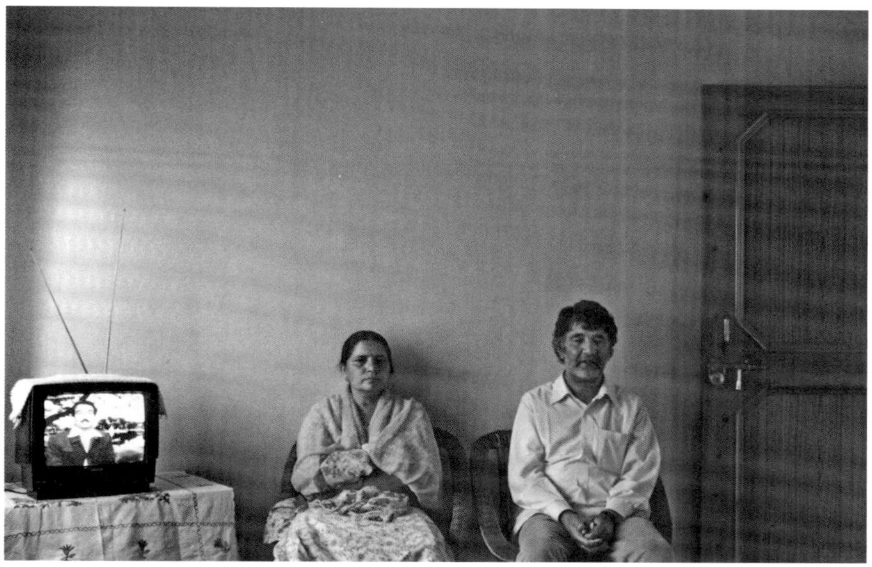

Roshan Sharma and his wife live in the heart of Srinagar. Roshan has lived through the bad days of militancy with exhortation, threats and persecution. He and a few other Hindus stay in Abi Guzar gated colony along the Jhelum bund

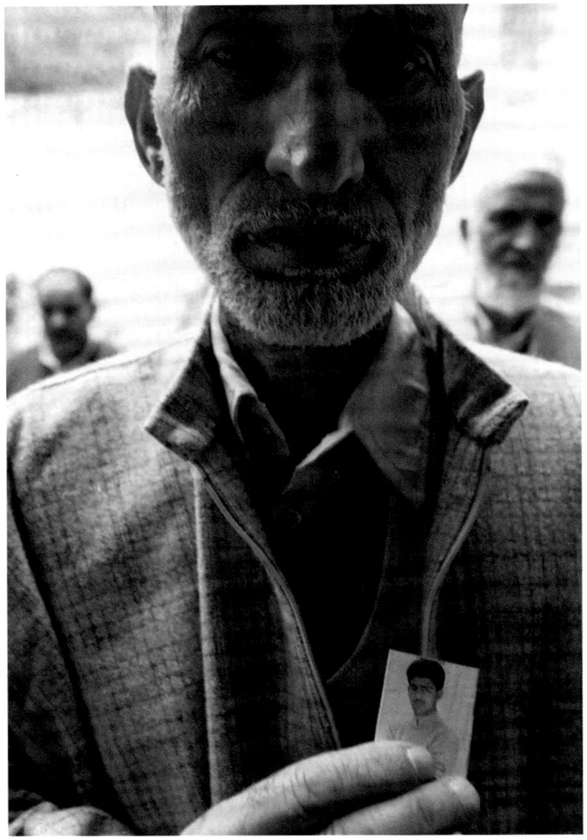

Javed was back from a trip to Jammu. He was a driver and he operated his SUV between Jammu and Srinagar. One day, when he had taken his two-year-old nephew to get some stationary he was killed in the police firing trying to quell a violent mob. His grandfather poses with his image, which says ' I lost my child....' Such instances are numerous in the Valley

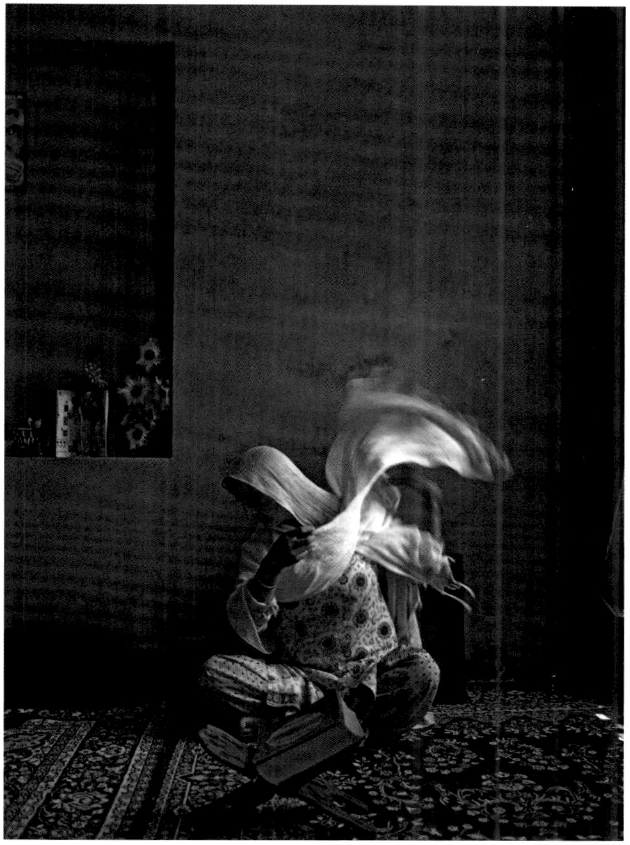

Hanifa's husband has been missing for a while and it is suspected that he may have been killed by the security forces or may have fled to Pakistan occupied Kashmir. Living in uncertainty, she spends her time alone at her home in Baramulla in north Kashmir, reading the Koran and leading a religious life. These women are called half-widows

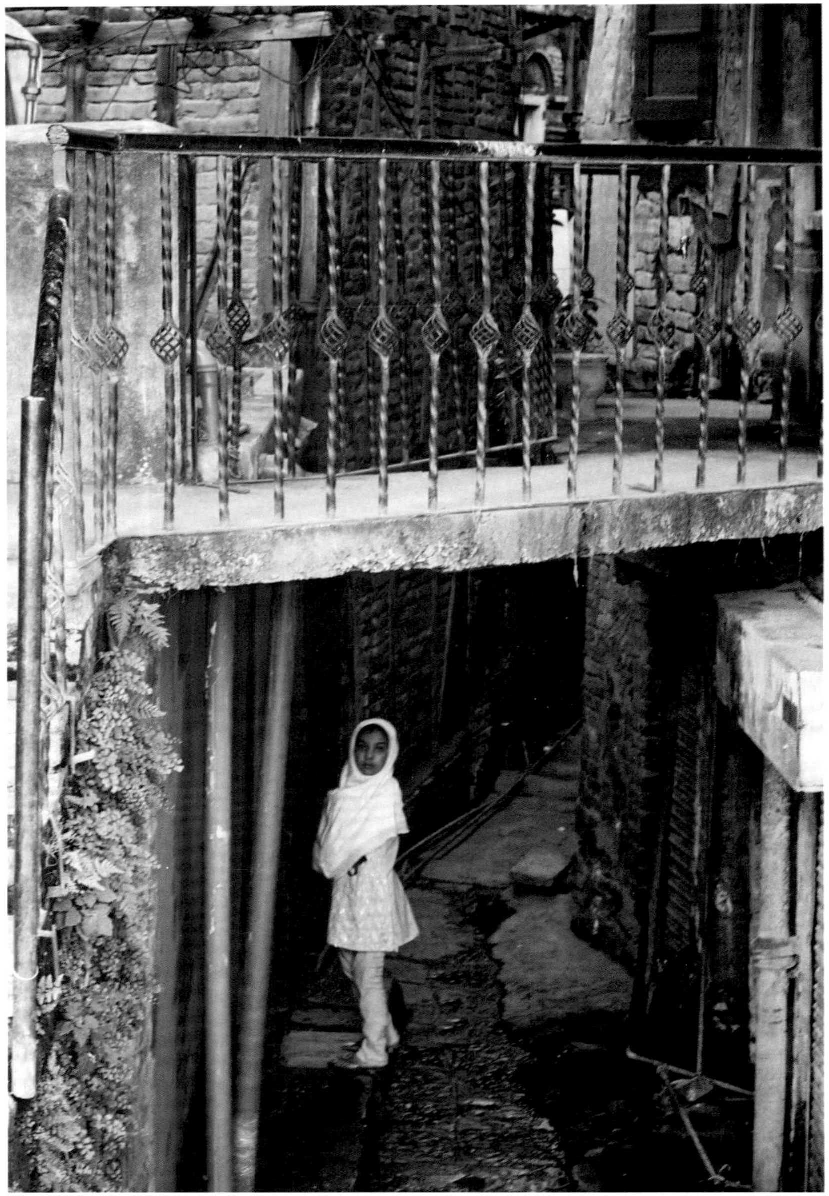

A young girl looks suspiciously at the camera. The people in the Valley are fearful of the security forces and the terrorists alike. Life of innocent civilians is very difficult, caught between the devil and the deep sea

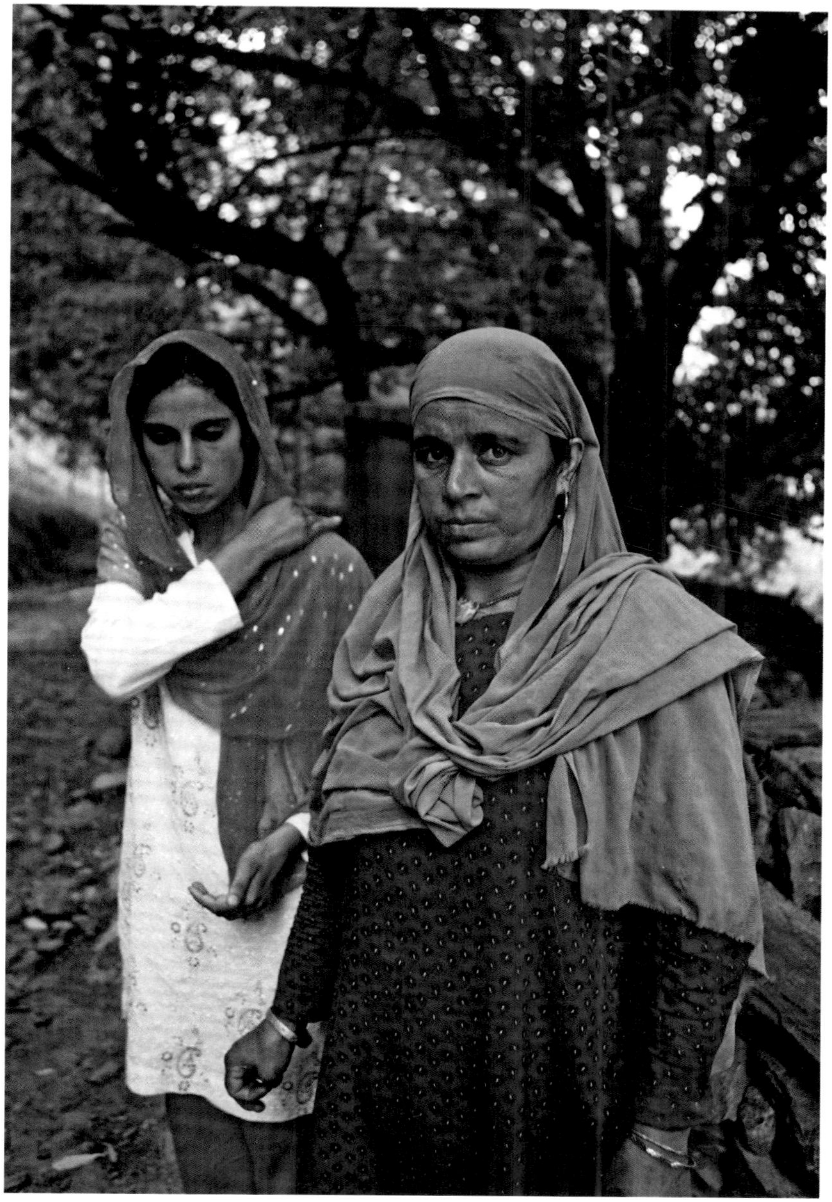

Hamida is still looking for her husband who has been missing for nearly 15 years. He too left for work and never returned. Hamida was pregnant at that time. Her daughter has not seen her father except in few photographs that this poor family preserved

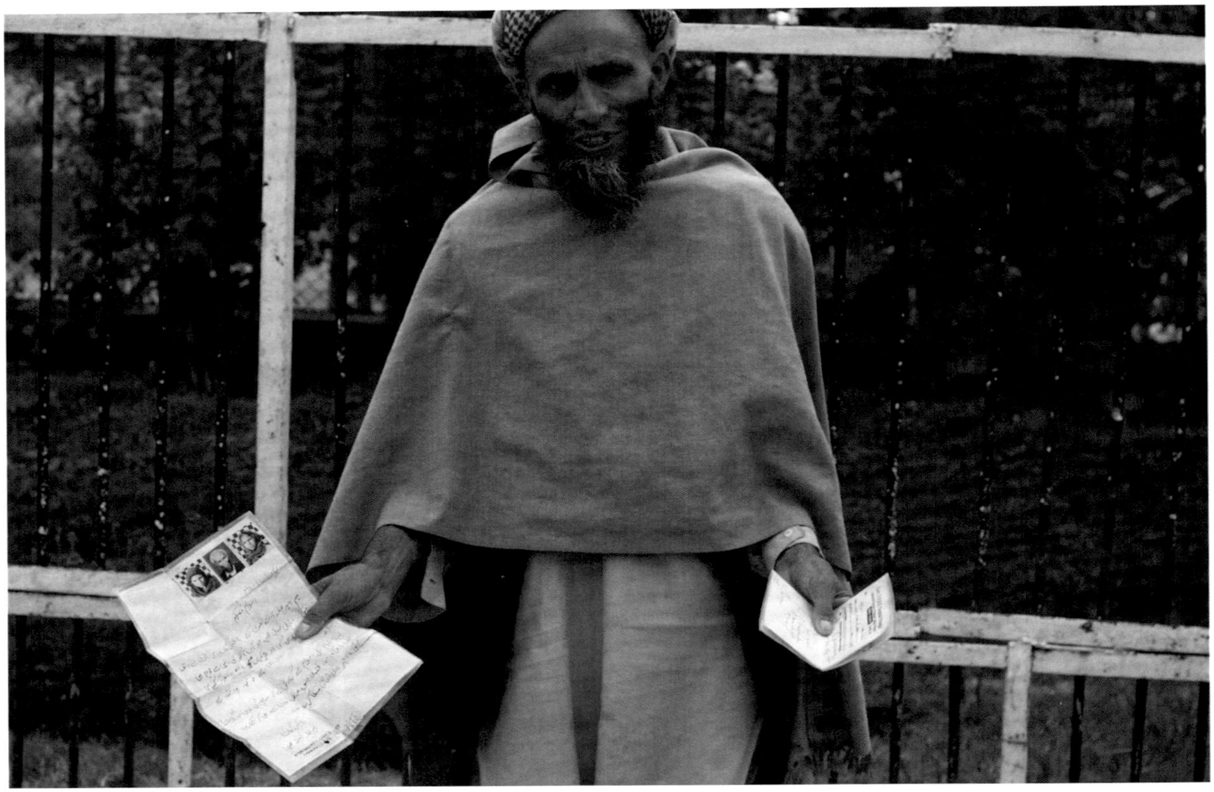

An old man, outside the city hospital in Soura, asking for donations to take care of his daughter

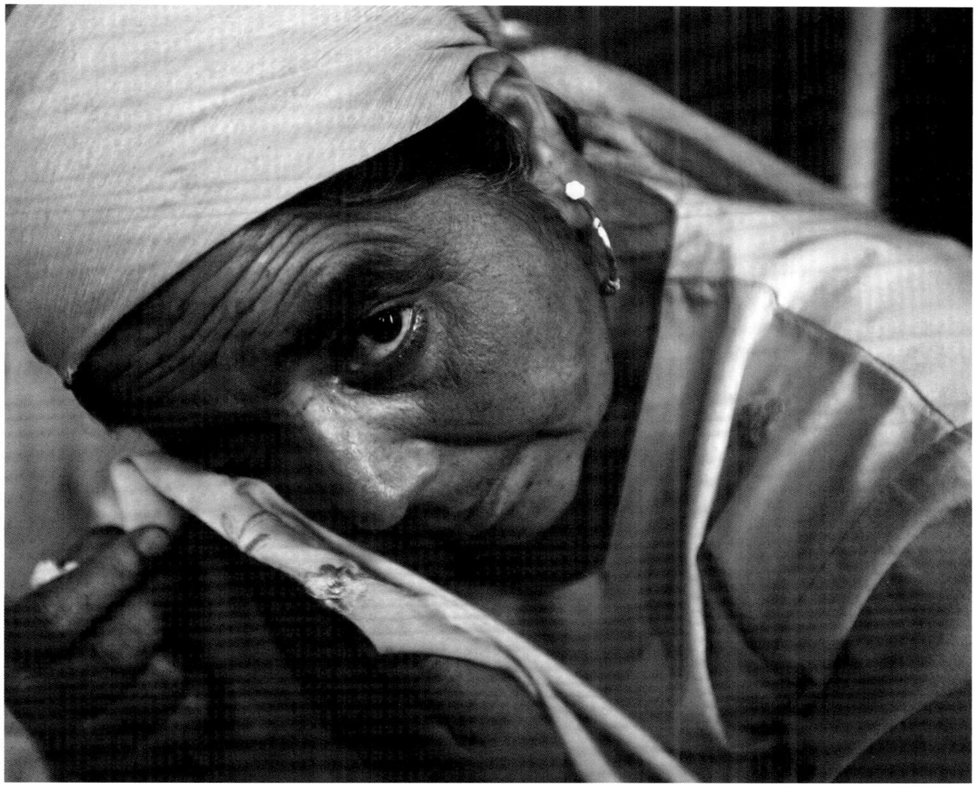

Atiqa is another half-widow. She is a mother of three daughters. Her husband used to work for the State Electricity Board as a linesman. One night, in the year 1994, some men in army fatigues took him for questioning. He has not been seen since then. Neither his body has been recovered nor has he been found in any of the Indian prisons. Atiqa's daughters are in their teens and have grown up without a male member in the family. There are around 10,000 such men missing from the Valley

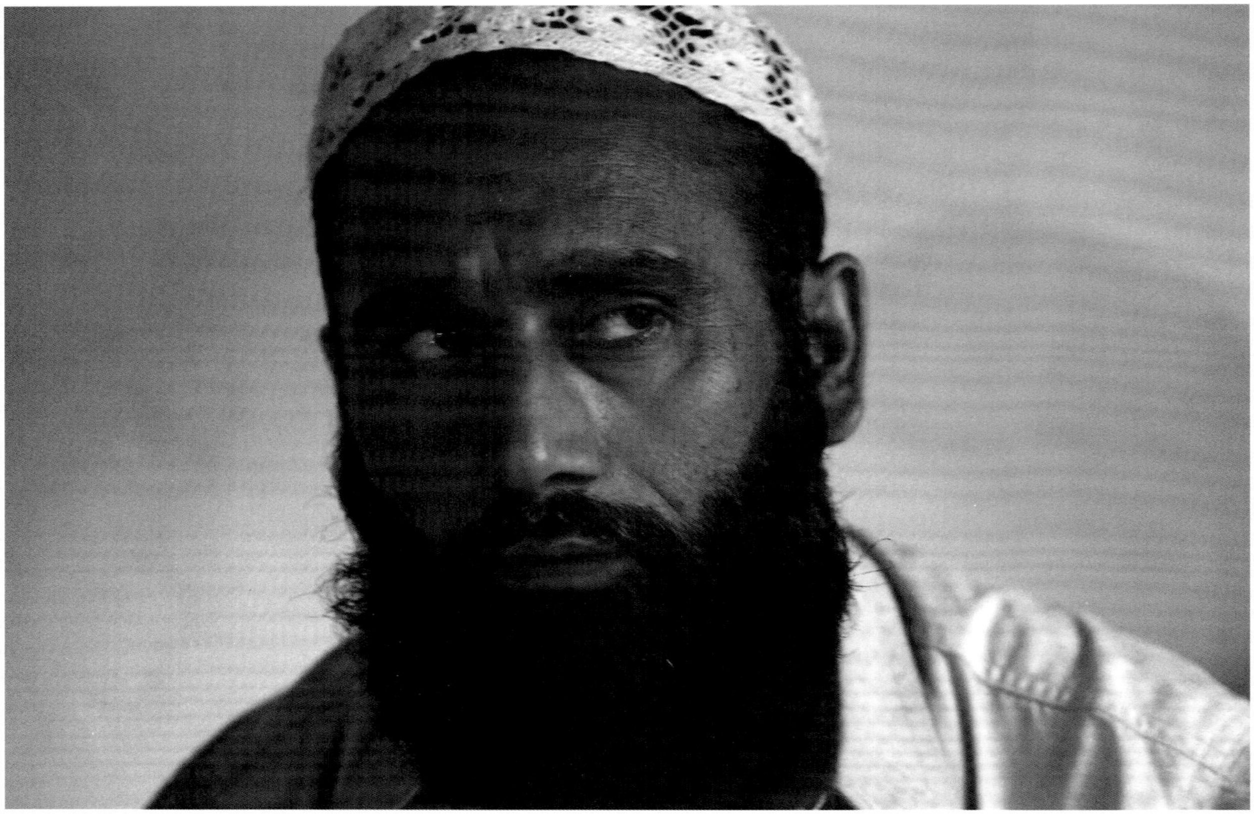

Gulam Md was the top commander of a militant outfit. He was a one of the militants released in exchange of the Indian Oil Executive Director, K. Doraiswamy. Today semi-immobile, due to the torture faced at the jail, he lives in Sopore under the strict vigilance of army and local police

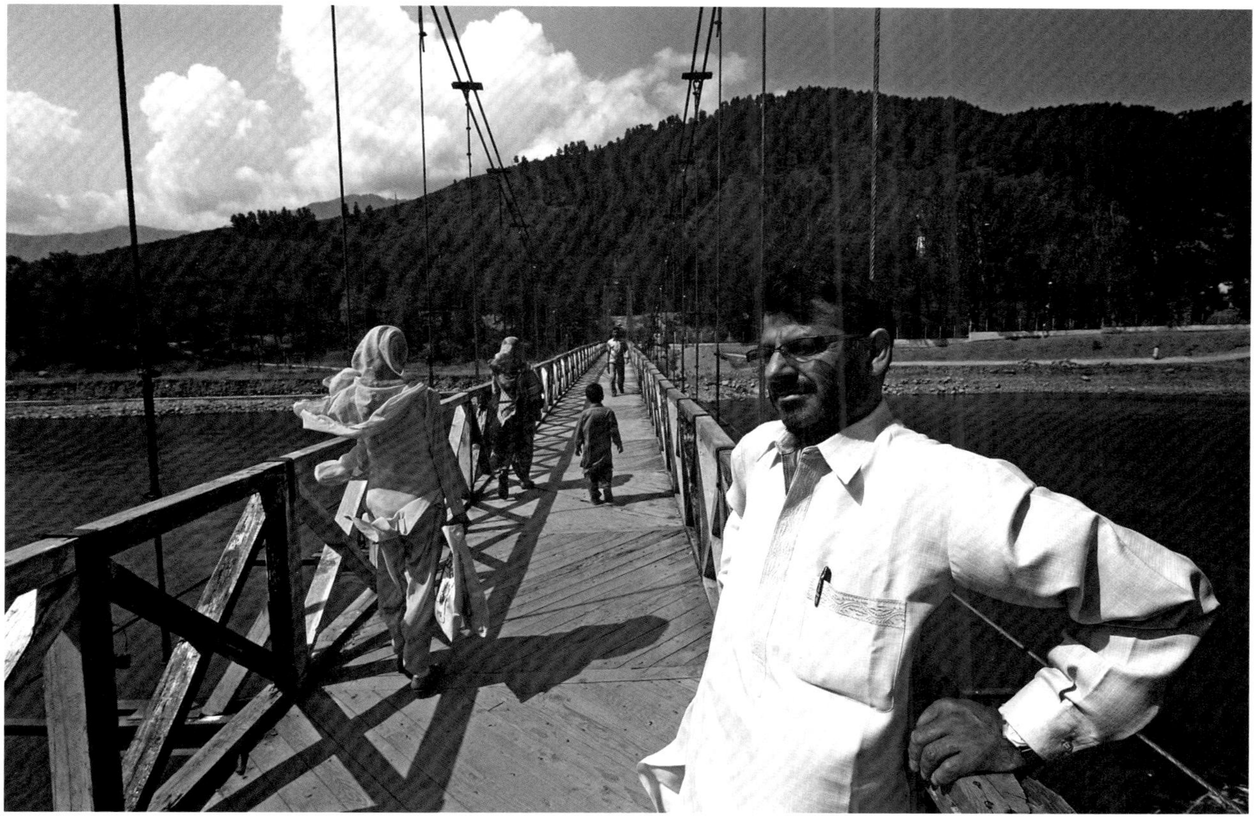

An ex-militant poses for a picture. Bhatt was with a militant group called Hizbul Mujahideen (HM) with its Amir, Yusuf Shah alias Salauddin operating from Pakistan Occupied Kashmir (POK). After surrendering to the authorities Bhatt now runs a construction business, but along with other surrendered militants he has to report to the army camp every week to mark attendance, to make sure he does not stray back into militancy

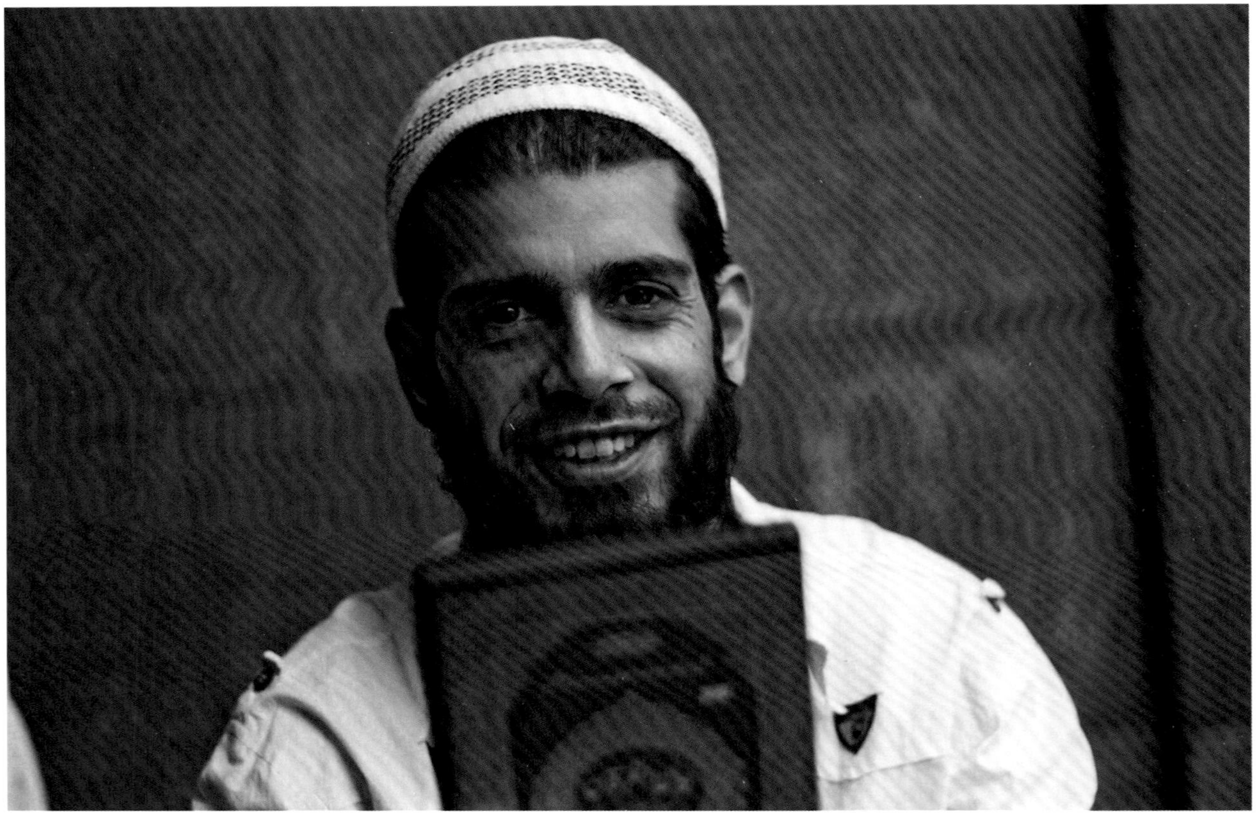

DVDs and CDs propagating Islamic ideology being sold in downtown Srinagar

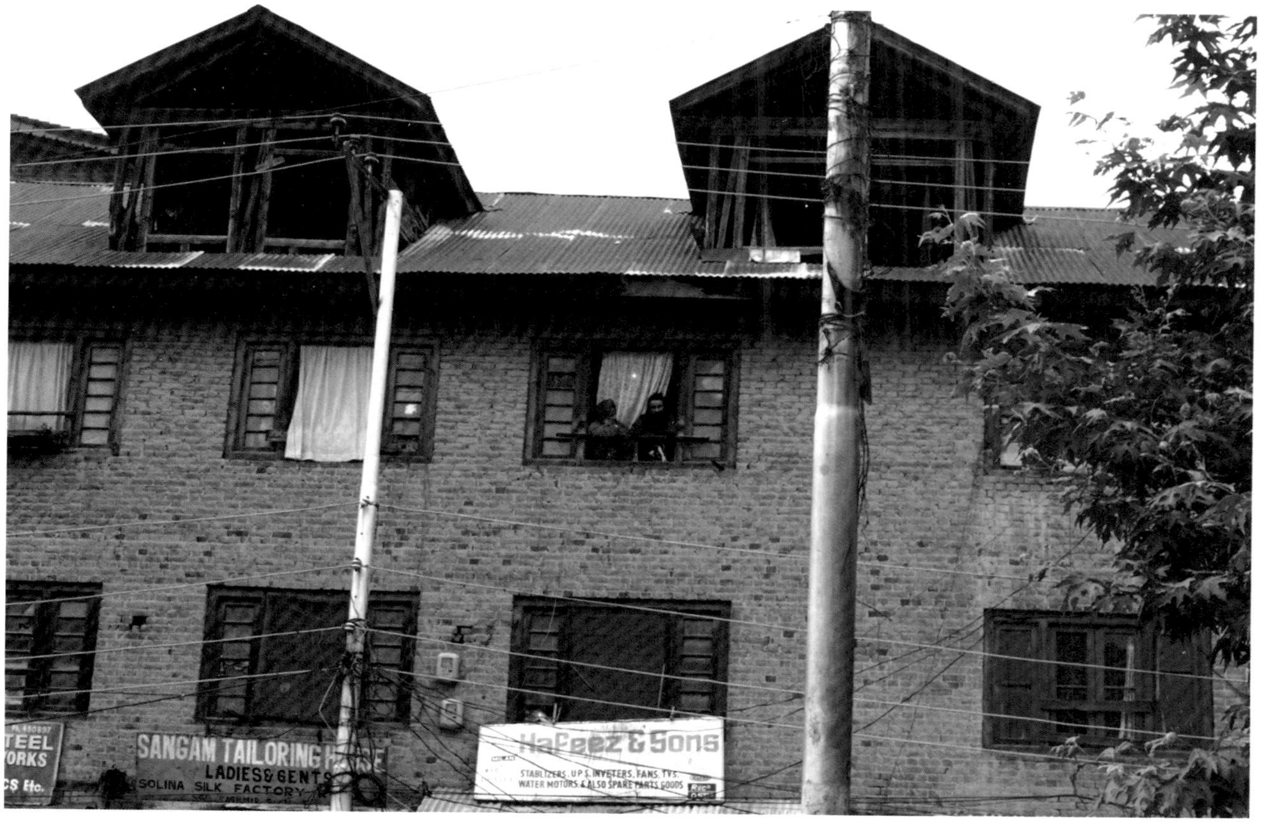

Two Sikhs in Hyderapora. The Chittisinghpura massacre, which saw 36 Sikhs killed in March 2000, in the Anantnag, has left this community fearful of the Islamic fundamentalist militant groups

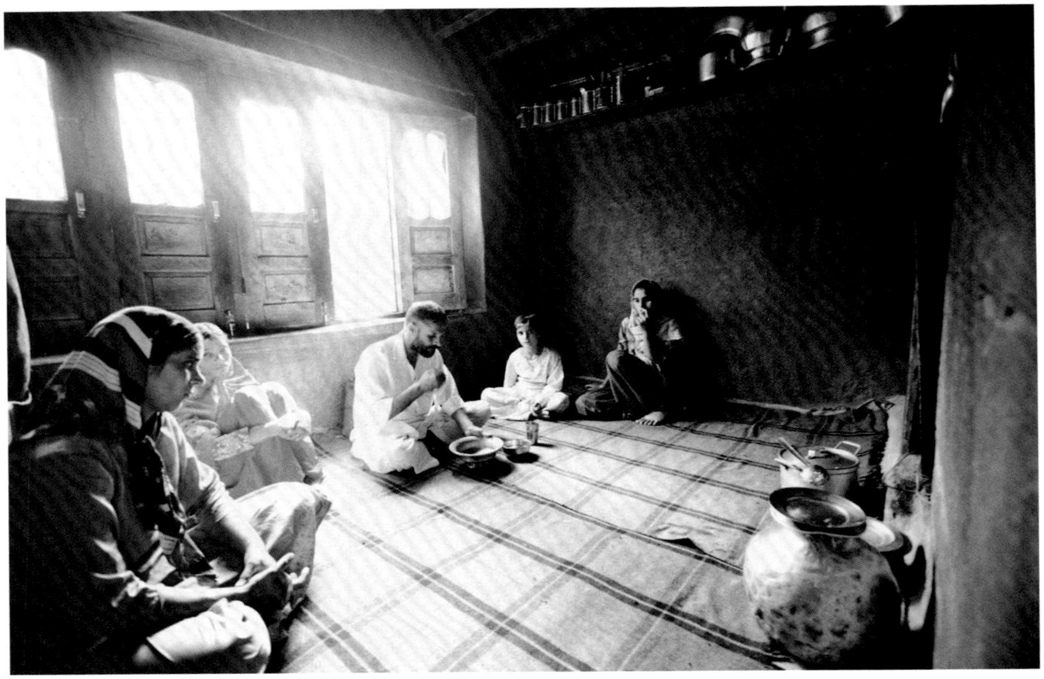

Abdul Ali Bhatt was a militant. After bring captured he was tortured and jailed and finally released in 2007. He is ill, semi-paralytic and suffers from temporary amnesia. While once upon a time he could fire an assault rifle with one arm, today he cannot even lift a feather. He had contemplated suicide because supporting his family, comprising his wife, three daughters and a son, has become more and more difficult. He has to still report to the security forces for routine interrogation

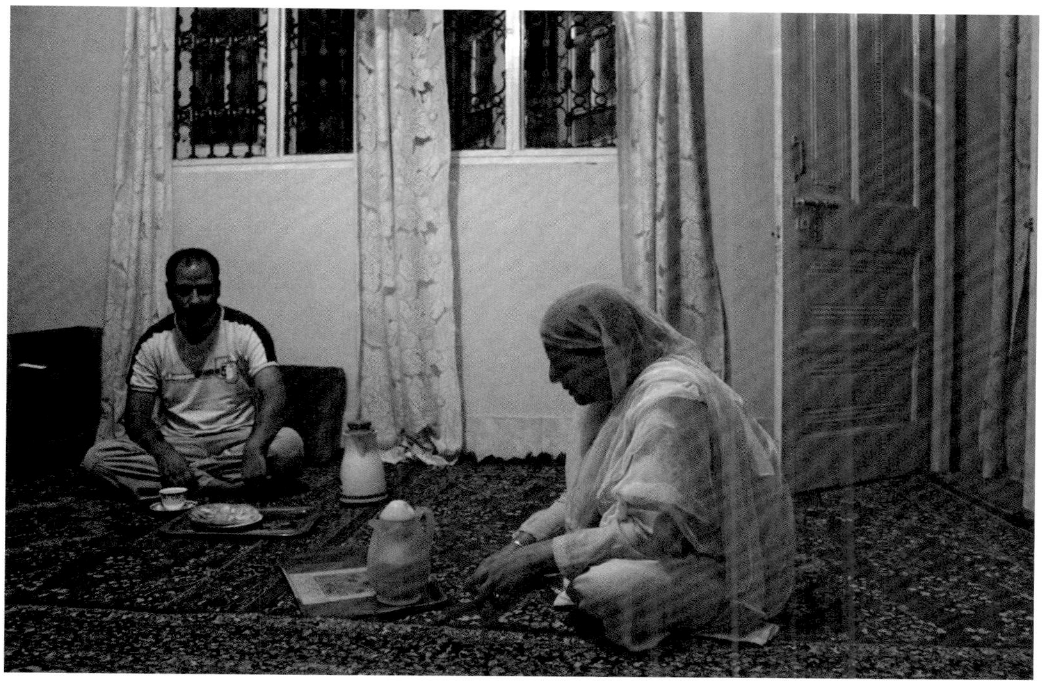

A family enjoying kawa or local tea, traditionally served in a samovar

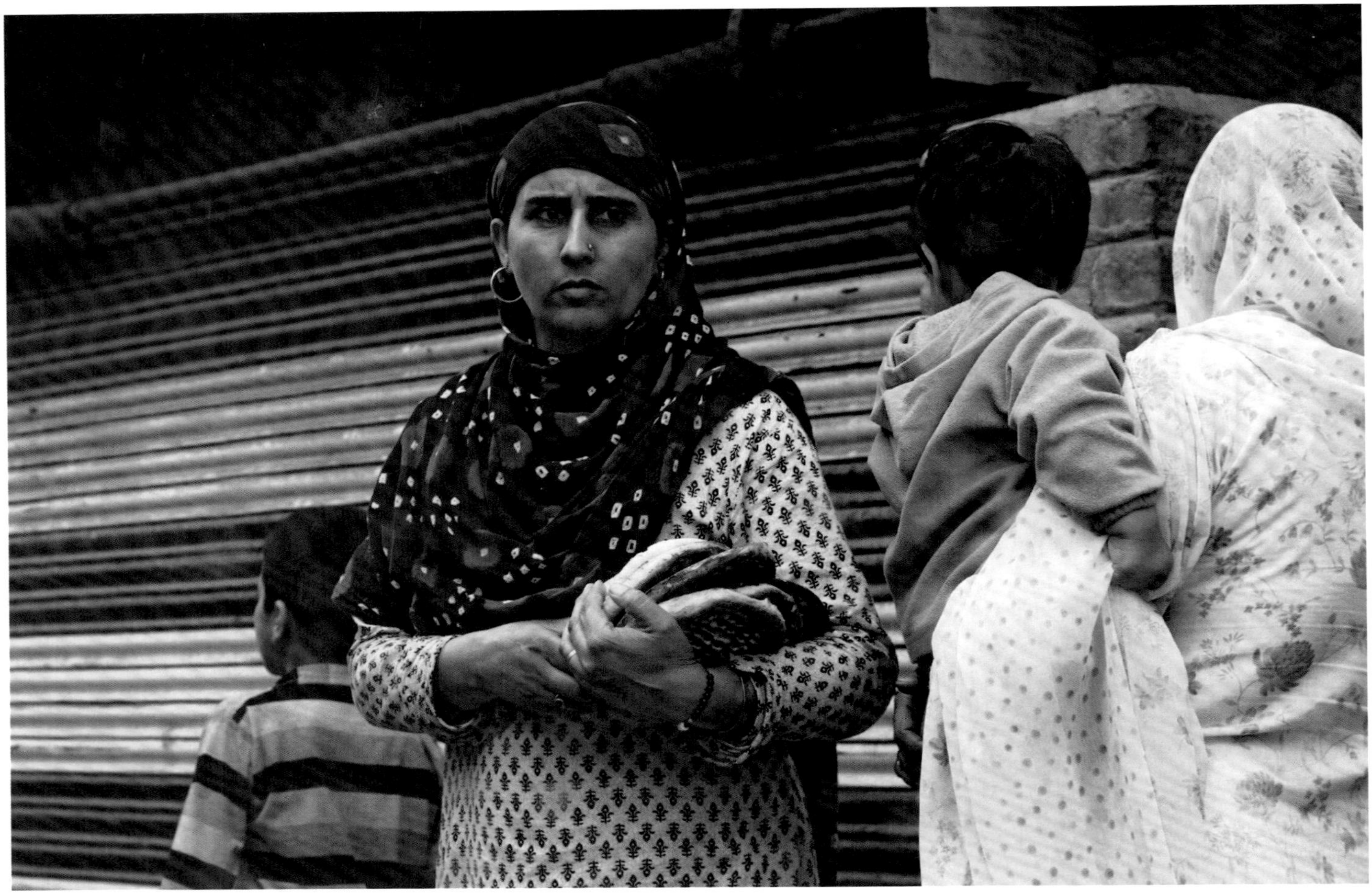

The staple diet of every Kashmiri is rice, but the Valley is otherwise famous for its bakeries

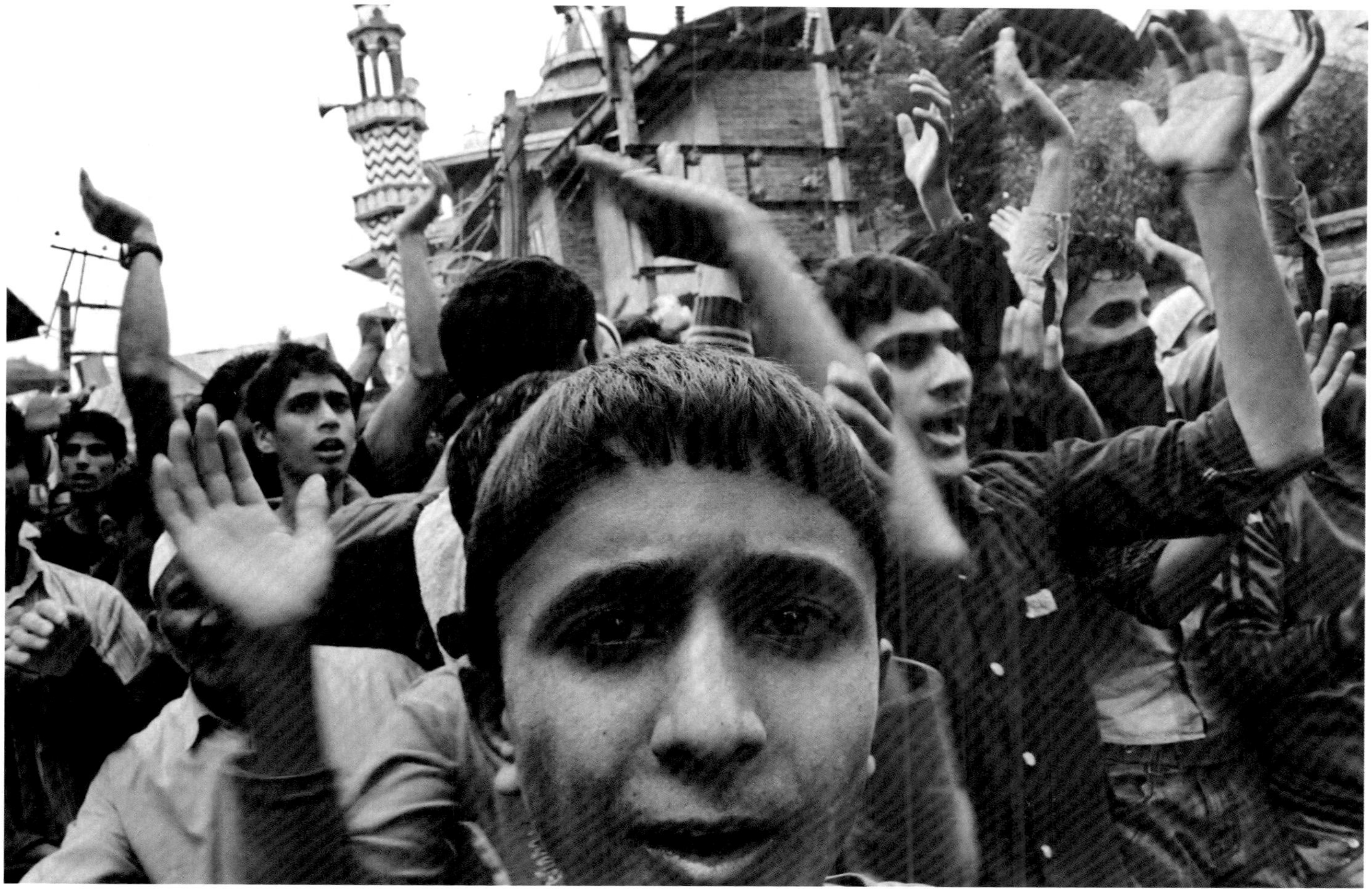

Juvenile protesters are increasingly seen in pro-separatist protests

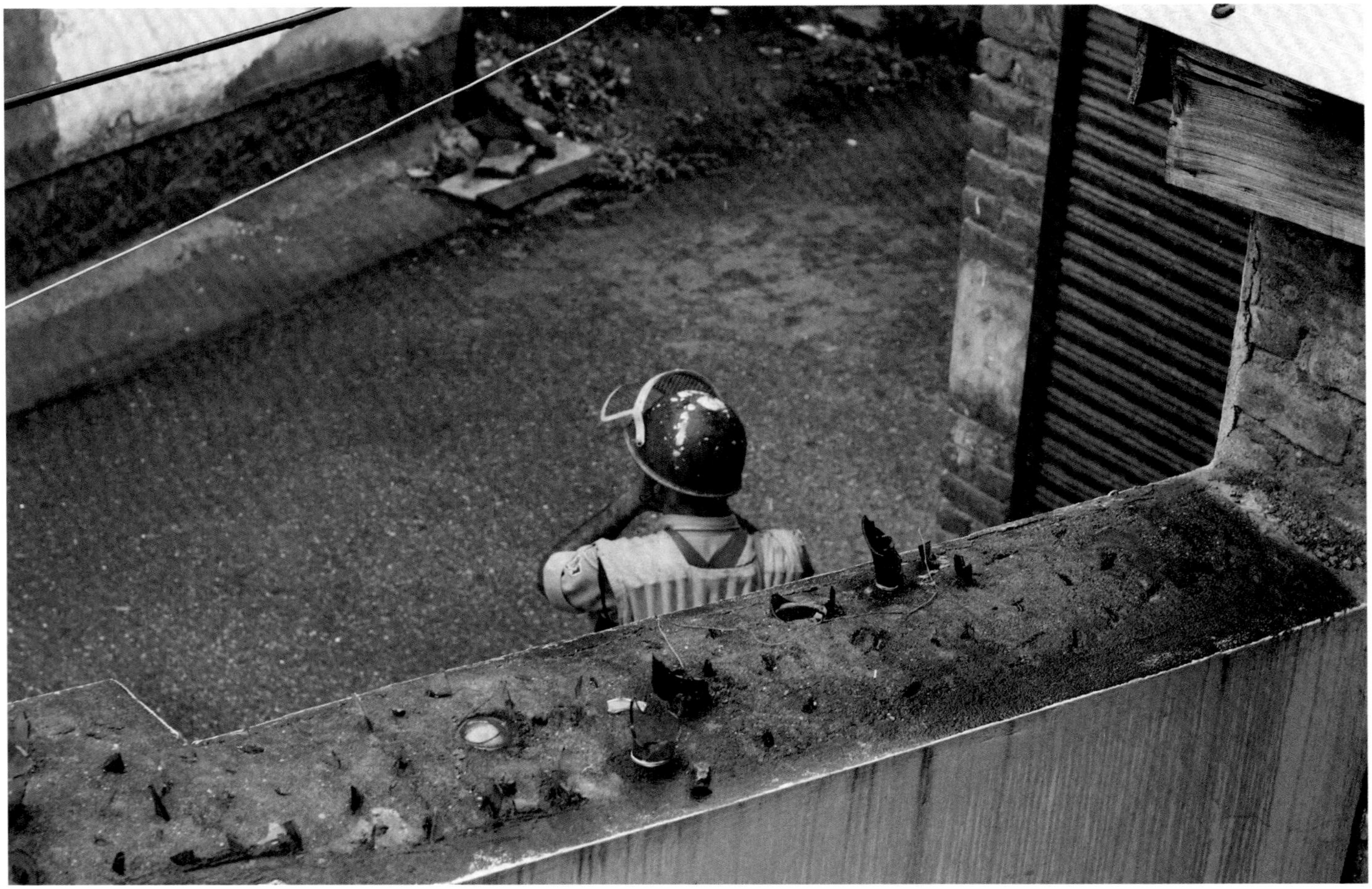

A paramilitary personnel patrols on full alert. Any laxity could be a matter of life and death

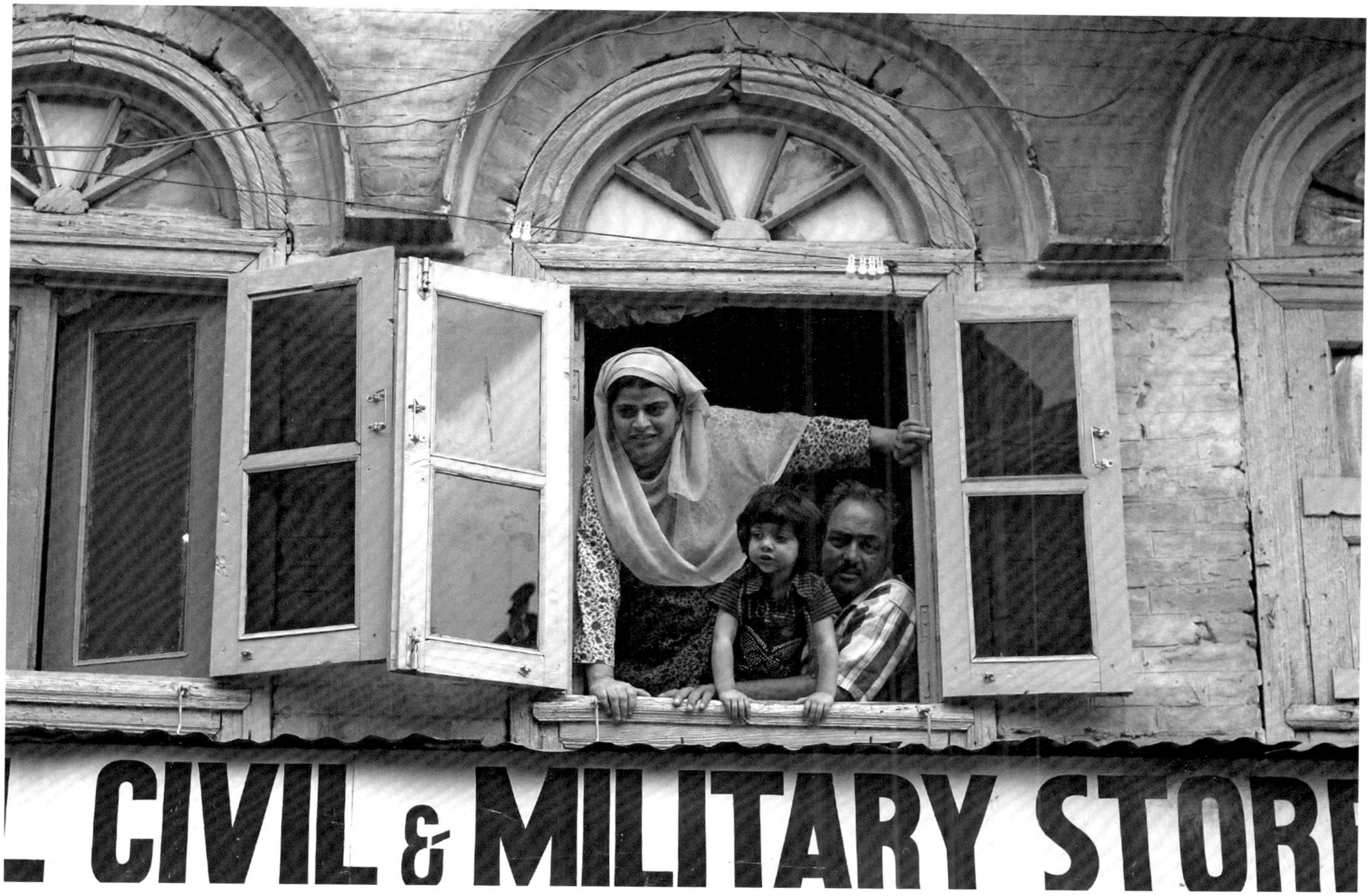

From above a shop, selling civil and military supplies, a family looks down at a massive protest in downtown Srinagar

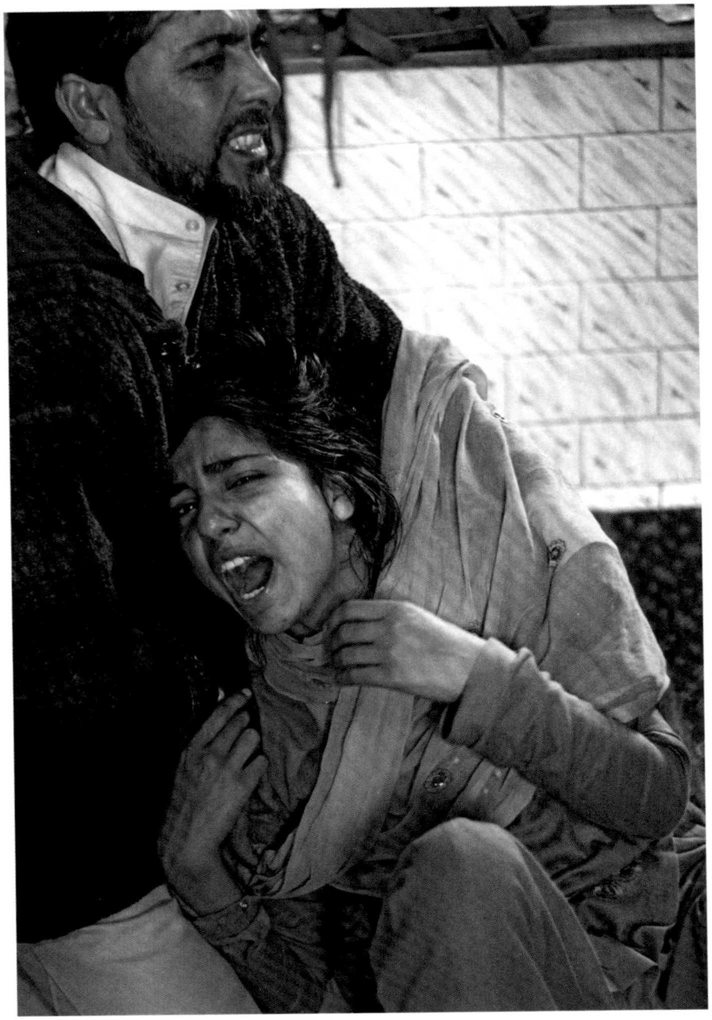

Nahida breaks down. Her brother, a juvenile protester, was caught pelting stones at the security forces in Soura. He was arrested and thrashed by the police. He could not take the torture and succumbed to his injuries. He was only 14 years old

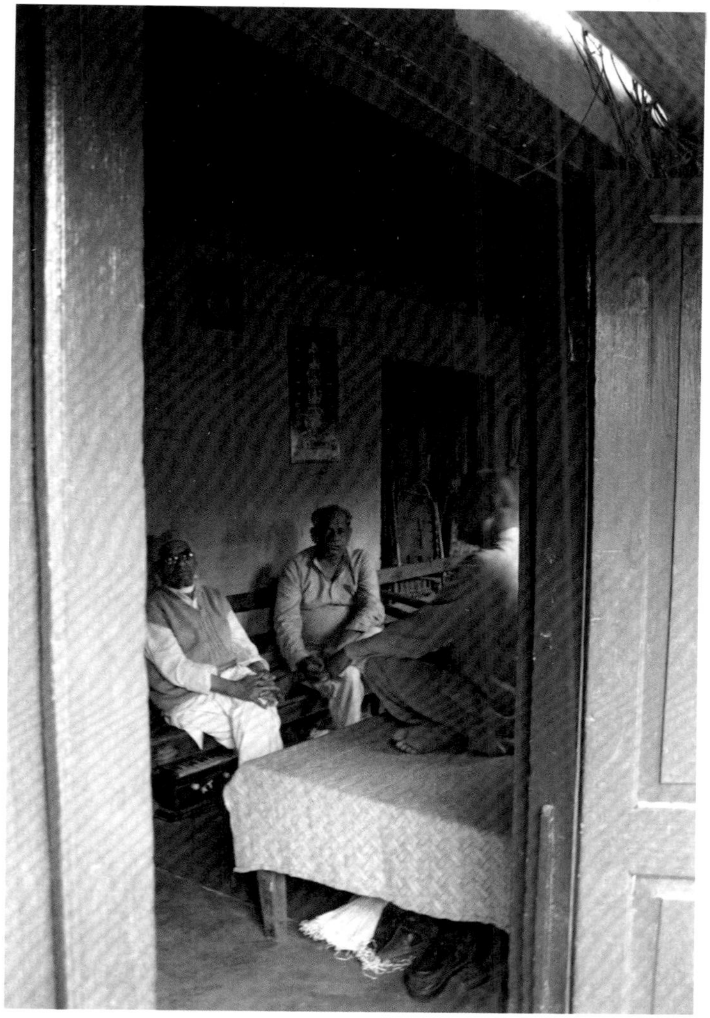

A Kashmiri Pandit taking a break while at work at the Abi Guzar Shiva temple. This is one of the few Hindu places of worship left after the outbreak of militancy. Hindus, their homes, and places of worship have been systematically targeted and burnt to the ground by separatists

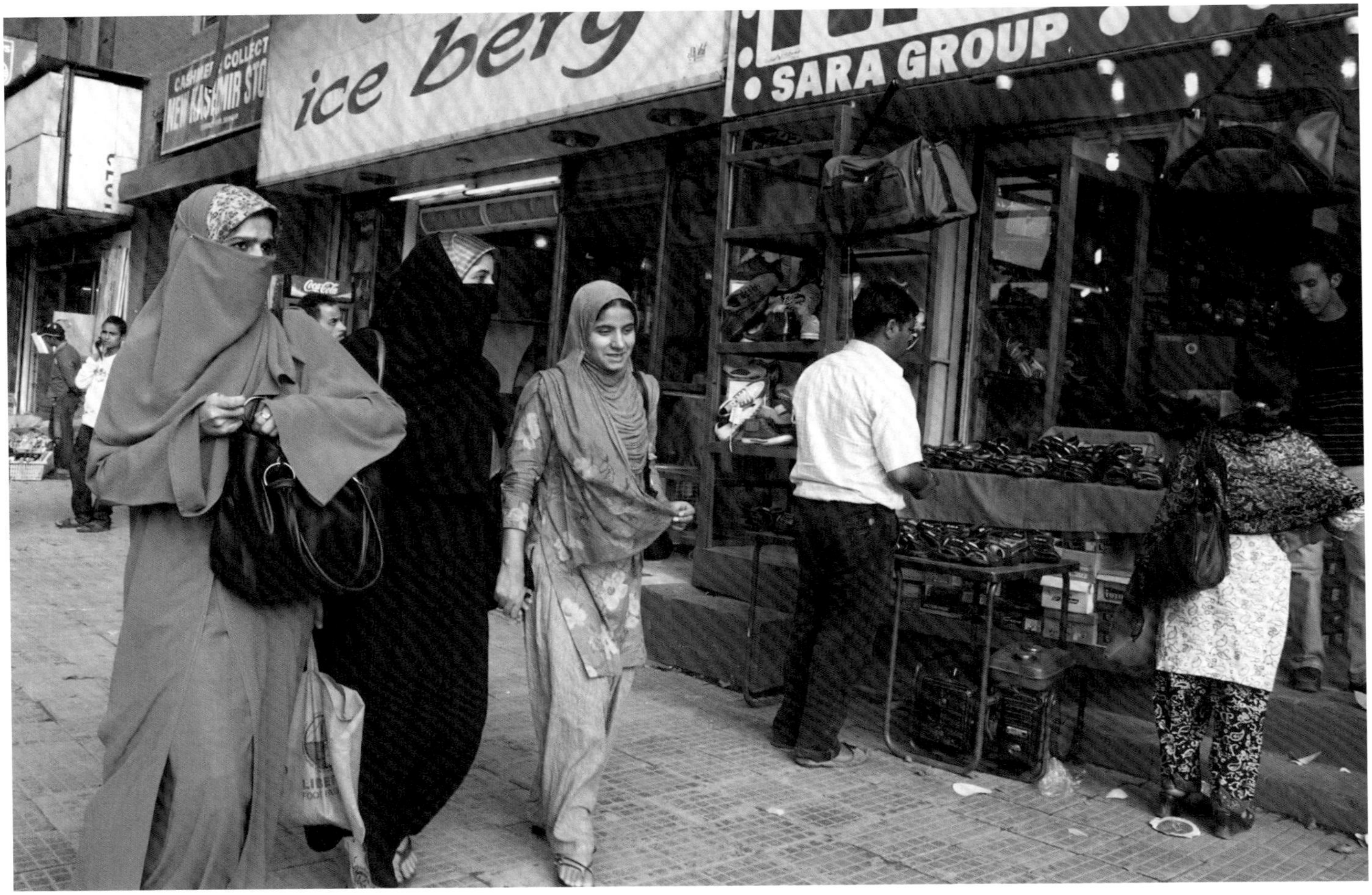

After Muslim fundamentalist organisations and their militant arms put out fatwas that women will not be allowed to wear pants, jeans or T-shirts, women have resigned themselves to wearing hijabs and burquas. Disobedience of the fatwa could lead to being assaulted or killed by militants. Though the grip of the fatwa is not so strong at present, burquas and hijabs continue to exist

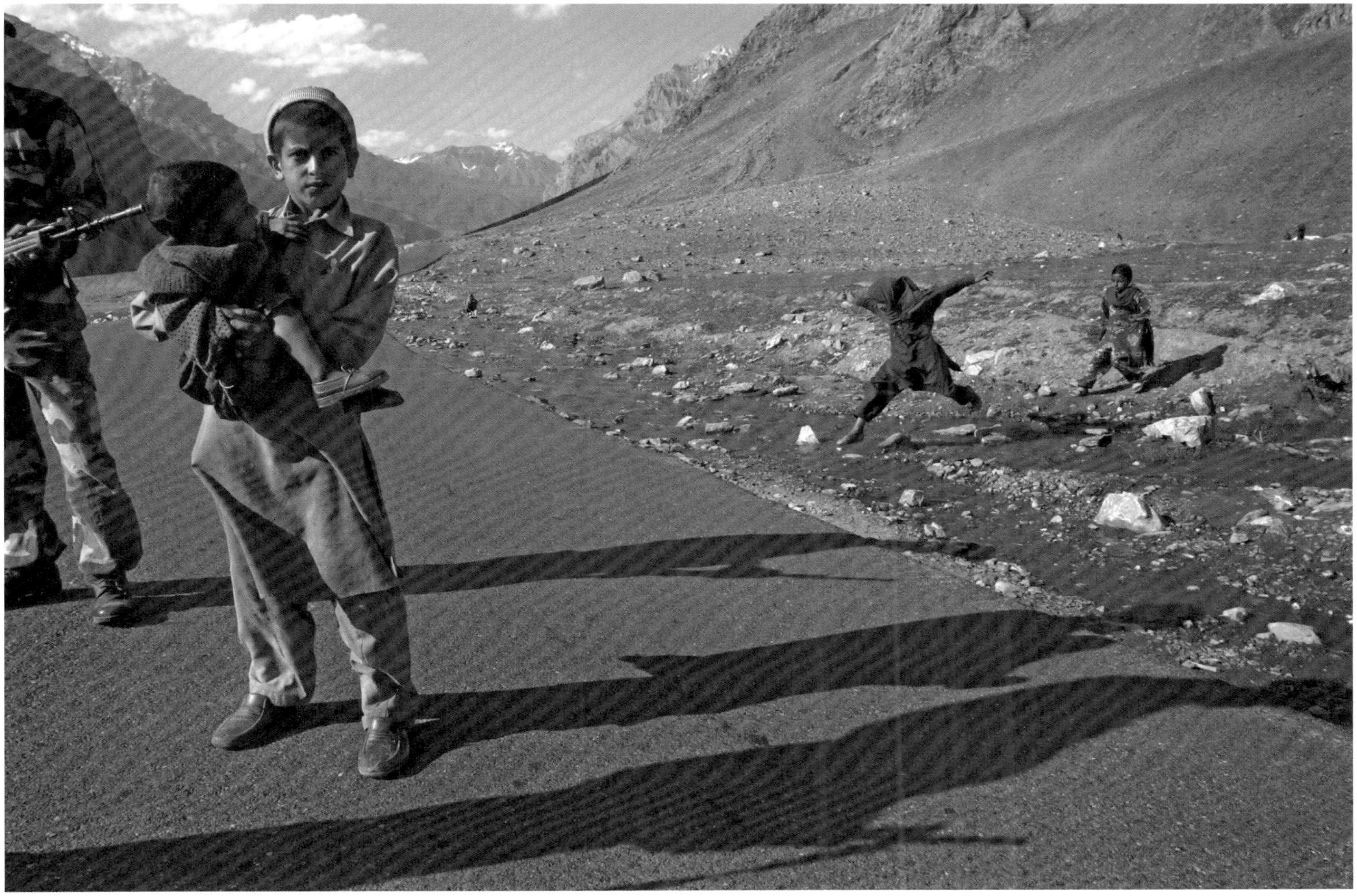

A Muslim boy with his infant brother live in the shadow of war, with POK across the hills to the left. For these villagers living close to the LOC, life is on the brink of uncertainty at all times. Sporadic shelling from Pakistan can cause damage to life and property, with very little warning

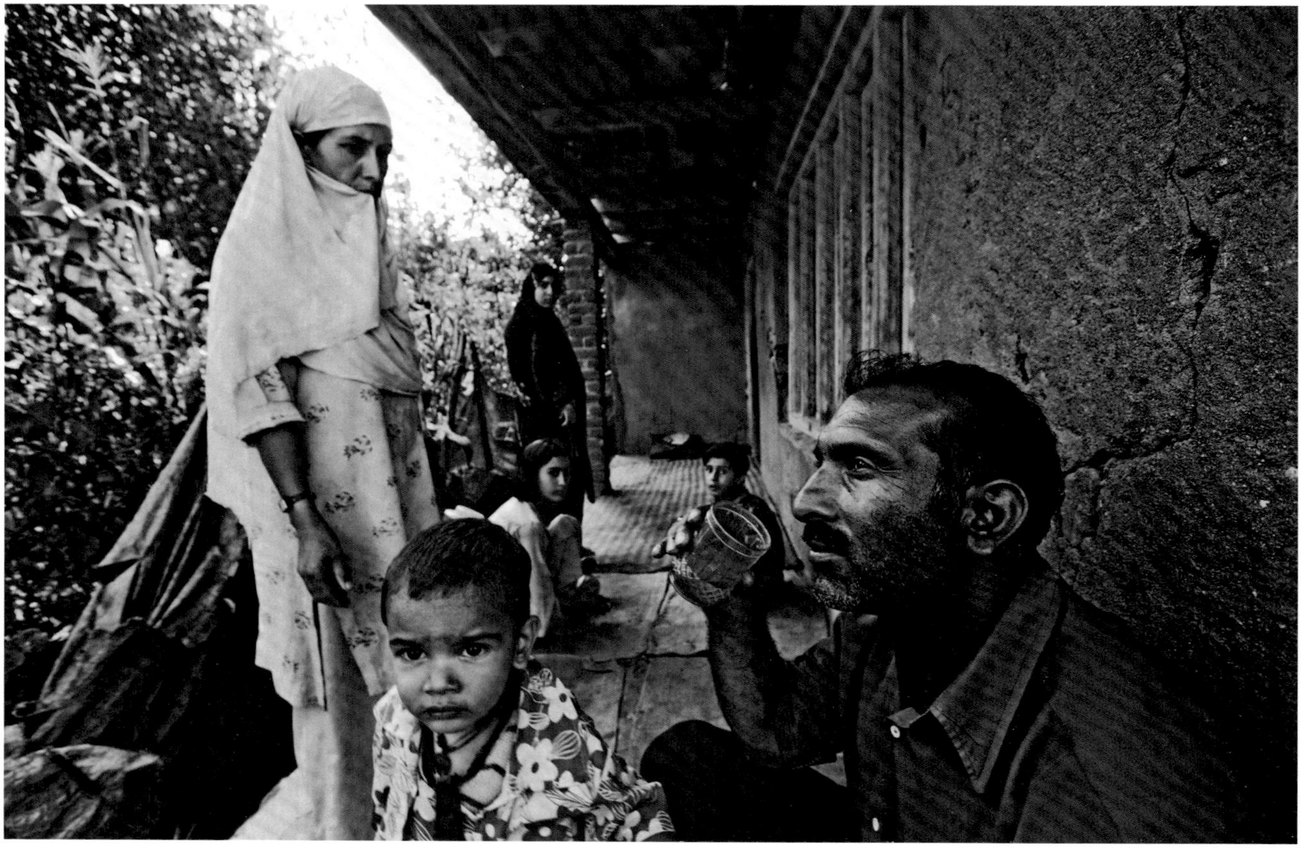

This man does not want to be named. He is an ex-militant. After his jail sentence, he now works as an intelligence agent for the security forces. His life is not smooth, but not as bad as other militants who do not believe in the Indian constitution, he says

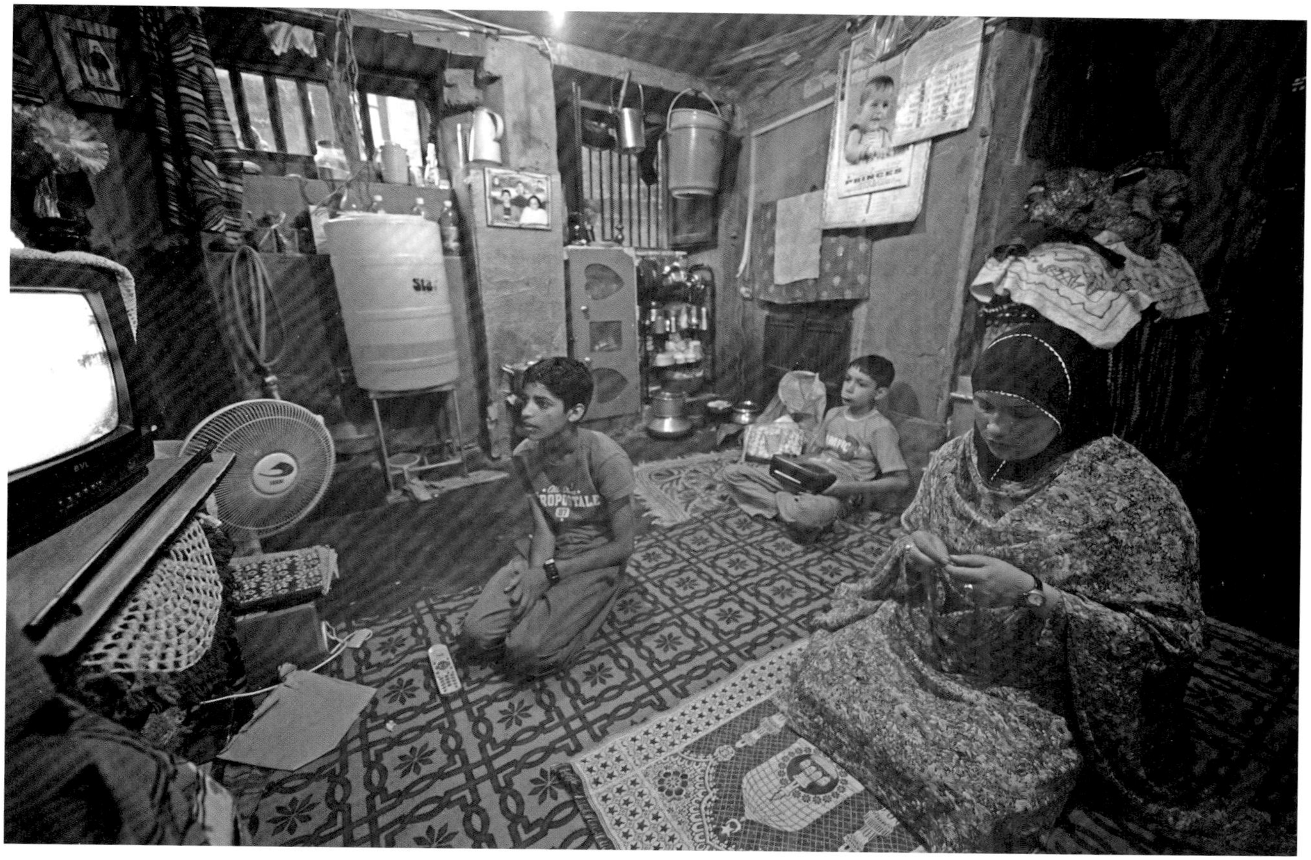

Tahira, a half-widow, lives downtown Srinagar with her three sons. Her husband vanished in 2007, on his way to Delhi to look for a better job

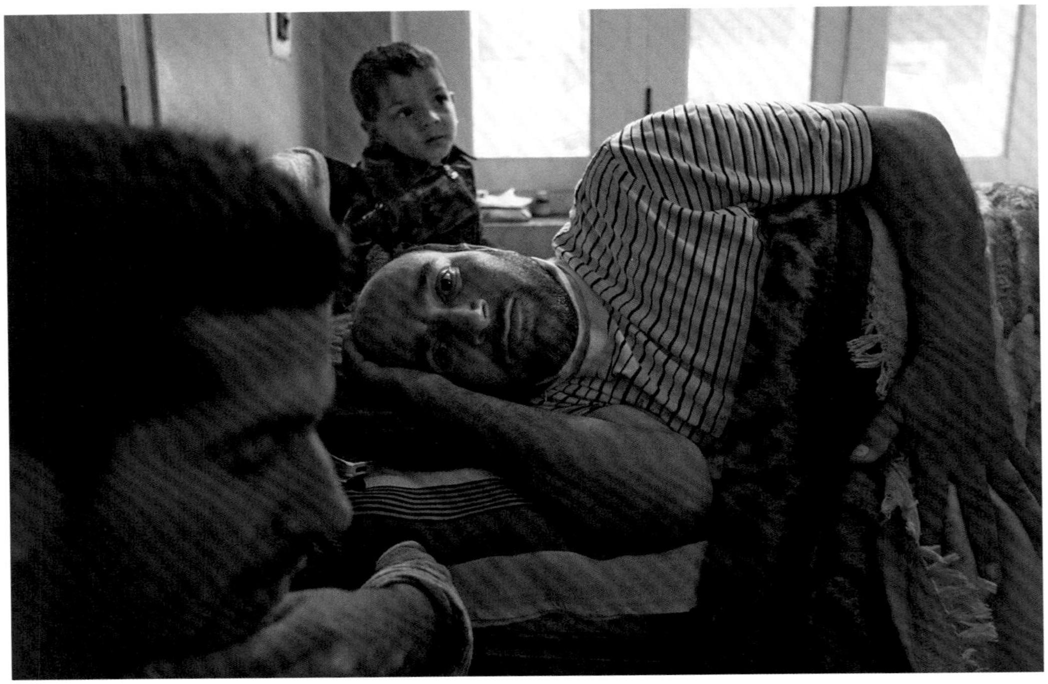

Majid was hit by a bullet during police firing and has become paraplegic

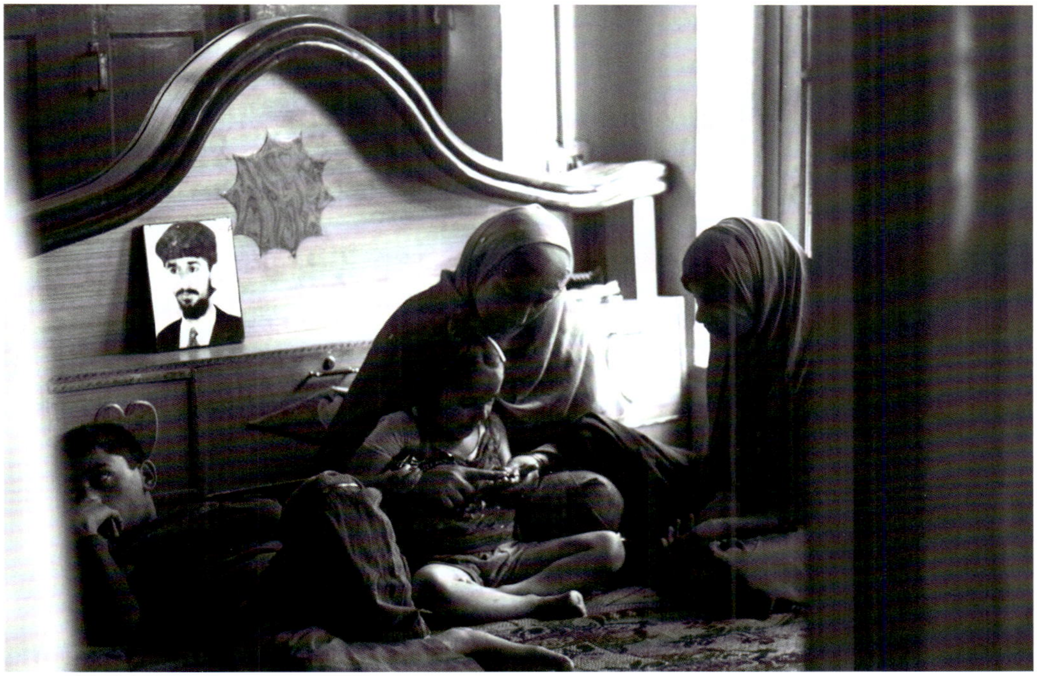

Naseem is a half-widow form Srinagar. Her husband Miraj Dar was taken away by the security forces and never returned. She can barely manage to raise her three children so the older ones have dropped out of school to ease her burden

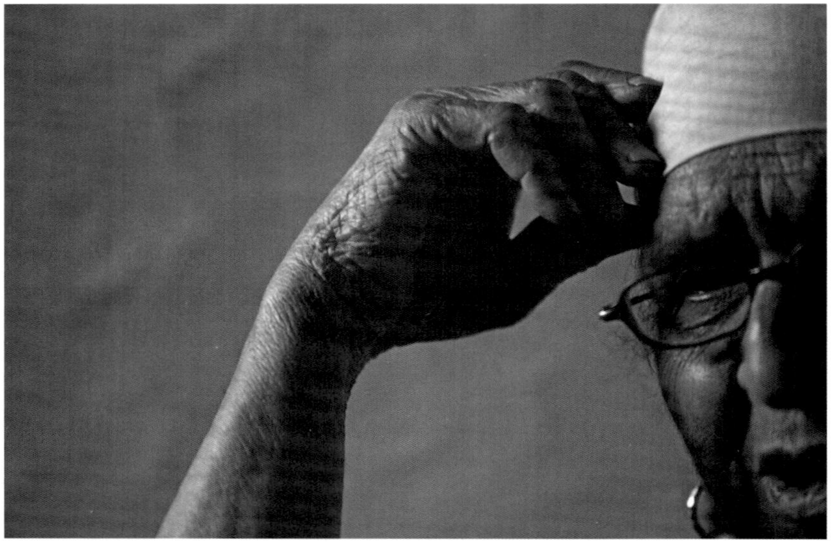

Moguli Begam is no more. She died in 2011. Some say she was over 90 years of age. In the year 1992 her son went out to work. He was a chemistry teacher. The day he left he had promised to take his mother to an ophthalmologist after work. That never happened. He just disappeared. His mother waited for 20 years, hoping her son would come back. It is suspected that her son must have been taken away by the security forces on suspicion of being a militant and killed thereafter, without leaving a trail

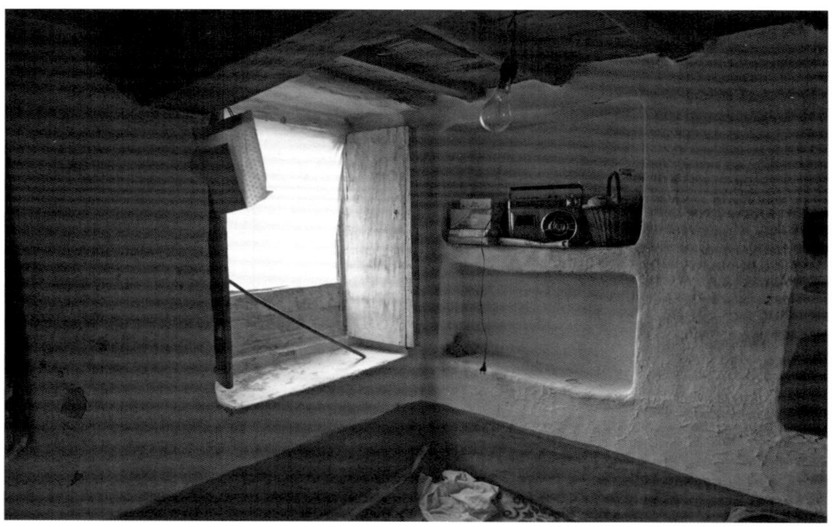

The room of Moguli Begam in Habba Kadal in Srinagar

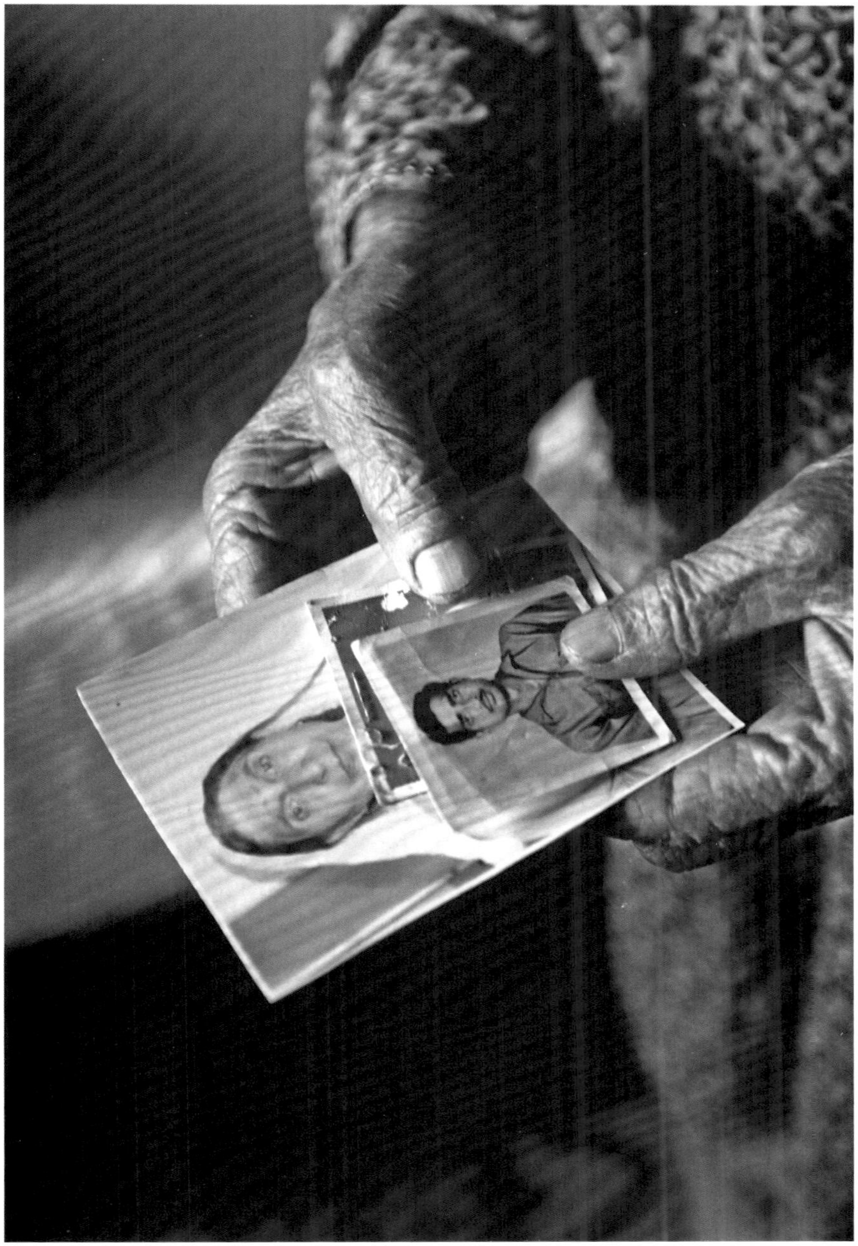

Moguli Begam holding a photograph of her son who disappeared in the 1990s during the militancy era

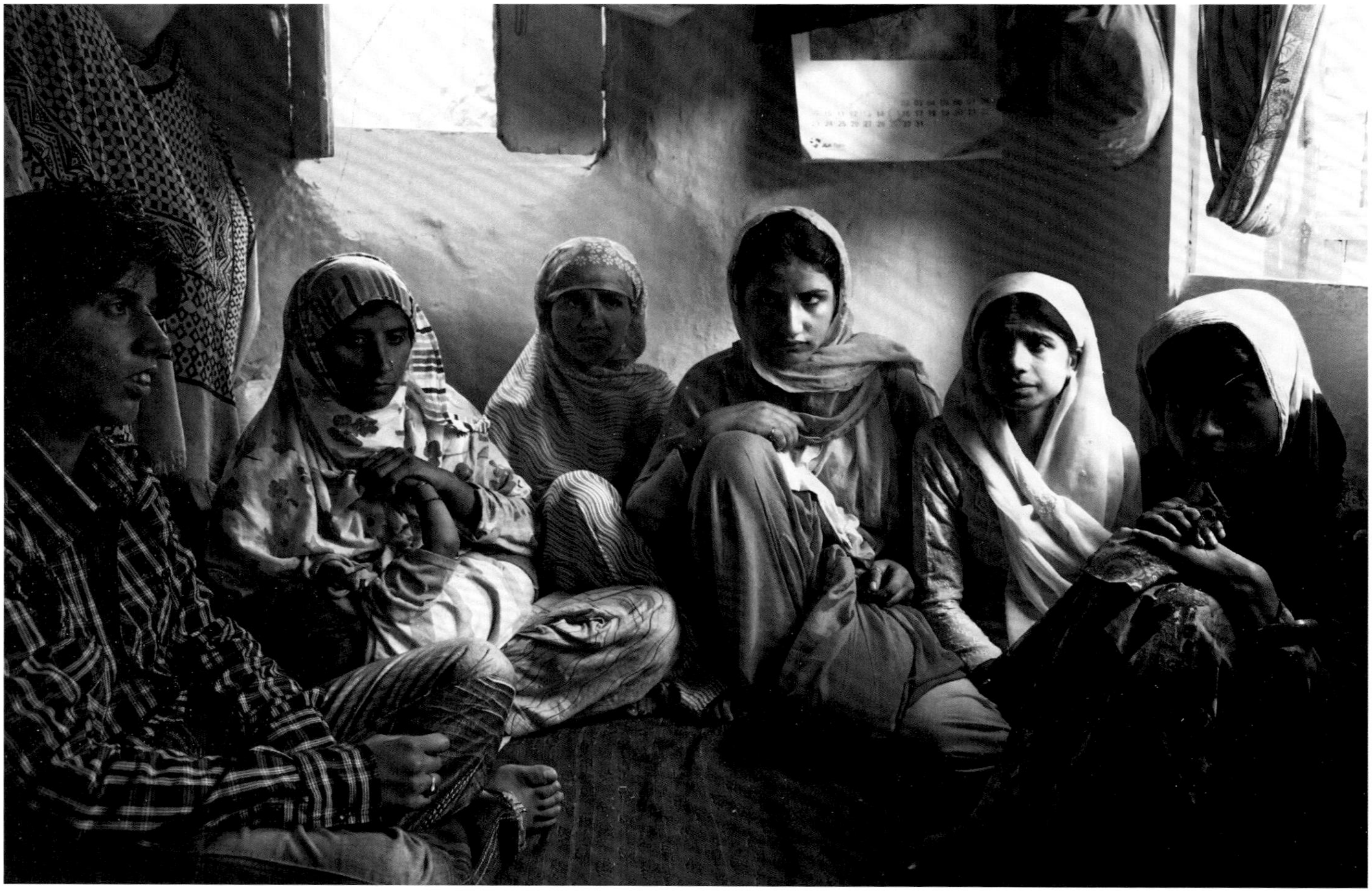

These sisters from Nowahatta mourn the arrest of their only brother, aged 17, under the Public Security Act of Indian government. There is no information available on him

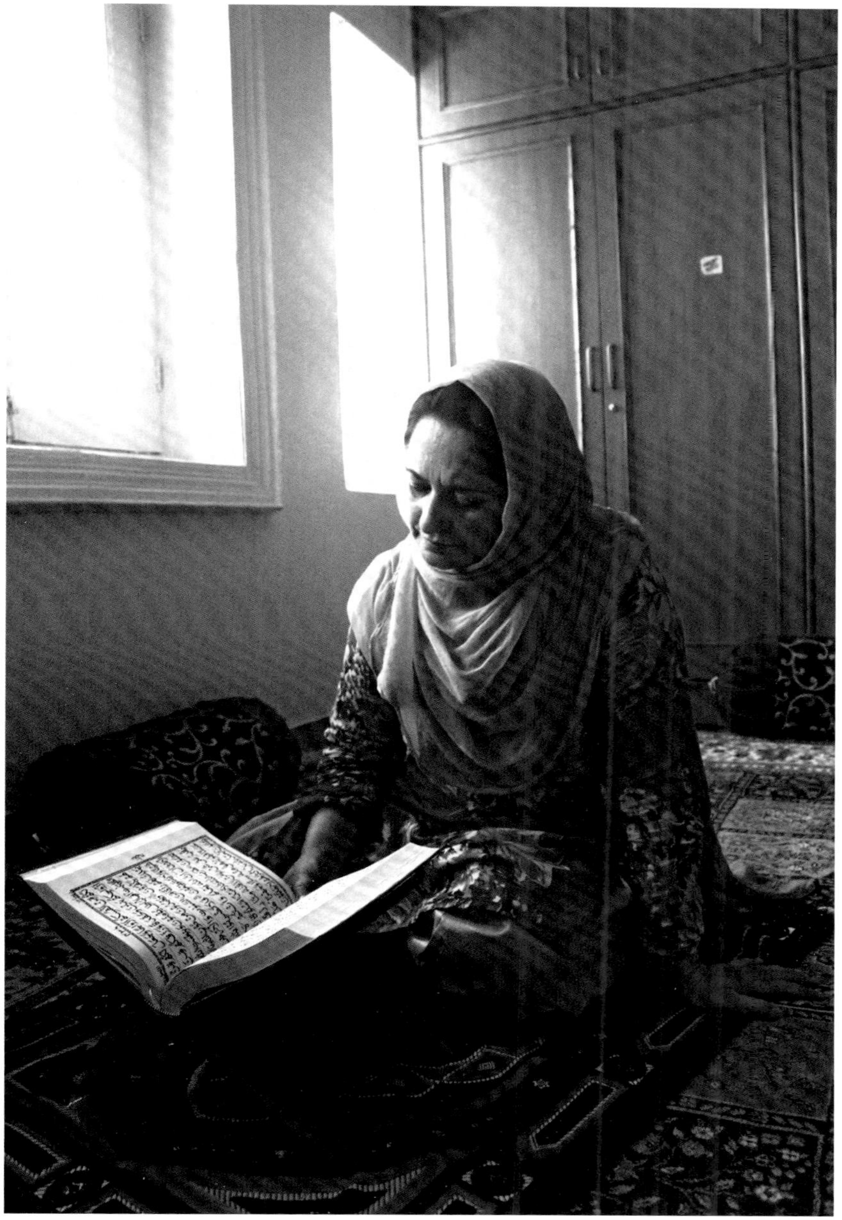

Muslim Fazli, a faculty member with the Kashmir University, does not advocate an independent Kashmir but she certainly wants it to be demilitarised at the earliest, or fears worse days ahead

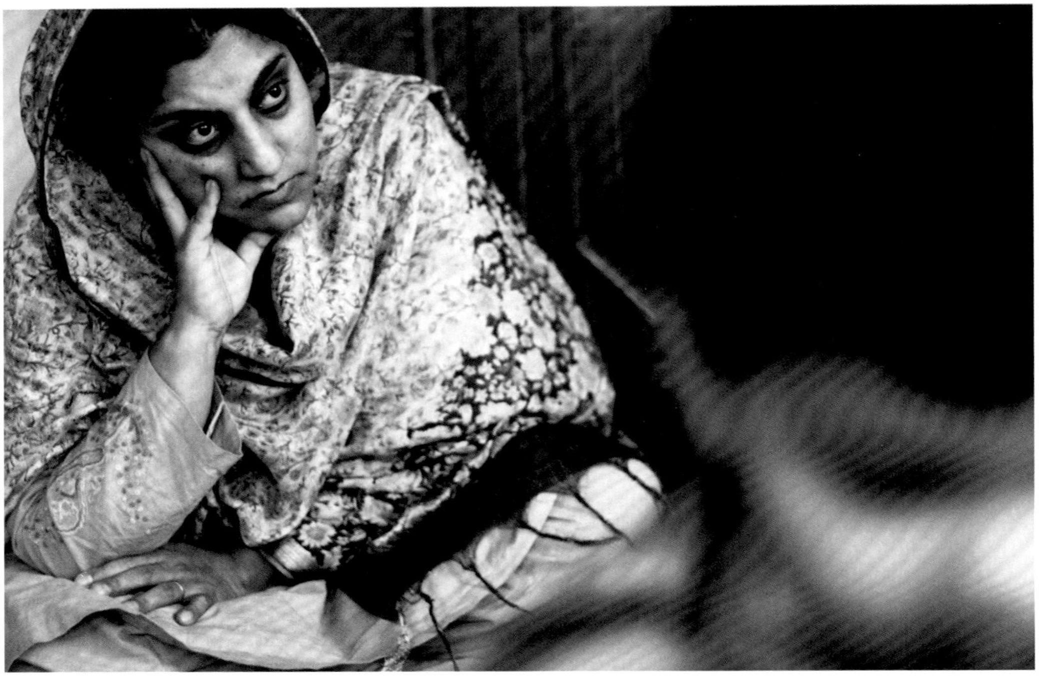

Afshana is a professor of Media Studies at the Kashmir University. She rues the appalling condition of media in the Valley where at the slightest sign of agitation, internet, cable networks and circulation of newspapers are shut down

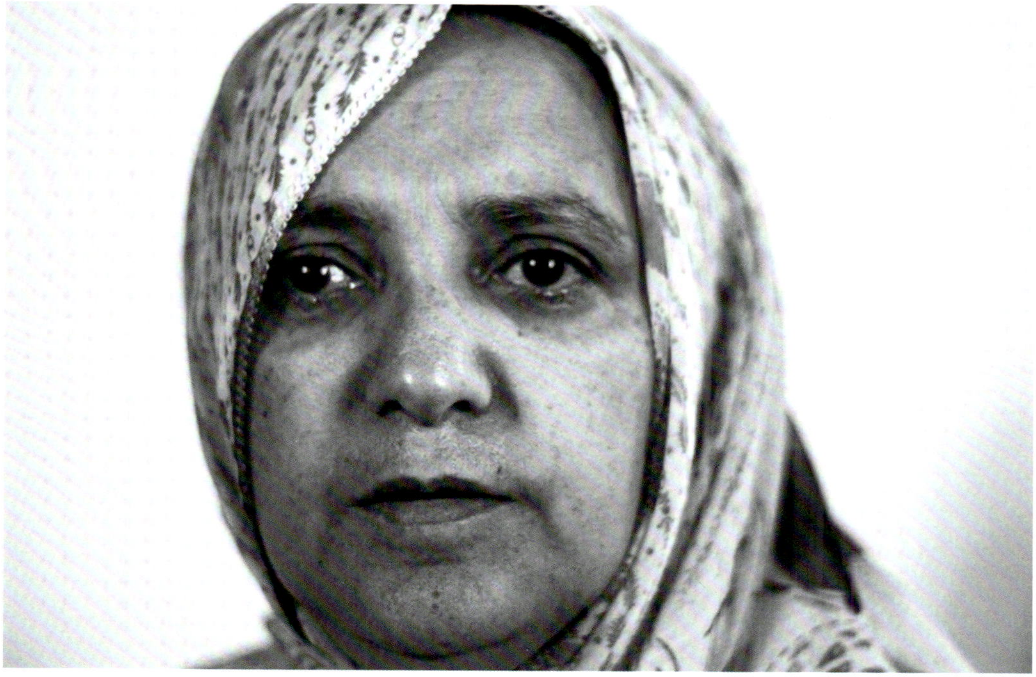

Parveena Ahangar, the chairperson of the Association of Parents of Disappeared Persons (APDP) in Kashmir, has been fighting an arduous battle for the last 24 years. Her son Javed Ahmad was 17 years old at the time of his arrest on 18 August 1990, during a raid in Batmaloo area of uptown Srinagar. He never came back. The illiterate Kashmiri mother continues to search for him in the prisons across Rajasthan and Kashmir

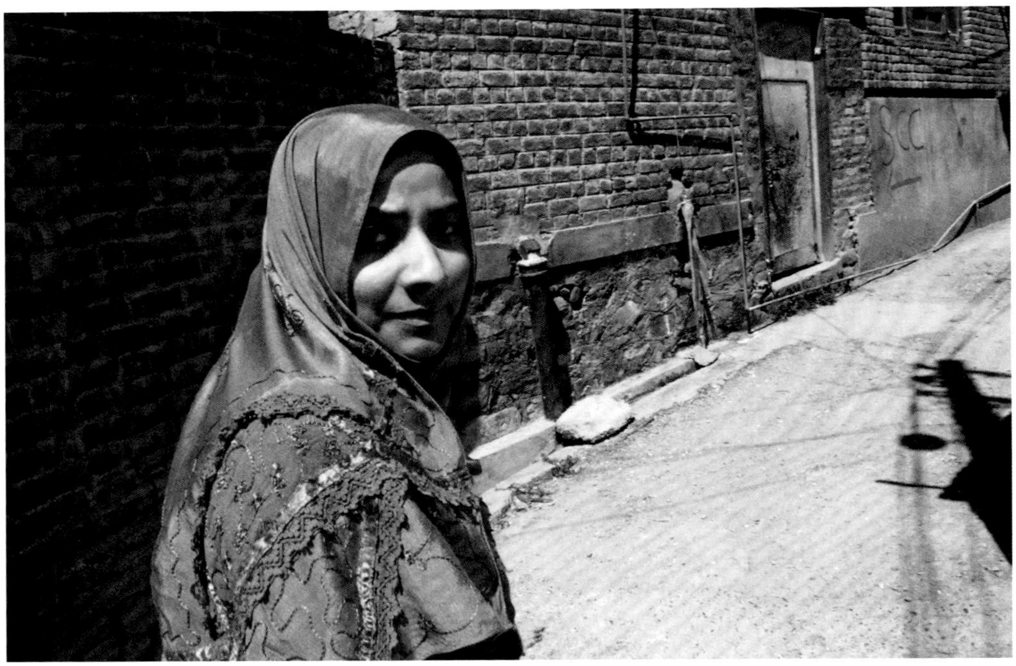

Uzma Falak, a journalist and an activist from the Valley, works on women issues specially on half-widows and half-mothers

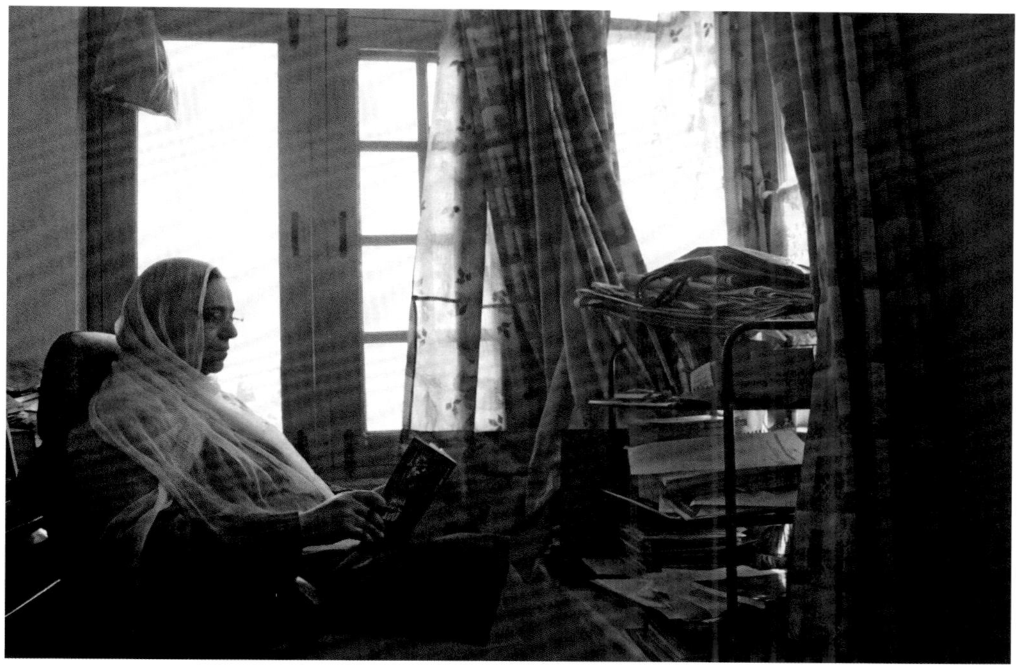

Zamruda Sheik, a separatist leader from the Valley, spent 100 days in Tihar jail. Now an author and a leader, she works for Kashmiri women in distress

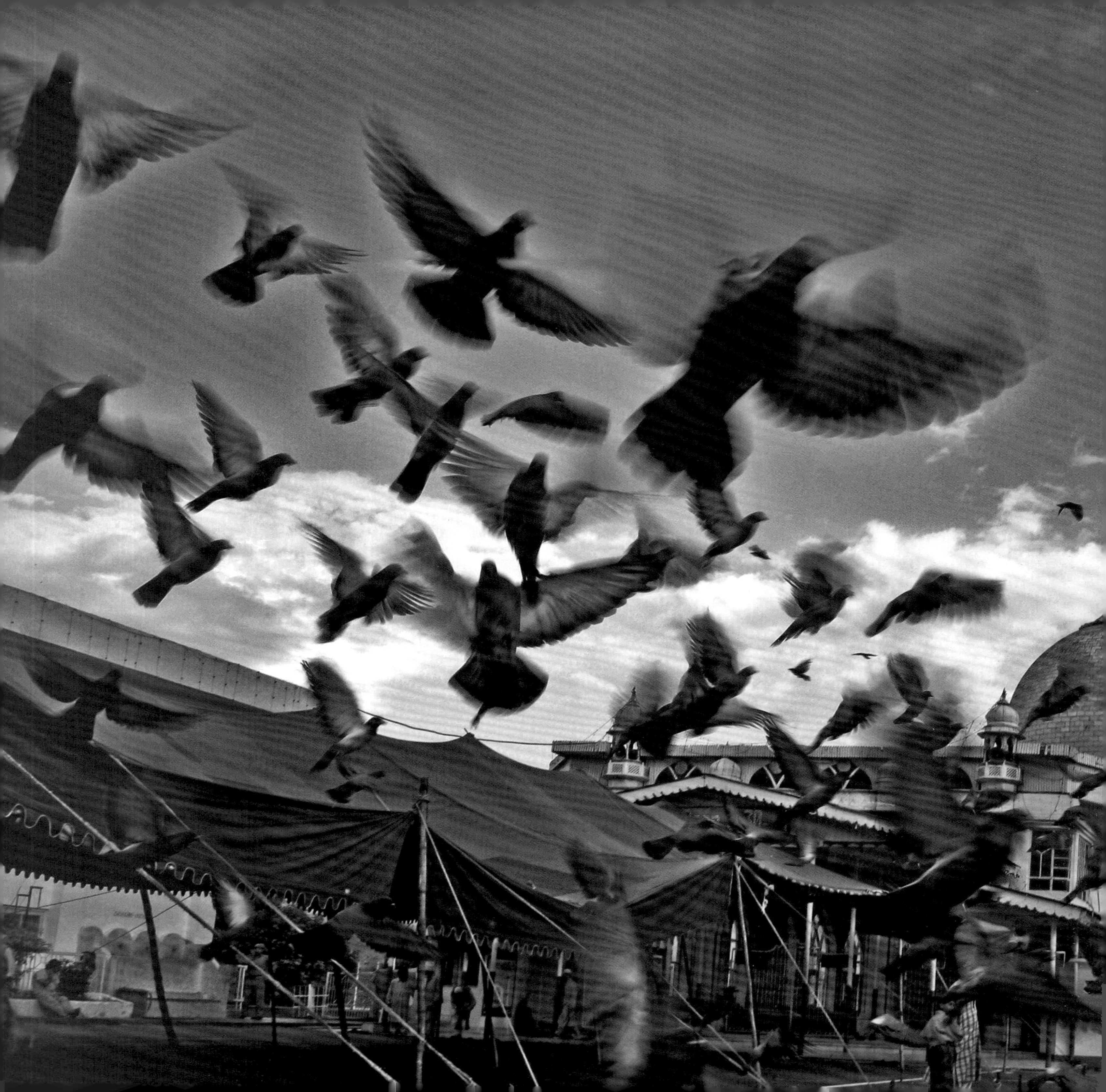

PROTEST

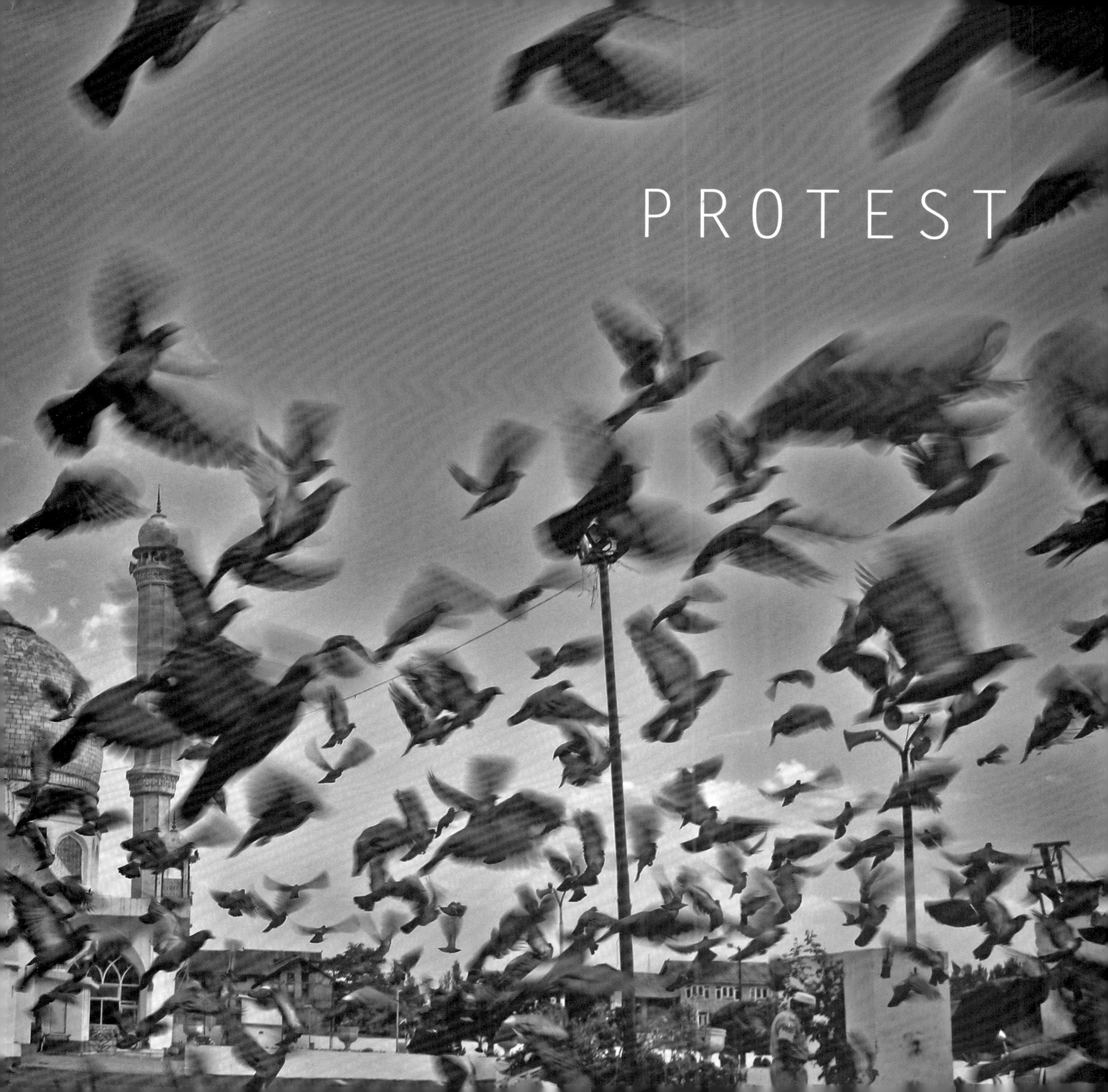

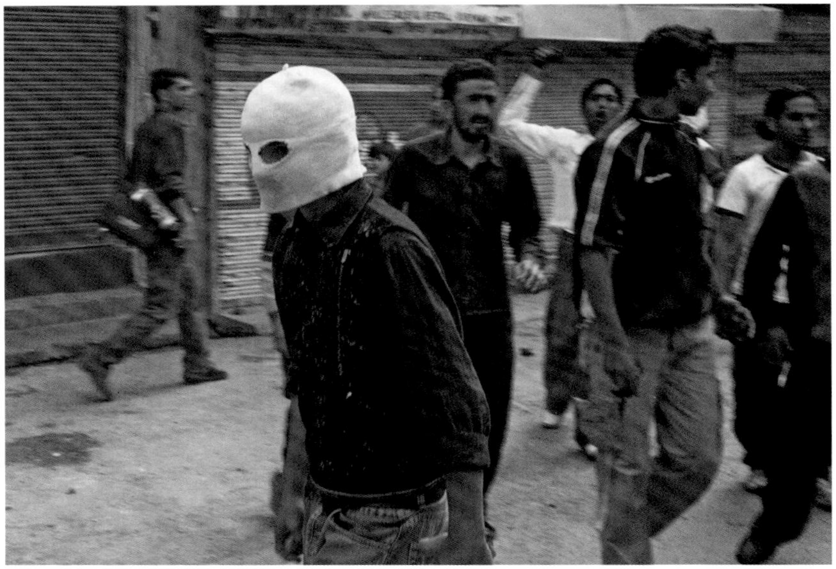

Taking a cue from the Palestinian militia, this Kashmiri boy wears a hooded mask—socks with three holes for breathing and seeing. Video footages and photographs of protesters are used by police to crack down and make arrests, which can amount to jail under PSA (Public Security Act). Such attire is to conceal the identity

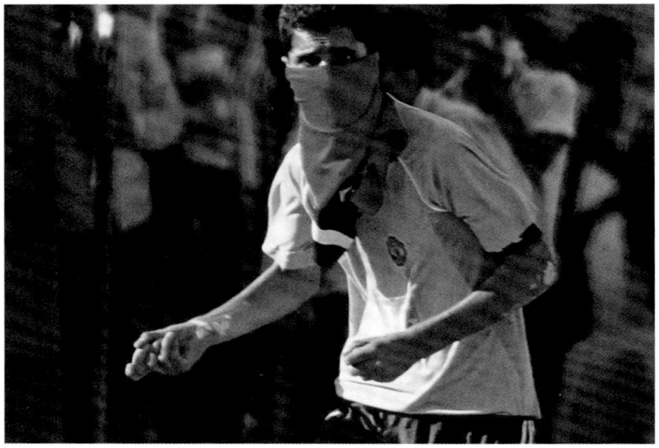

Masked men pelt stones towards security forces. Once in a while journalists get hurt and have to be hospitalised

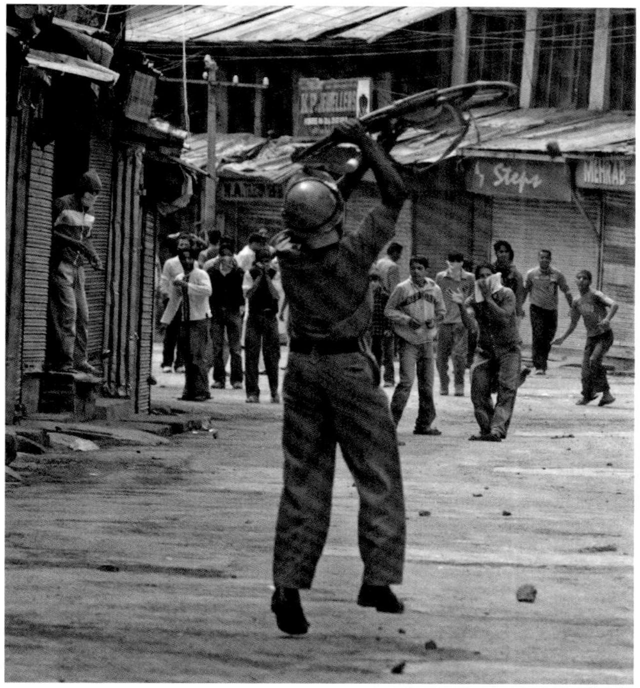

A state police constable tries to negotiate a rowdy crowd at Nowahatta in downtown Srinagar (old city). He uses a cane shield to stop the stones flying like cannon balls

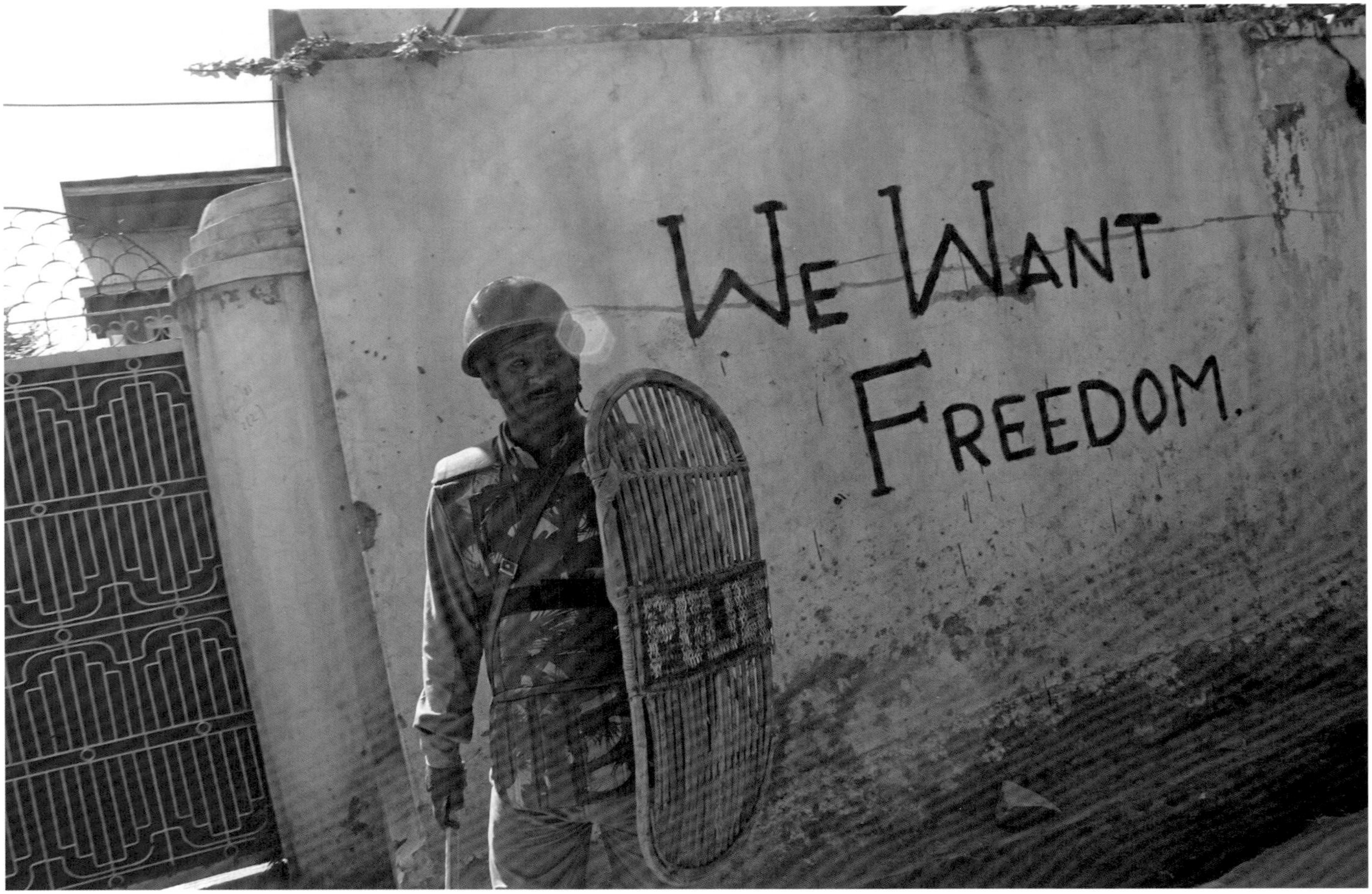

'We want freedom' written on the walls by the pro-Kashmir independence protesters during the height of riots that resulted in numerous arrests and many deaths. But separatist sections of the population continue to participate in sporadic incidences of violence and organised protests

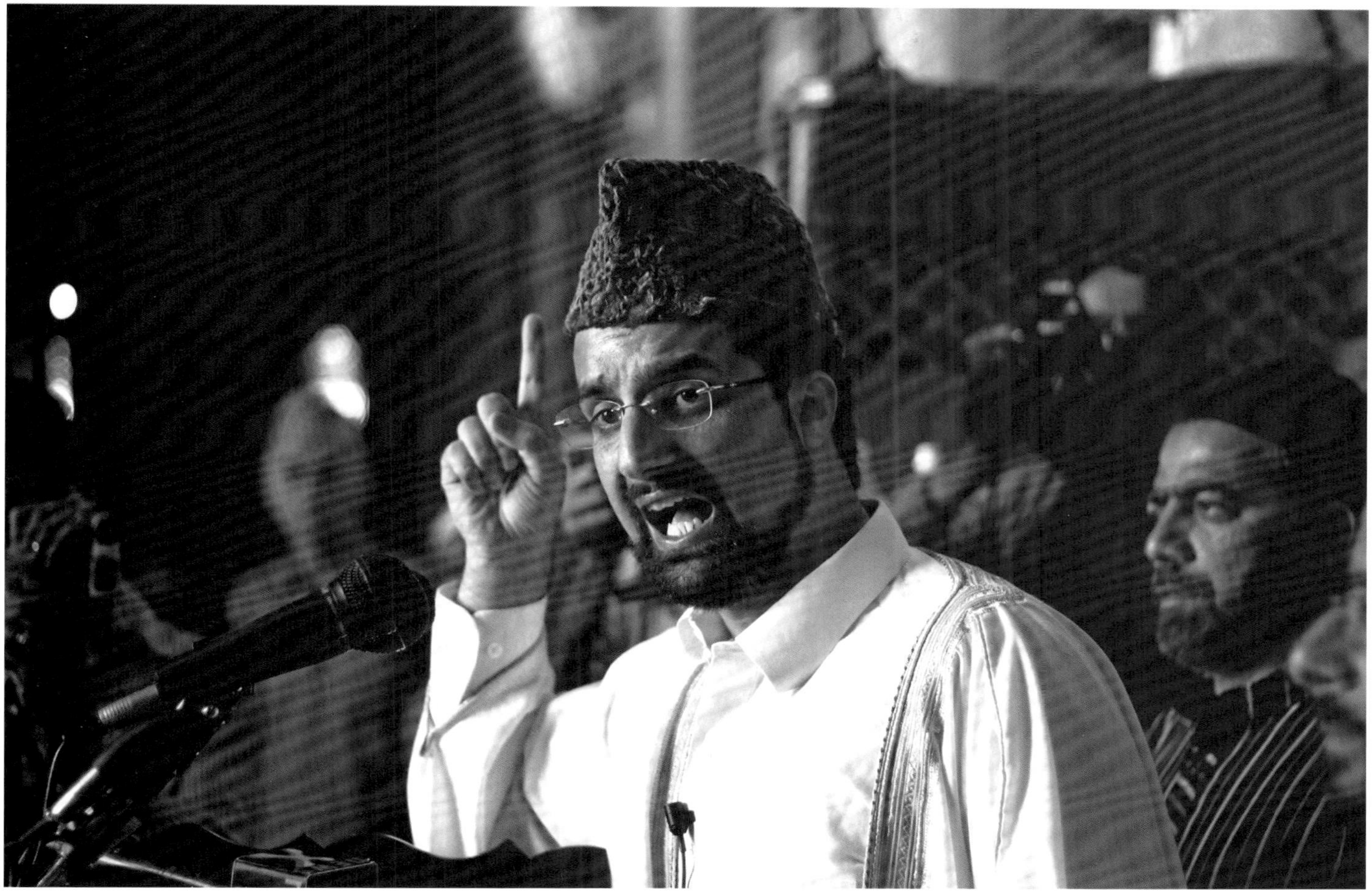

Mirwaiz Umar Farooq, an America-educated maulvi, delivers a sermon from the Jama Masjid. His father was gunned down by militants and he took over the legacy. He is one of the moderate leaders who can sway the crowd with his oratory

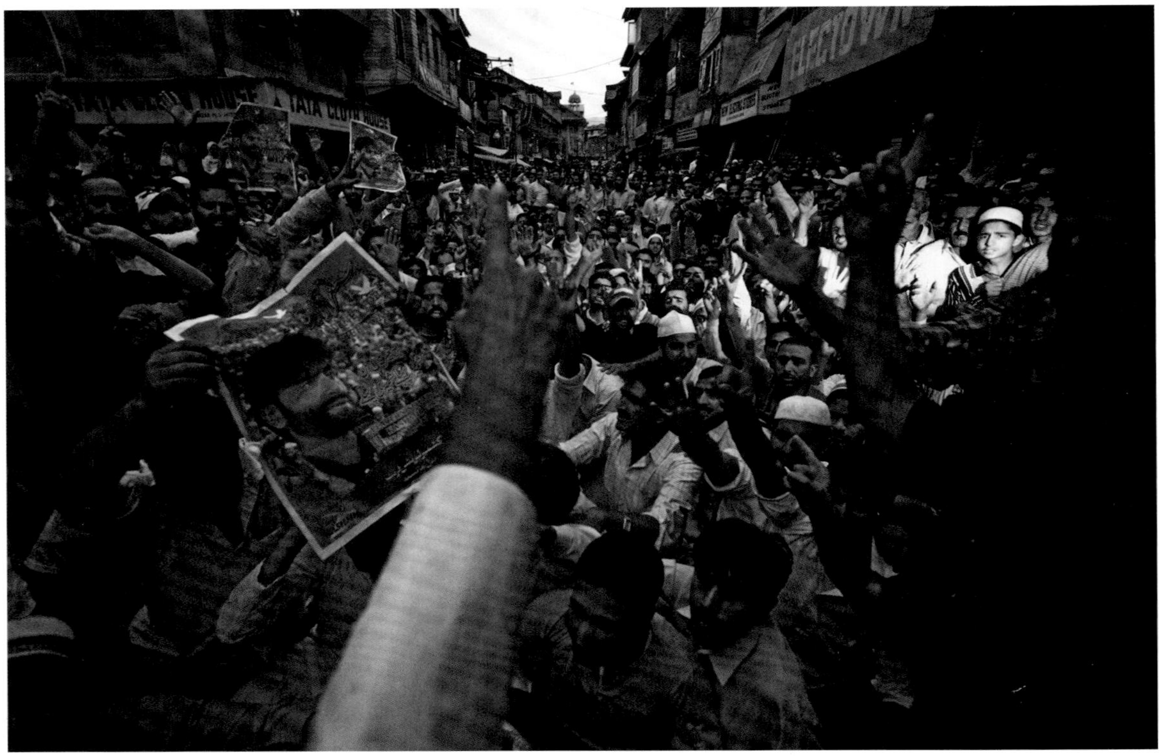

Protests in Maisuma, close to Lal Chowk in Srinagar, is mostly led by Jammu Kashmir Liberation Front (JKLF) supremo Yasin Malik. Now a Gandhian in thought, he too was involved in militancy in the '90s

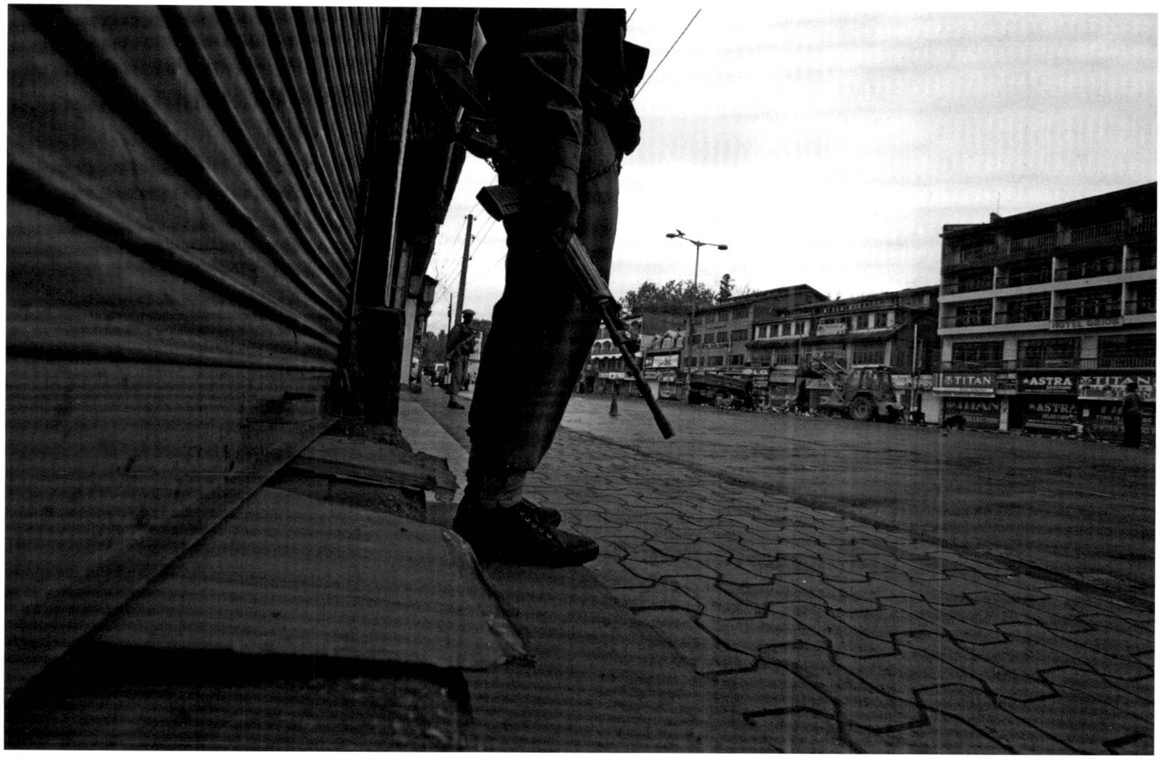

Shops closed on a day of 'hartaal'—a protest against the accession of Jammu and Kashmir to the Union of India

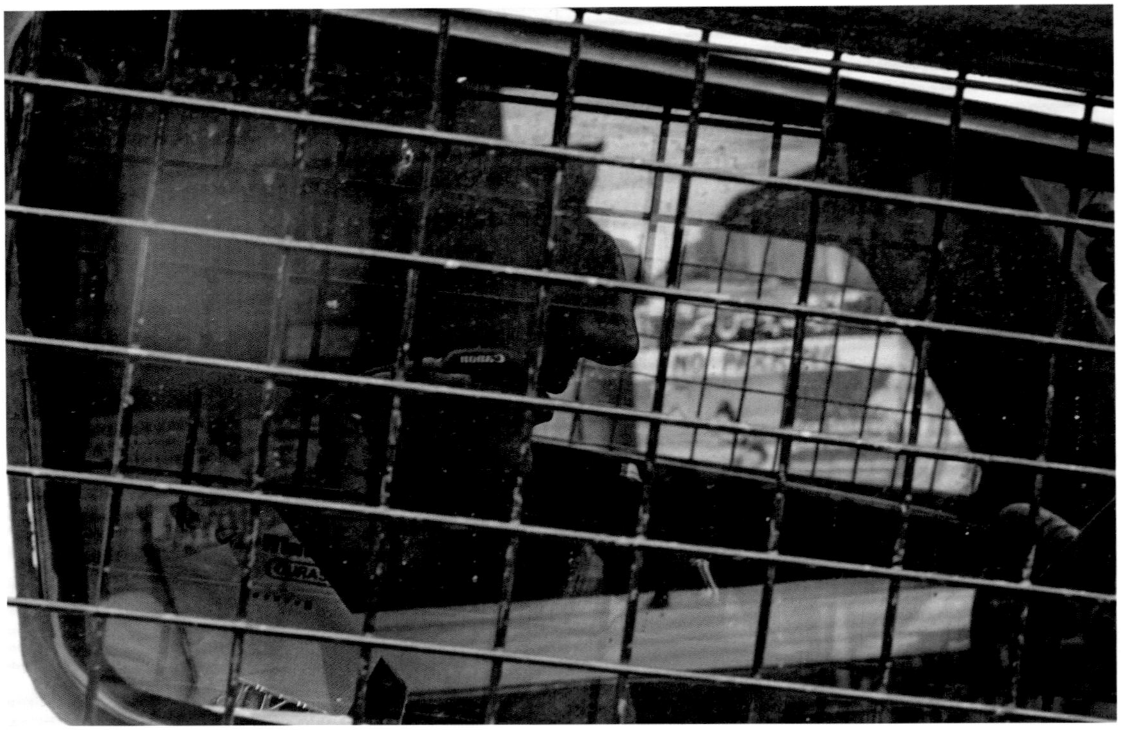

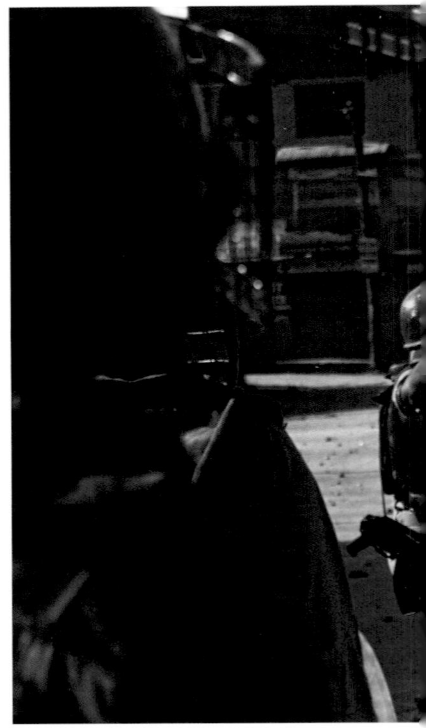

A police on alert in a riot-control van in downtown Srinagar.

CENTRE: A CRPF personnel uses a sling to throw back a stone towards the attacking crowd—a non-lethal weapon to tackle protesters

FACING PAGE: Protests flair up and gather momentum, in no time

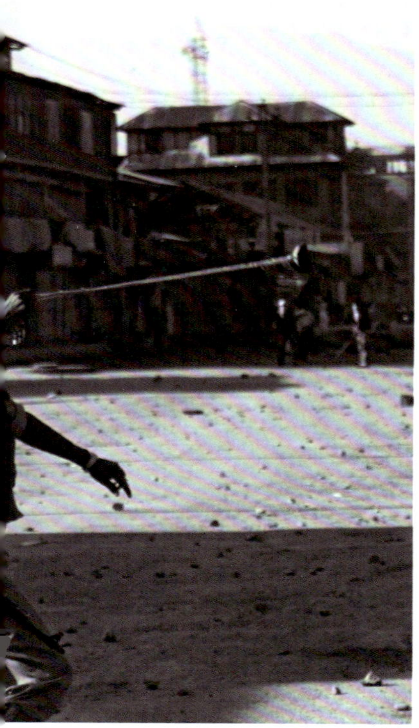

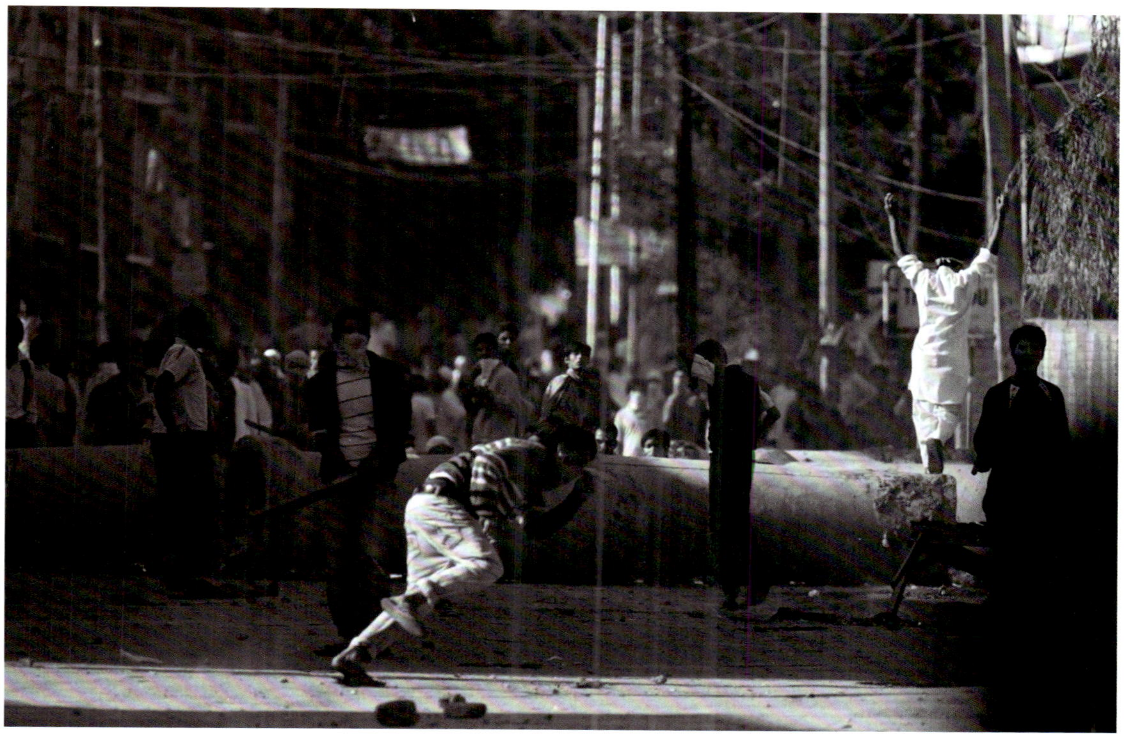

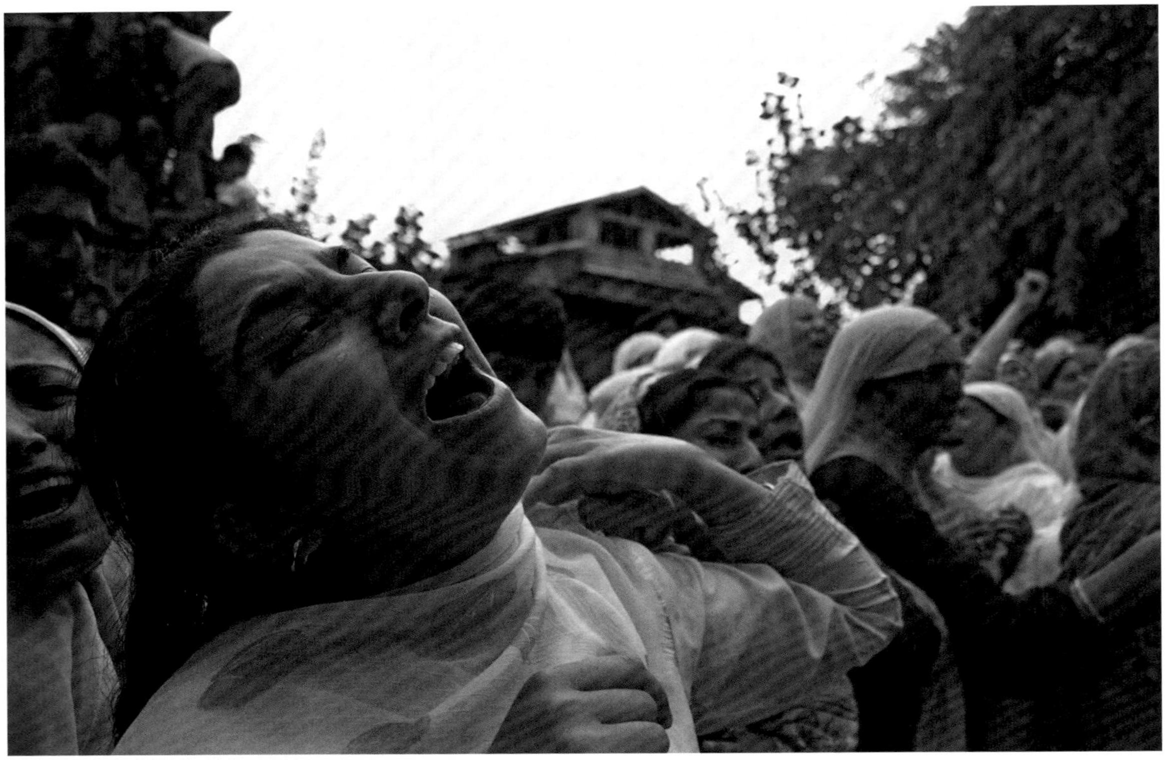

Aunts and relatives of Umer Bhutt mourn his untimely death

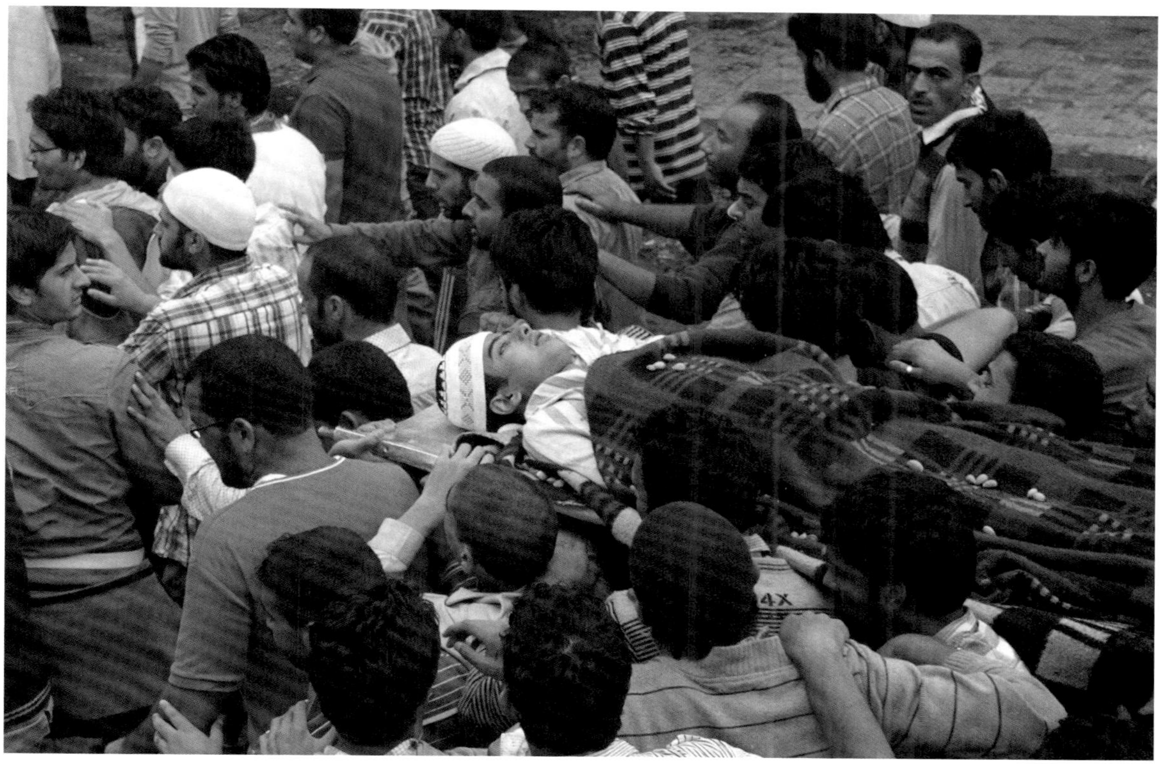

The death of Umer Bhutt, a boy of around 14 years, haunts the Valley. He was caught throwing stones during a protest and booked for vandalism and rioting under the PSA (Public Security Act); he was later beaten to death

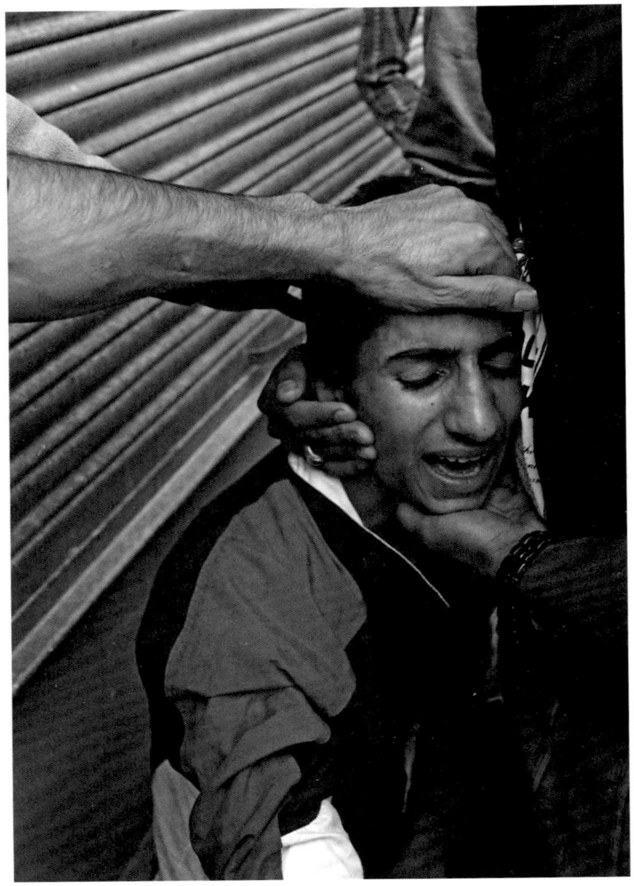

A young protester who has been hit by a tear-gas shell is being comforted by his comrades

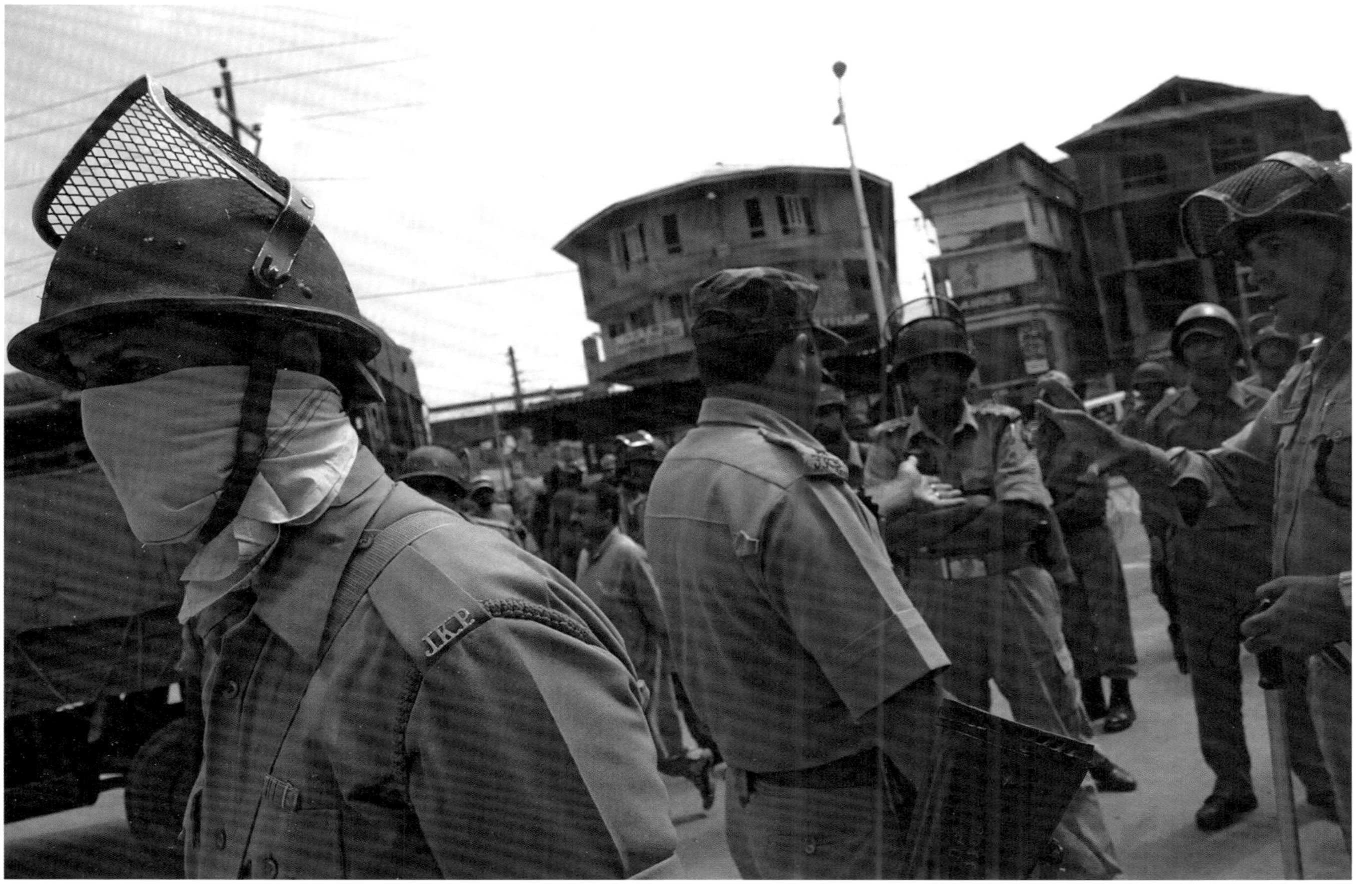

A policeman needs to cover his face sometimes to keep his identity secret from the local people, especially if he is a resident of that area. It is also a protection against the noxious fumes of the tear gas

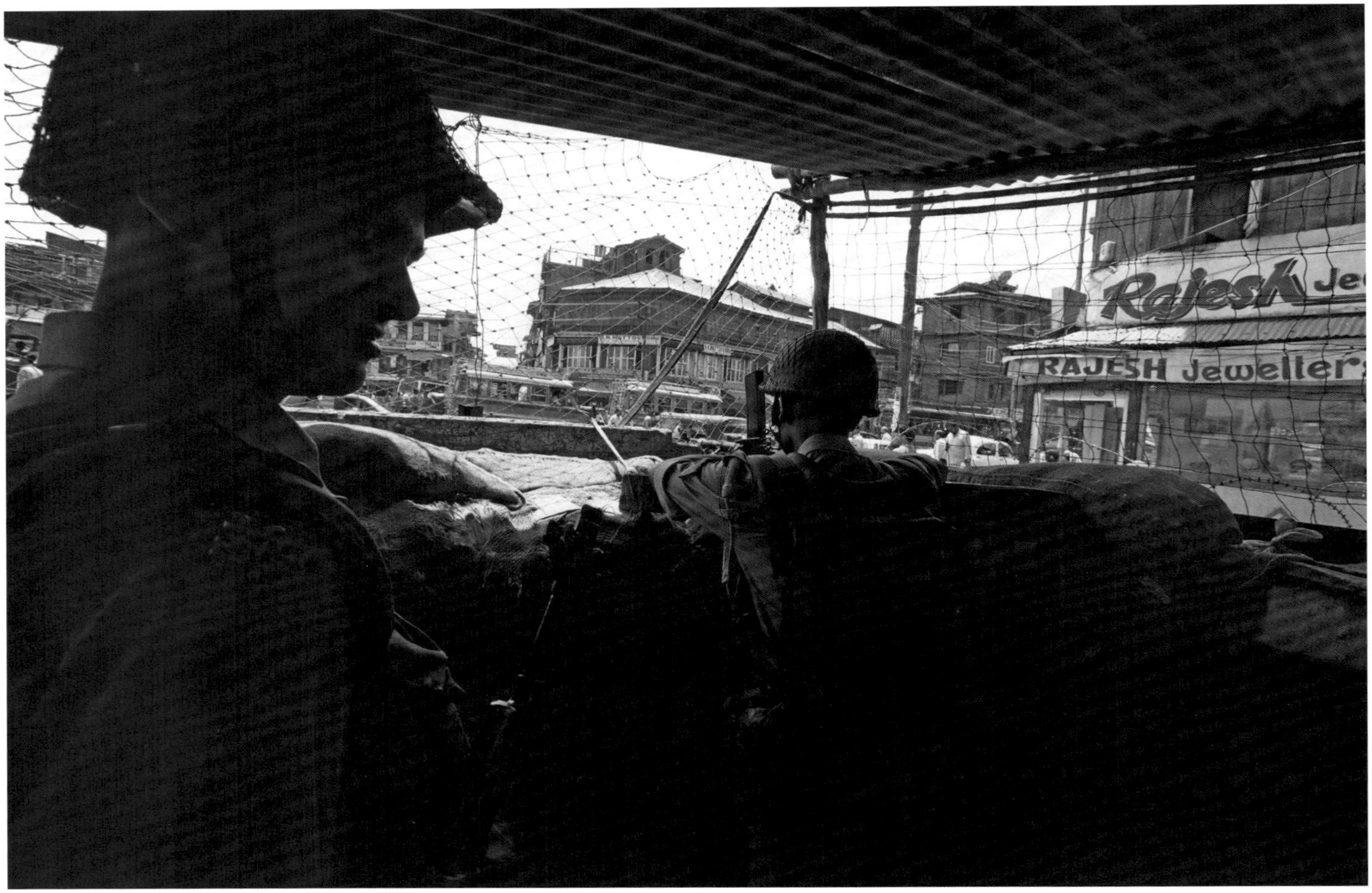

Security men keep vigil from a bunker. Sporadic violence can be expected anytime and they have to be on their toes

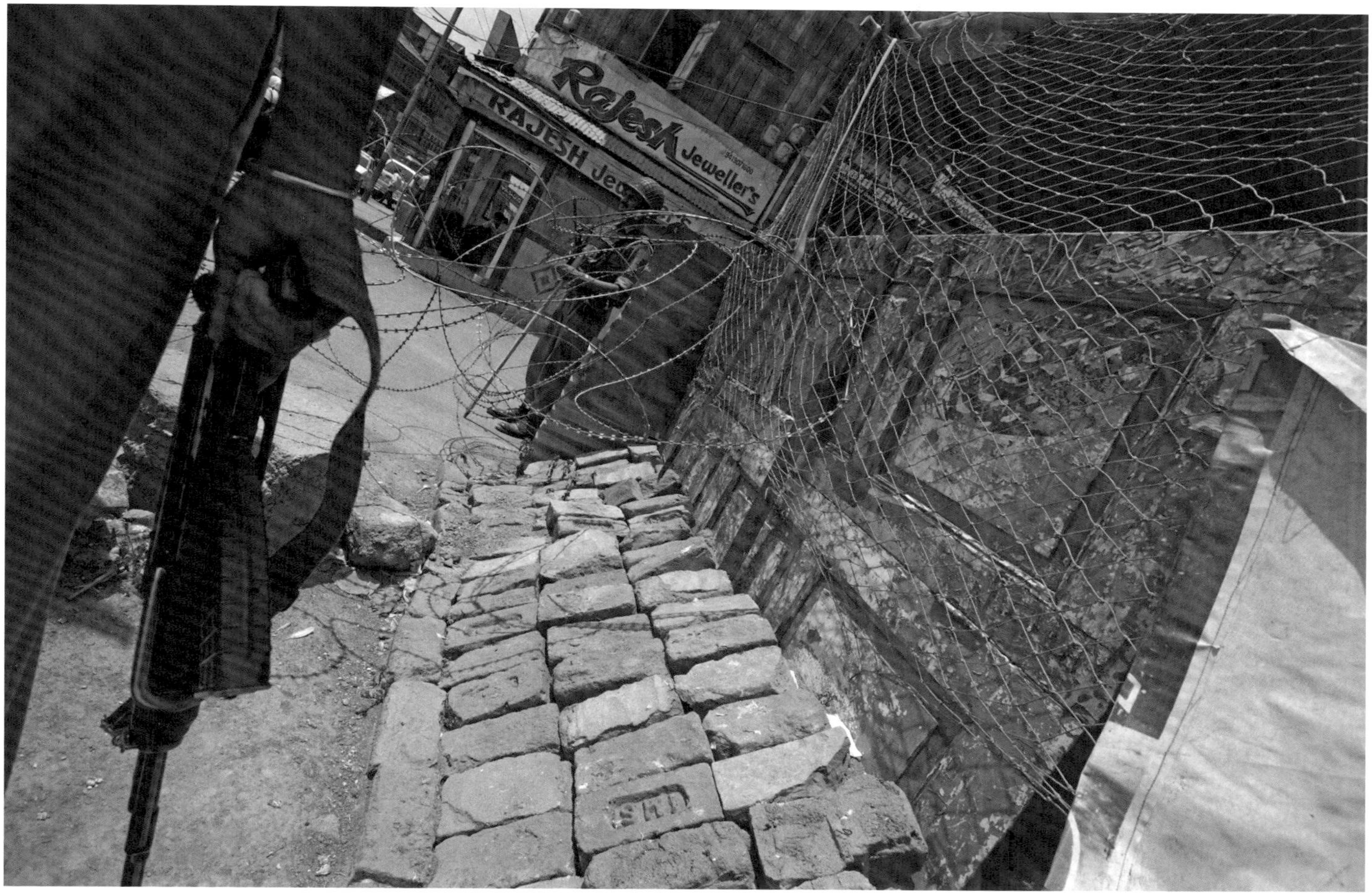

An Indian security man patrols with assault rifle

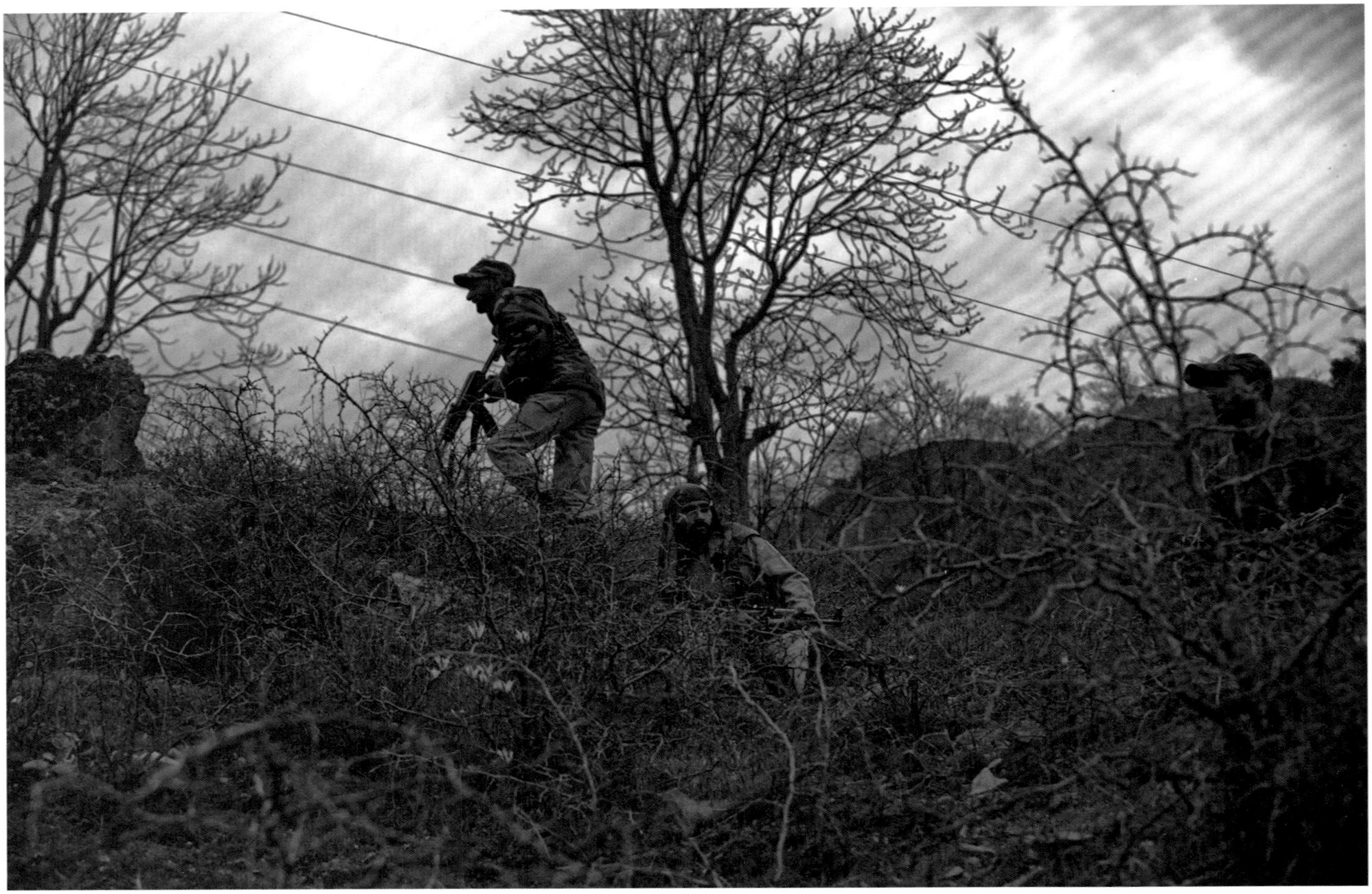

Security forces look for militants in Gandharbal district

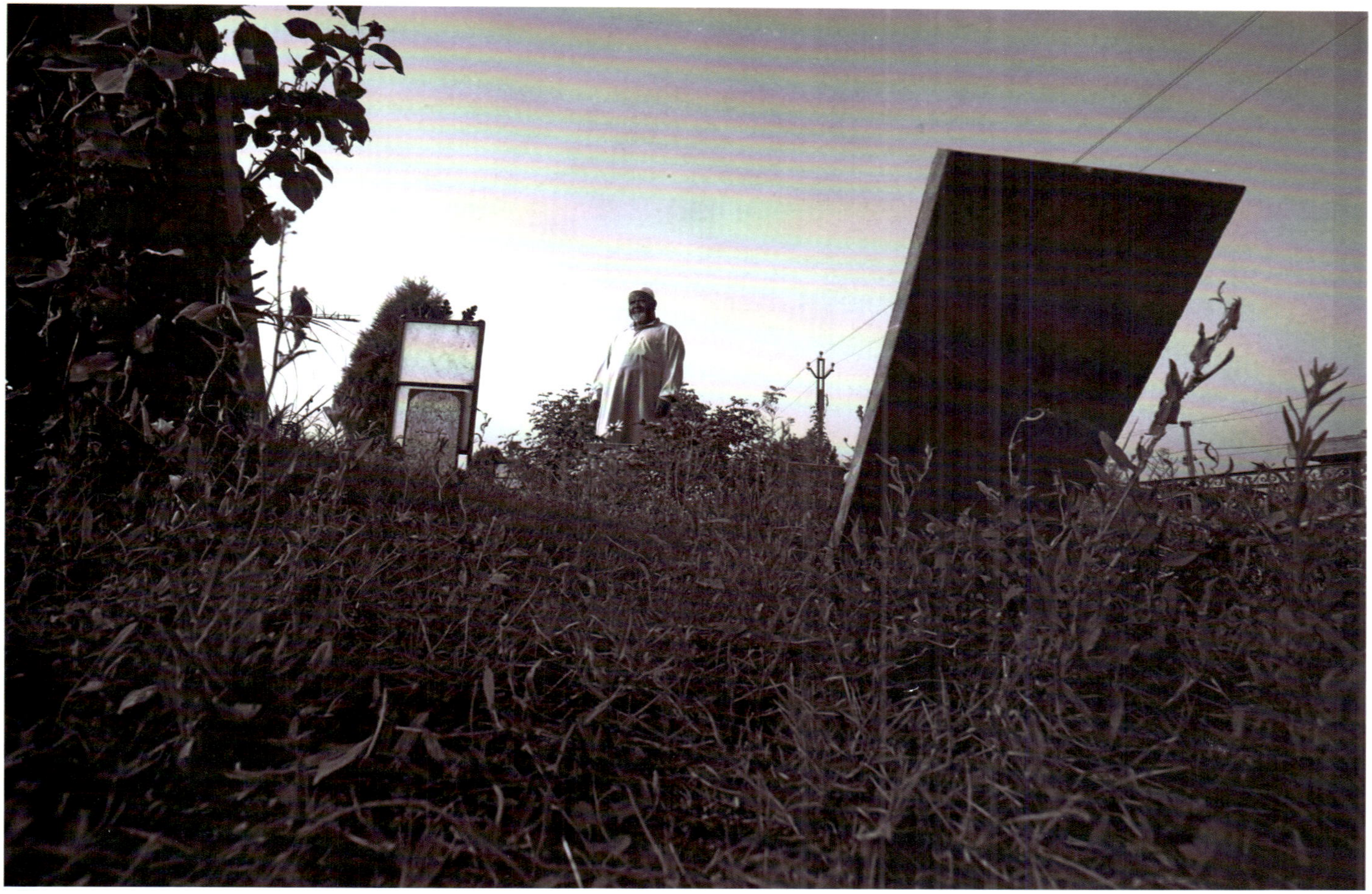

Father of a slain militant, Kabir Sheik, is now a grave digger for the martyrs. The first grave he dug was for his son Hamid, who was a militant, killed by the Indian Army

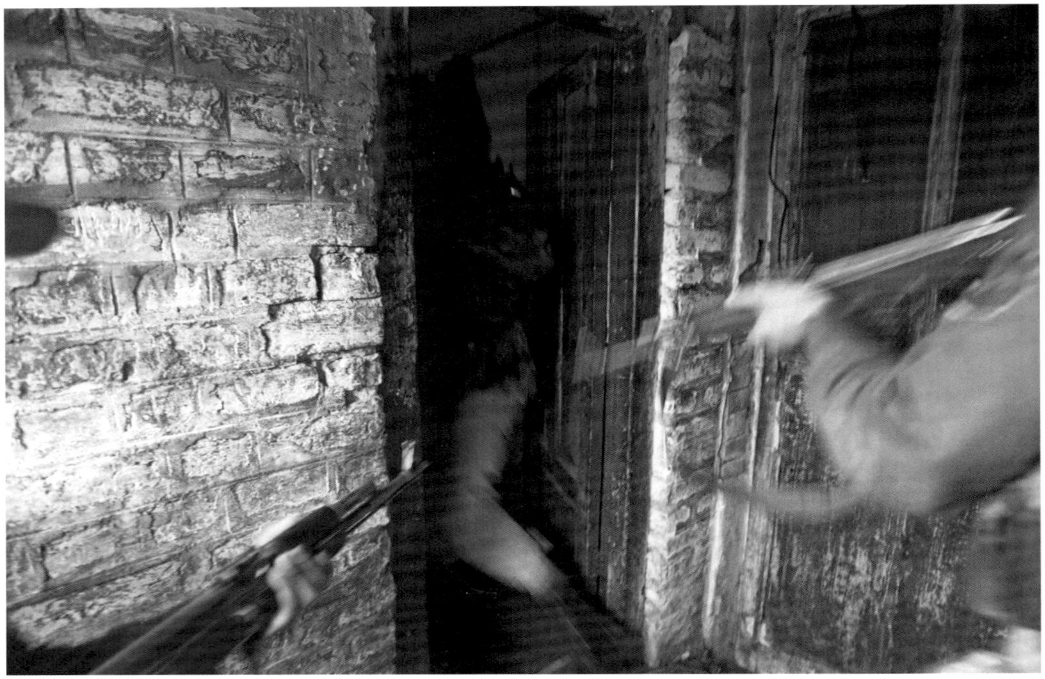

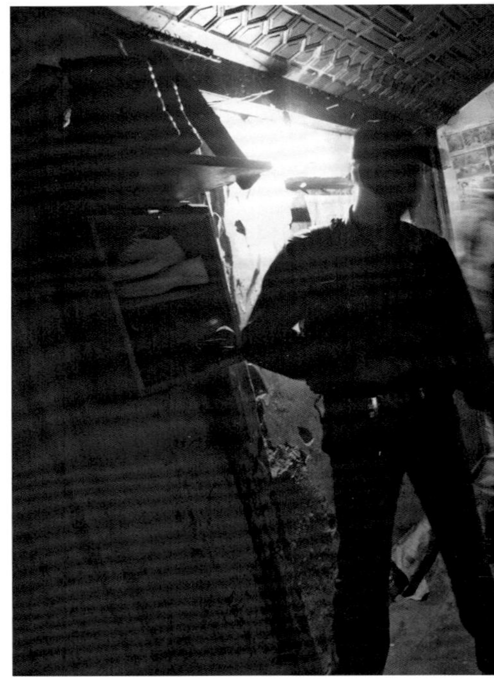

A search by the Special Task Force (STF) commandos for militant in hiding, in the district of Gandharbal. Such operations take place often with collateral damage. But without such searches militants easily escape and hide among the locals

FACING PAGE: Javed, a police officer, takes on militants in the jungle of Tral. Considered fearless and extremely efficient he has survived several encounters

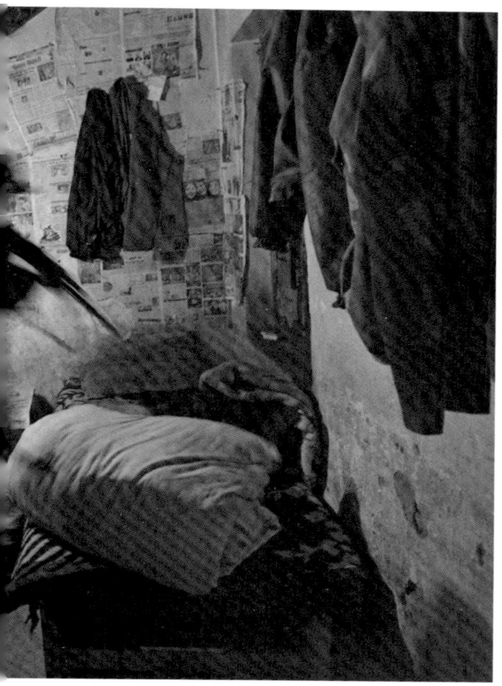

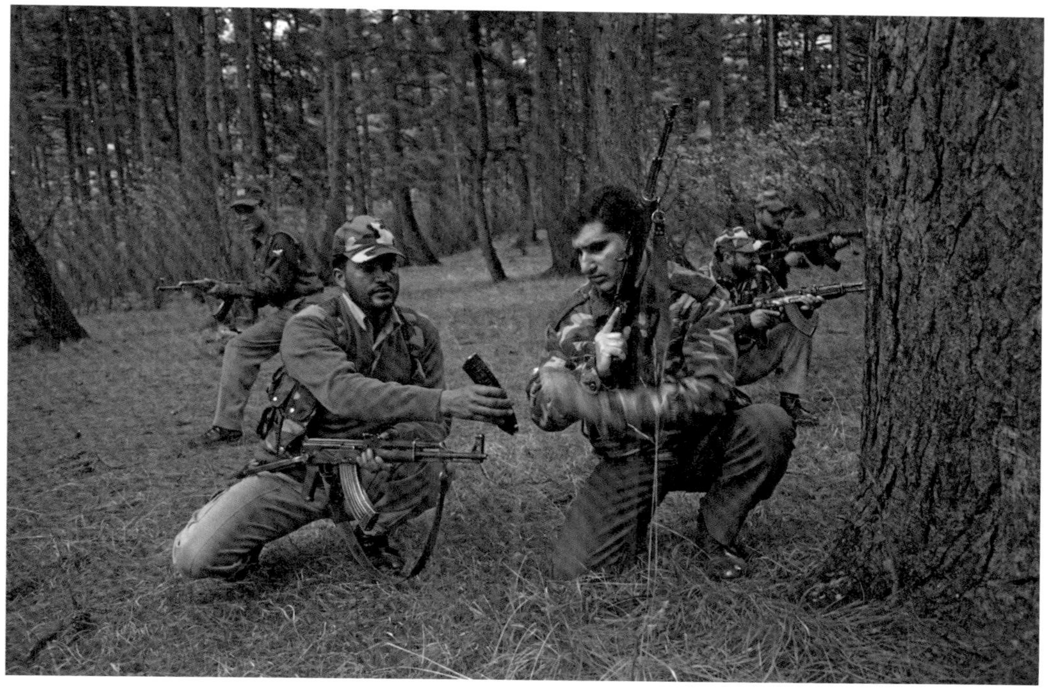

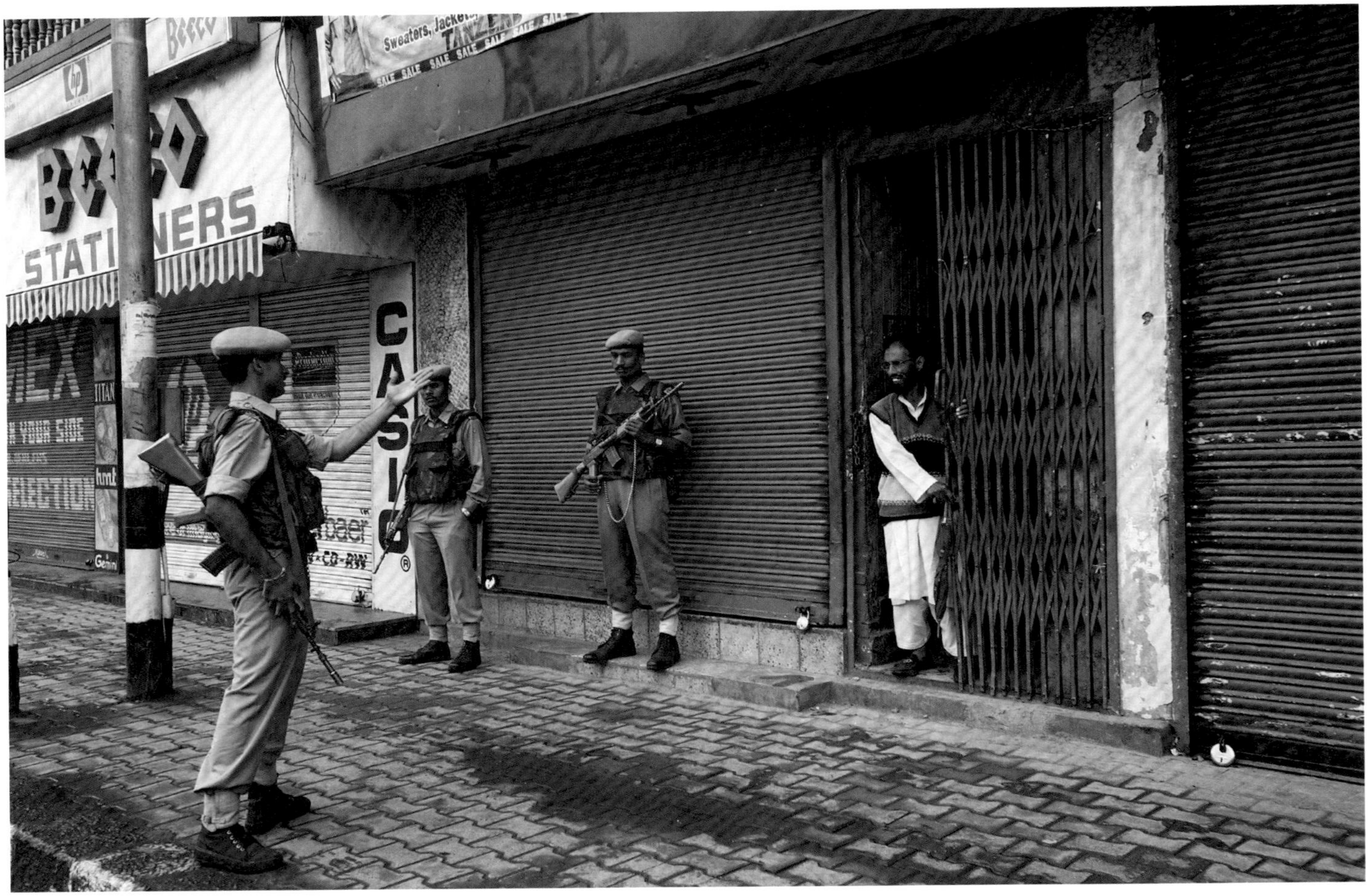

A paramilitary personnel questions a man who tries to sneak out during curfew—the sort of nuisance that jeopardise everyday life

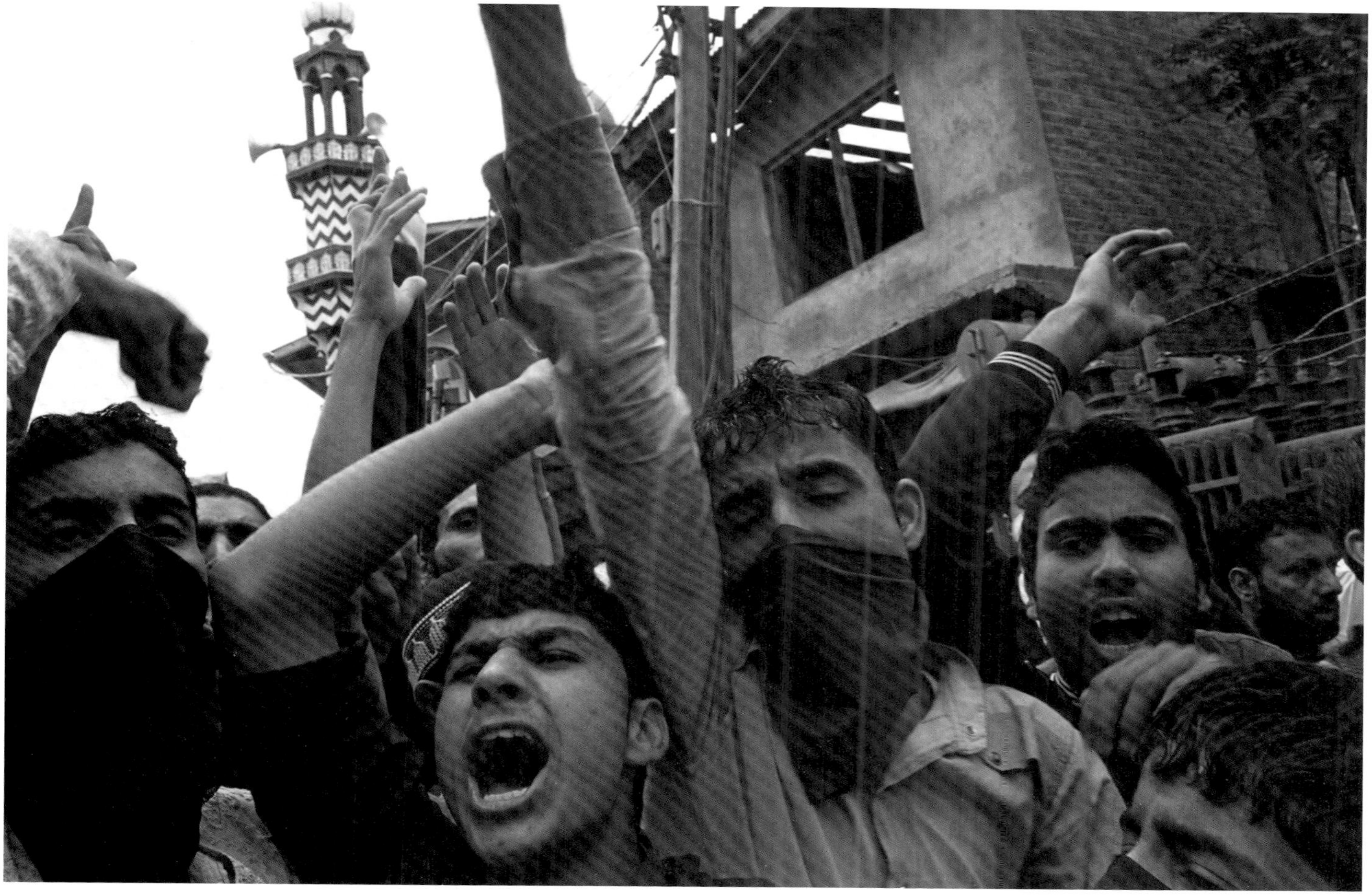

Protesting crowds turn ugly as they carry the body of an innocent victim

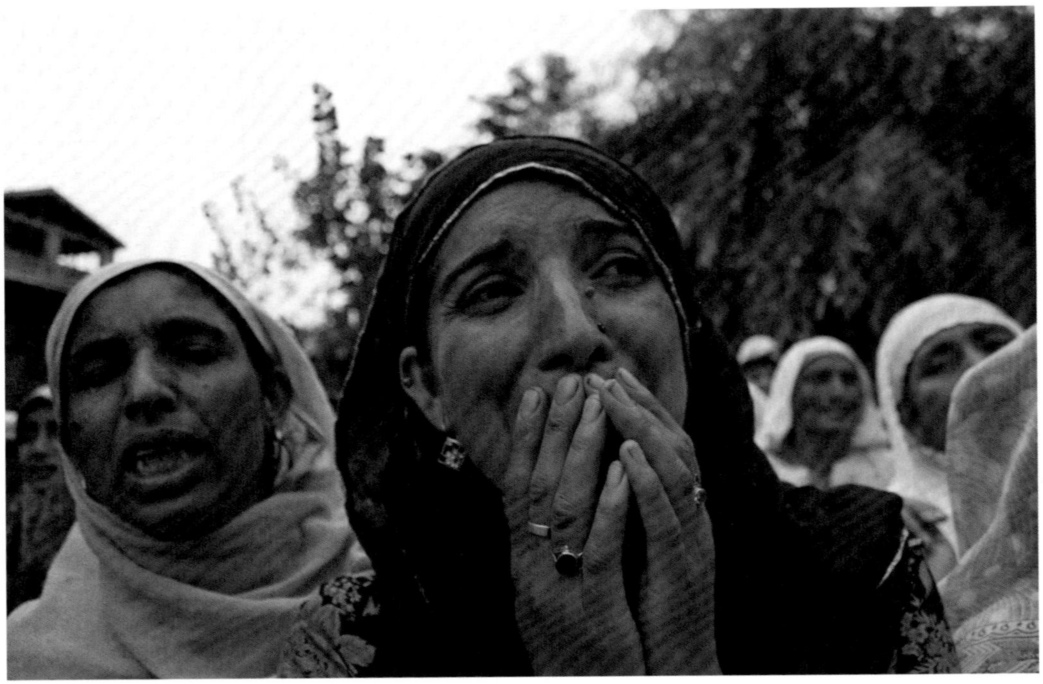

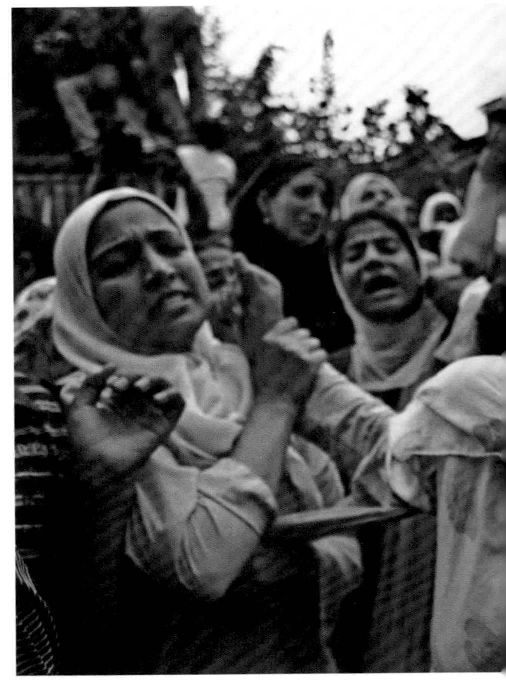

Streets filled with mourners after an encounter. Villagers mourn the death of a militant who they consider a patriot

FACING PAGE: Mother of a protester mourns at her son's funeral

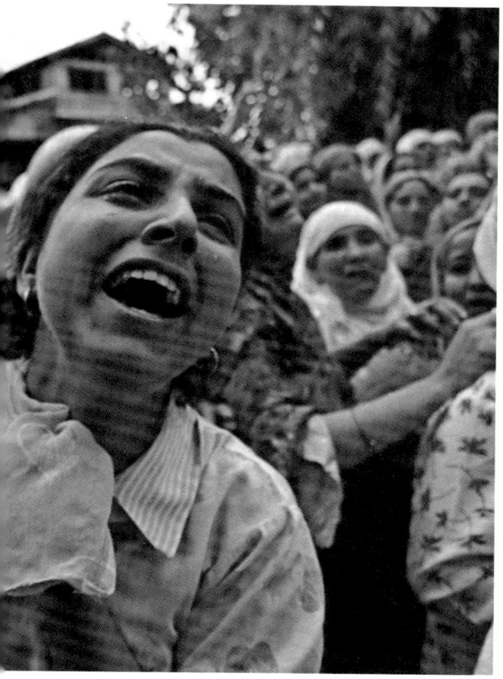

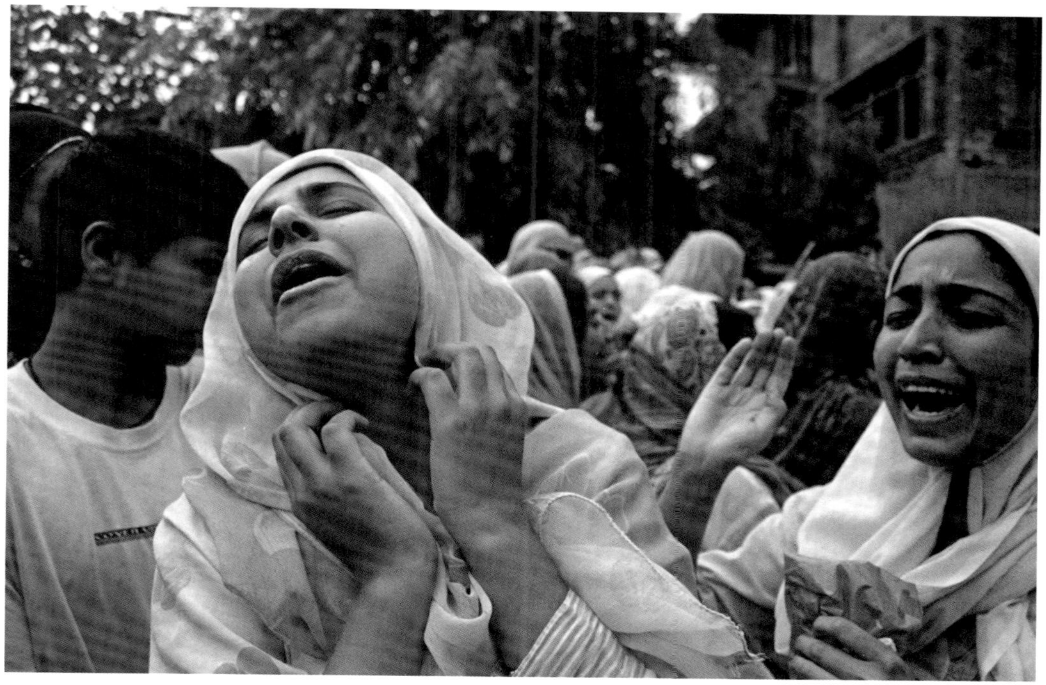

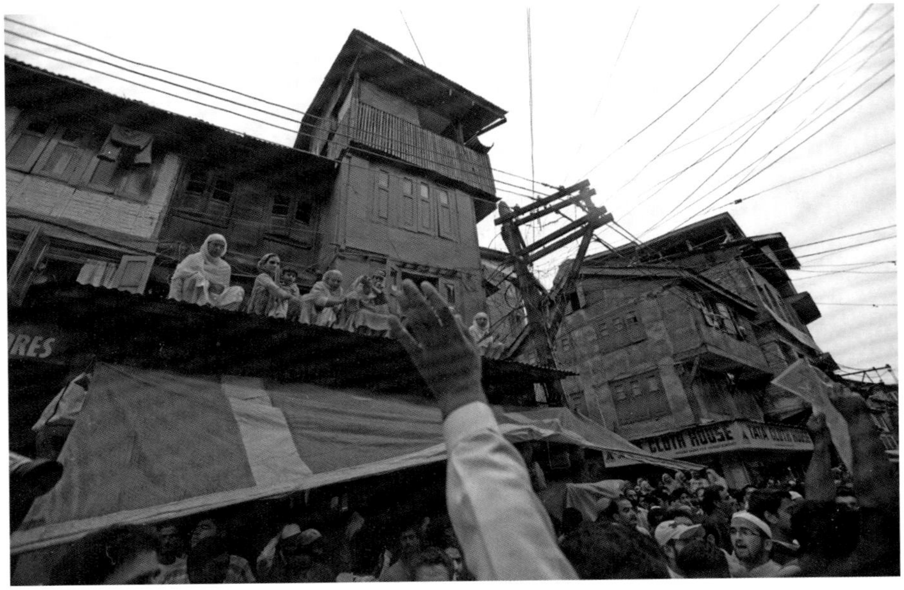

Crowds cheering from balconies during a protest

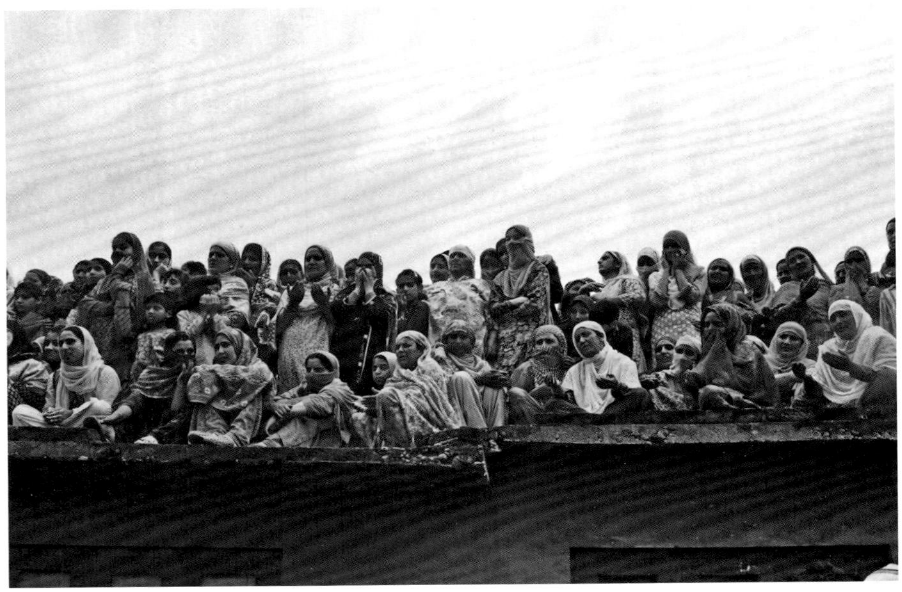

Women assemble at a rooftop to greet Hurryiat conference leader, Ali Shah Geelani, on the eve of a meeting to be held at Hyderapora

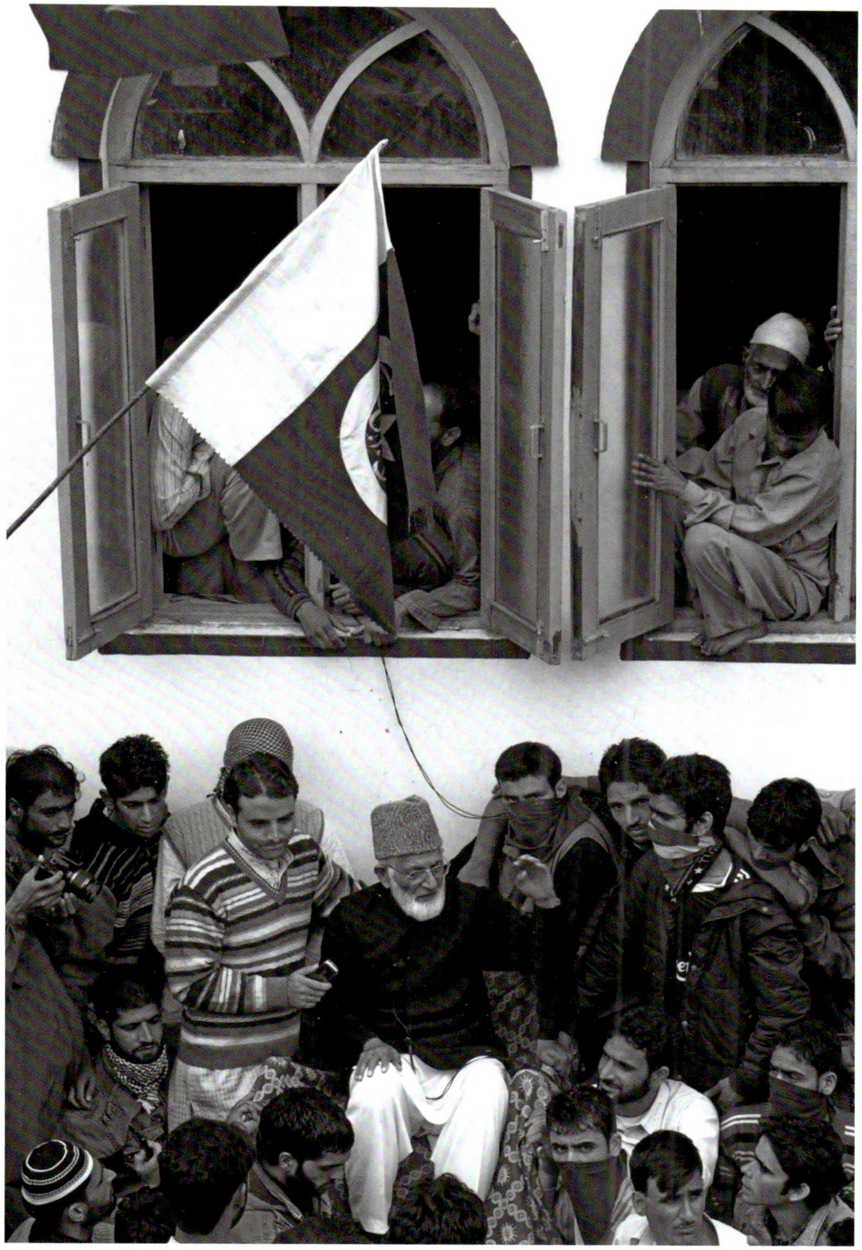

Sayed Ali Shah Geelani or the Wolf of Kashmir. A shrewd politician with high capabilities of mobilising a crowd he is a master of anti-Indian and pro-Pakistani thinking

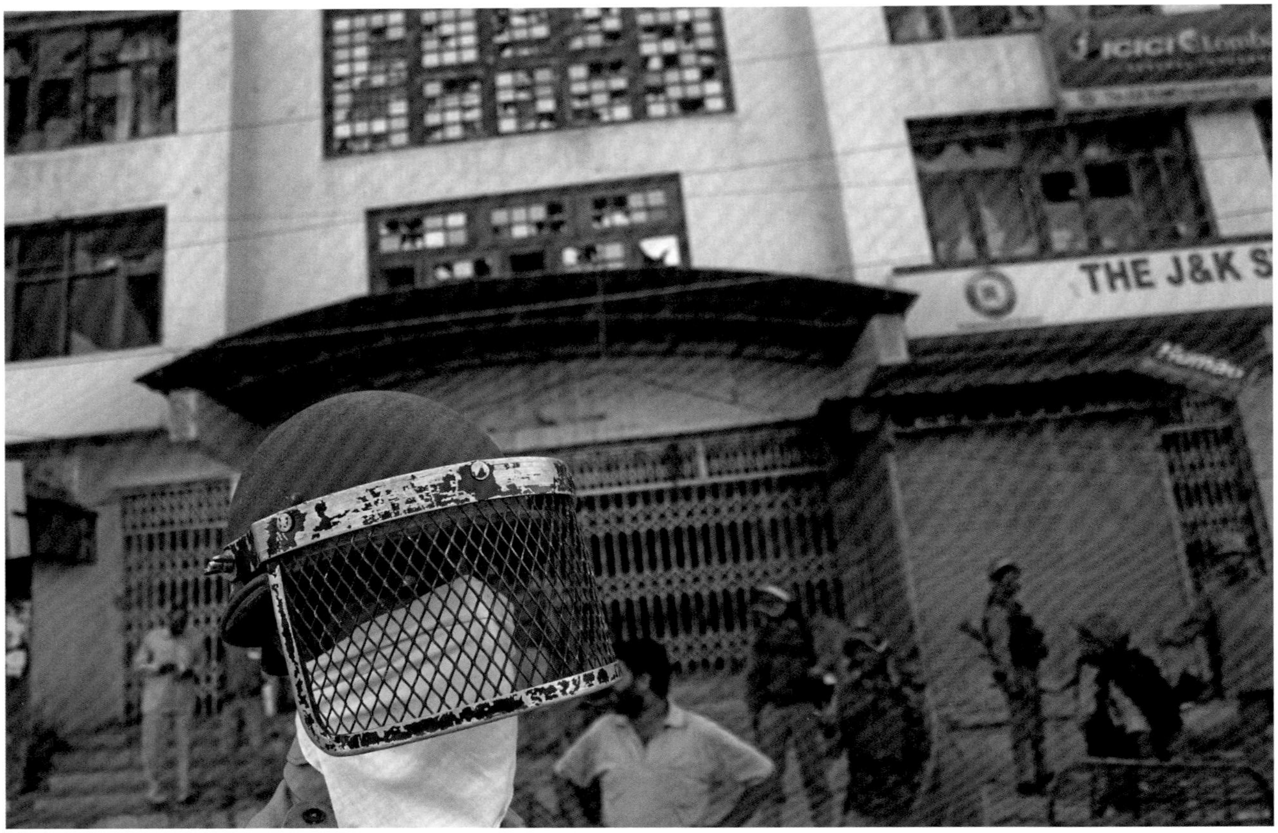

Policemen in riot gear

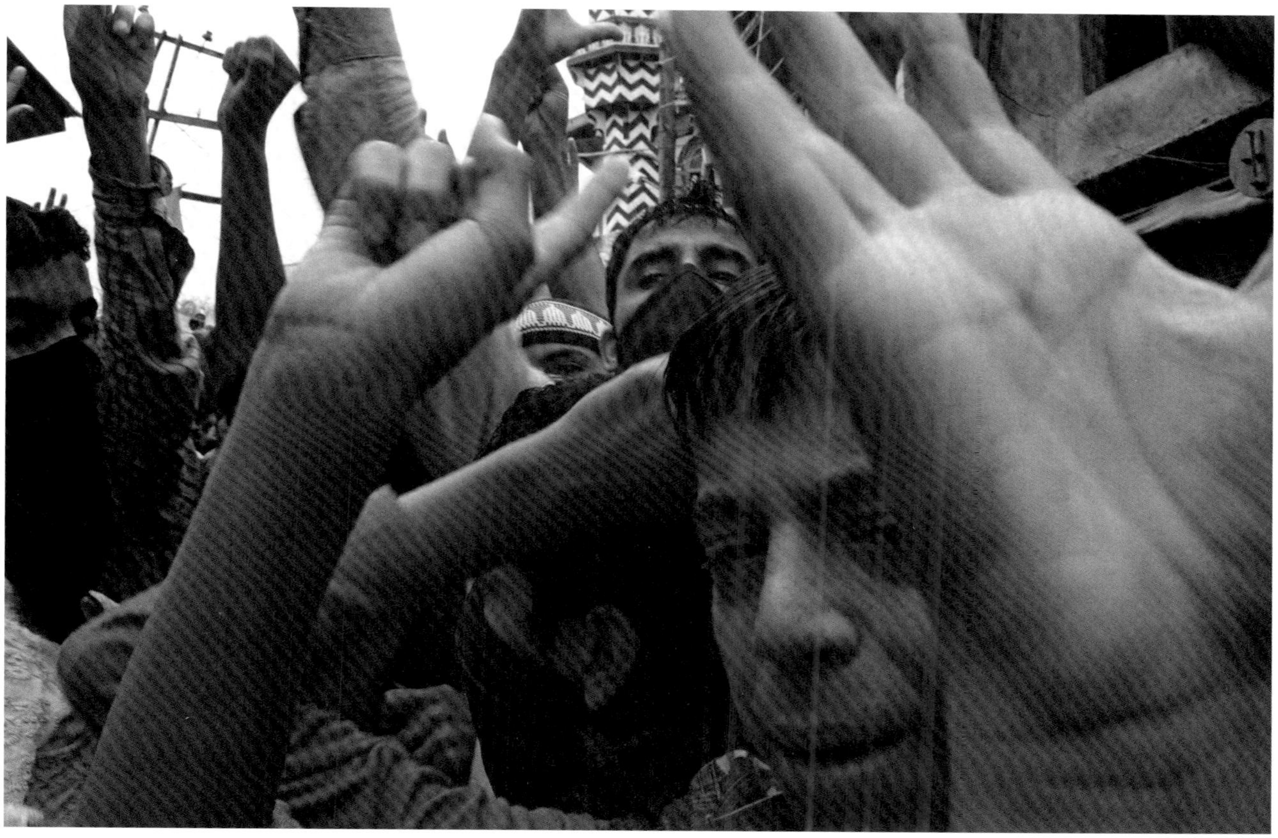

A child protester trying to get out of the mob which has gone crazy

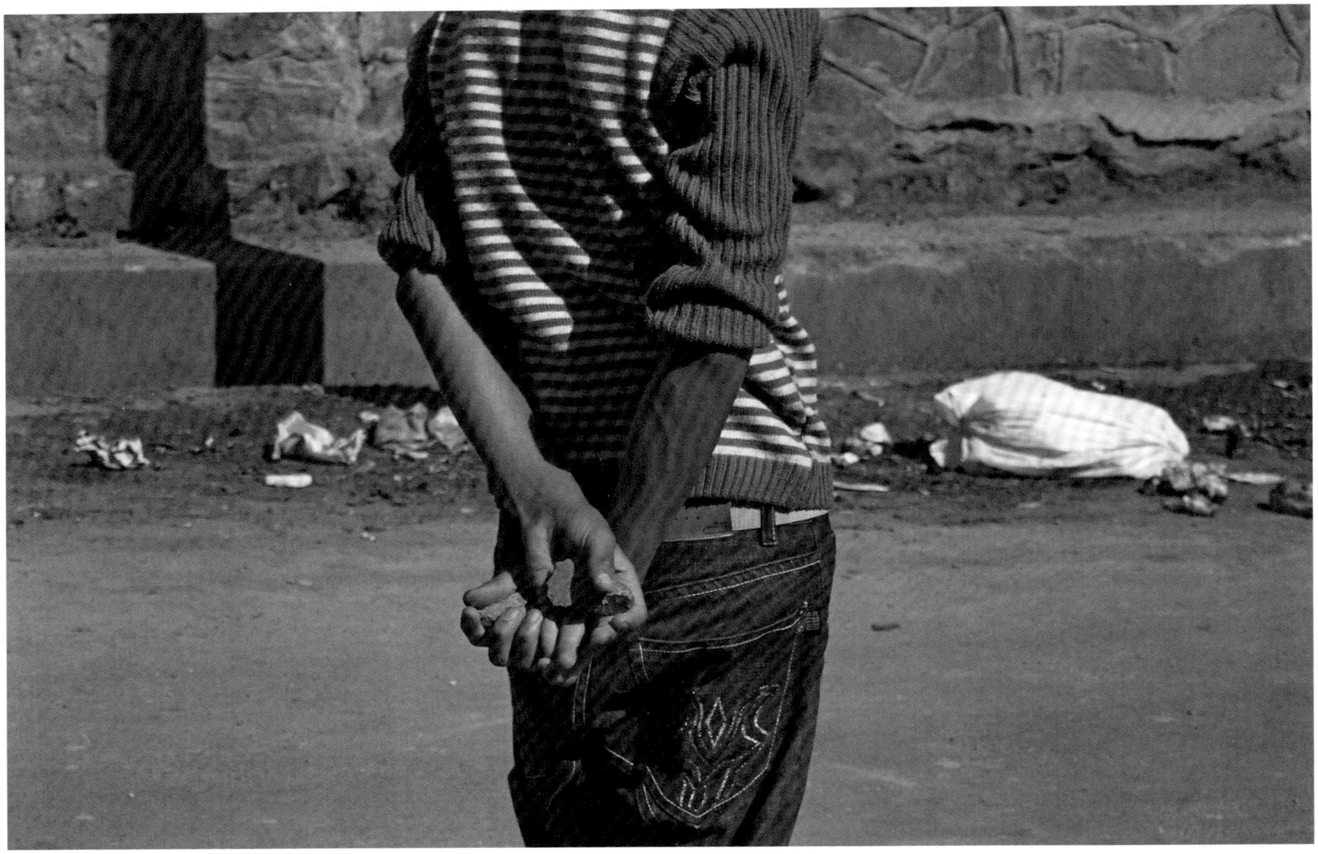

A riot monger readies himself with a stone hidden behind his back

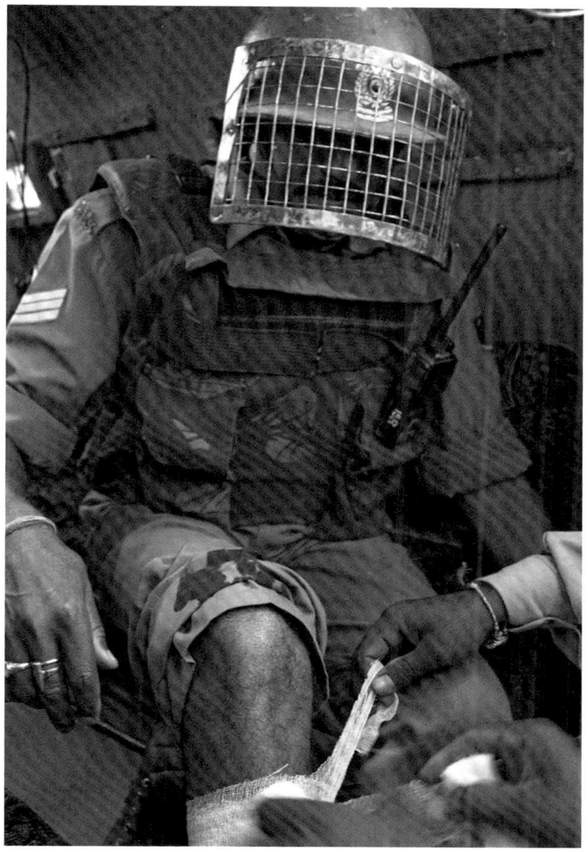

It's not only the civilians who get injured, security personnel get ambushed too

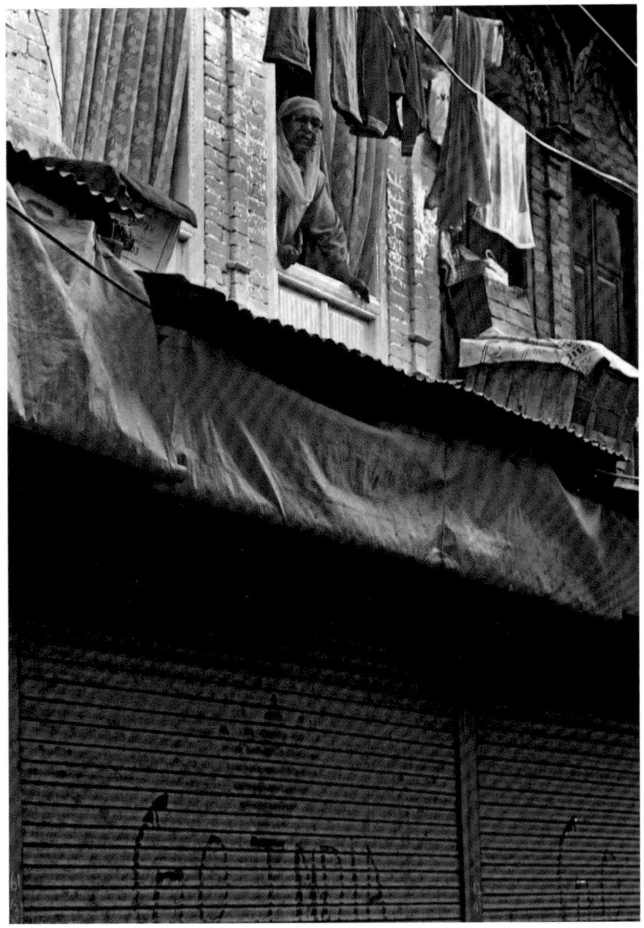

A woman looks from her window in Srinagar where anti-India slogans are written everywhere

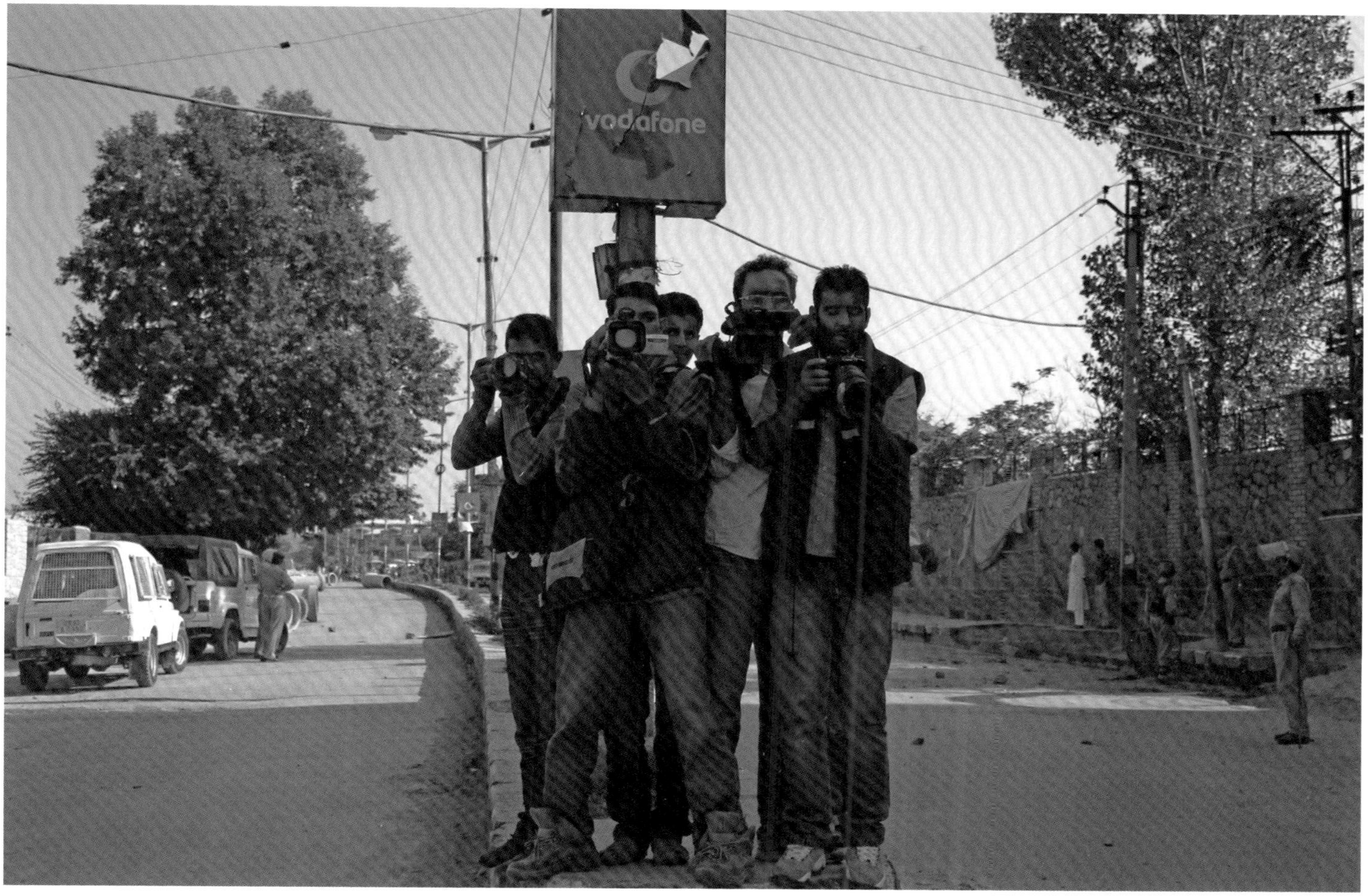

Photographers huddle together to cover street violence

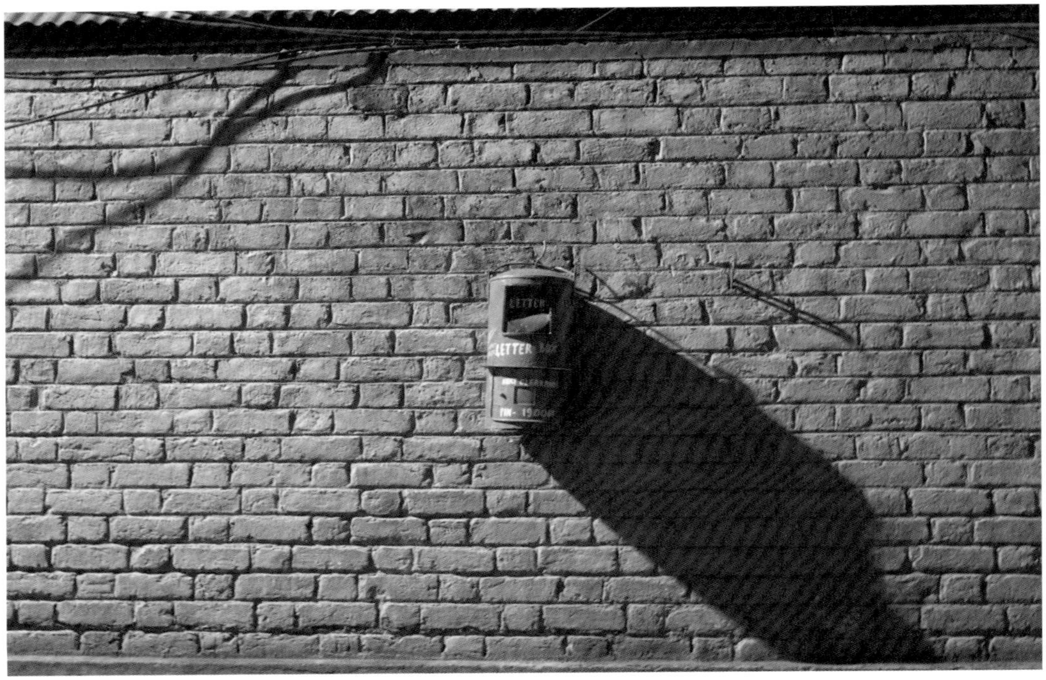

This is a postbox at a colony in Lal Chowk. Residents say letters have never been posted in this box but it remains an important address

CENTRE: An ambulance rushing to a casualty site during curfew hours

FACING PAGE: Shops close early as curfew nights draw no business. People stay at home while crackdowns take place

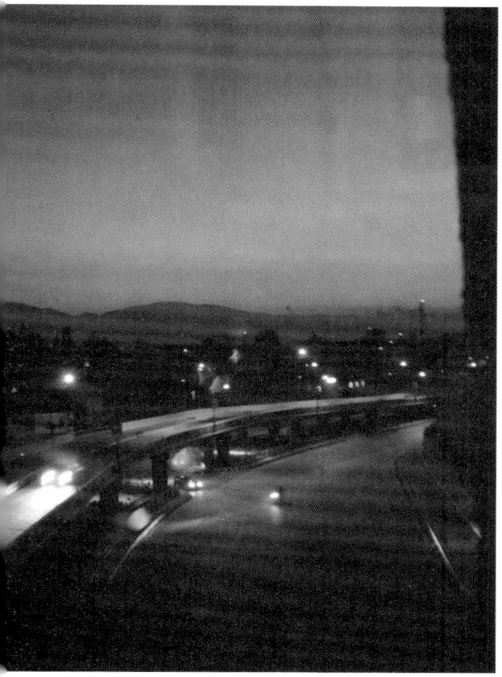

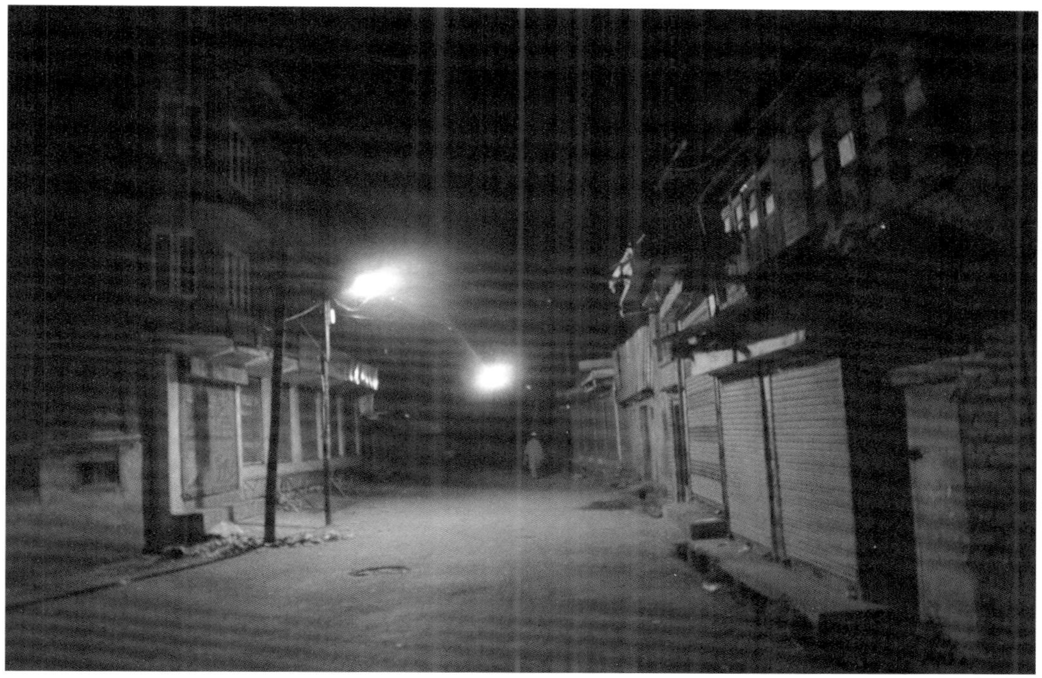

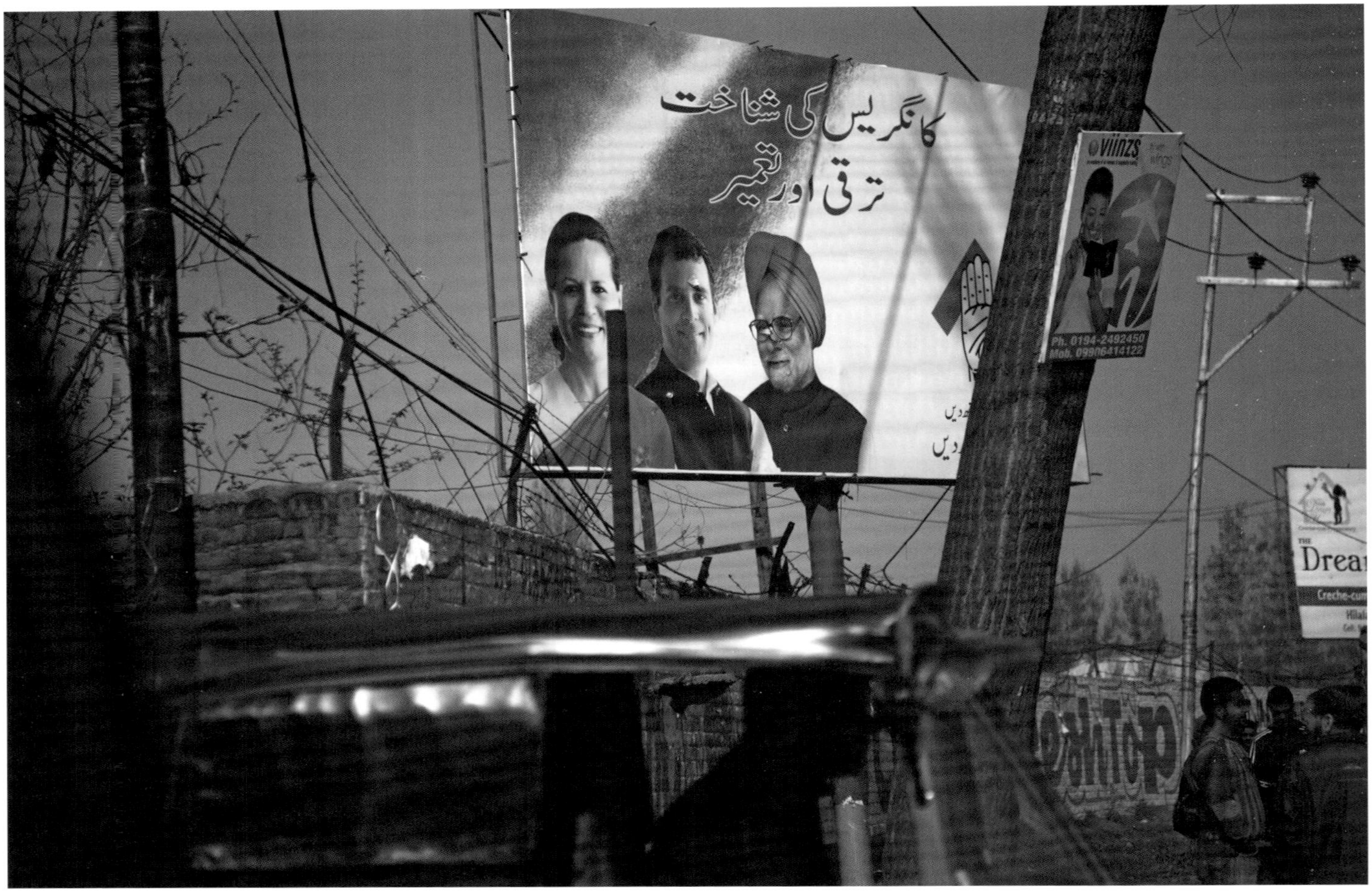

During the Indian elections in 2009. Only posters are seen here. There is very little physical presence of Indian politicians

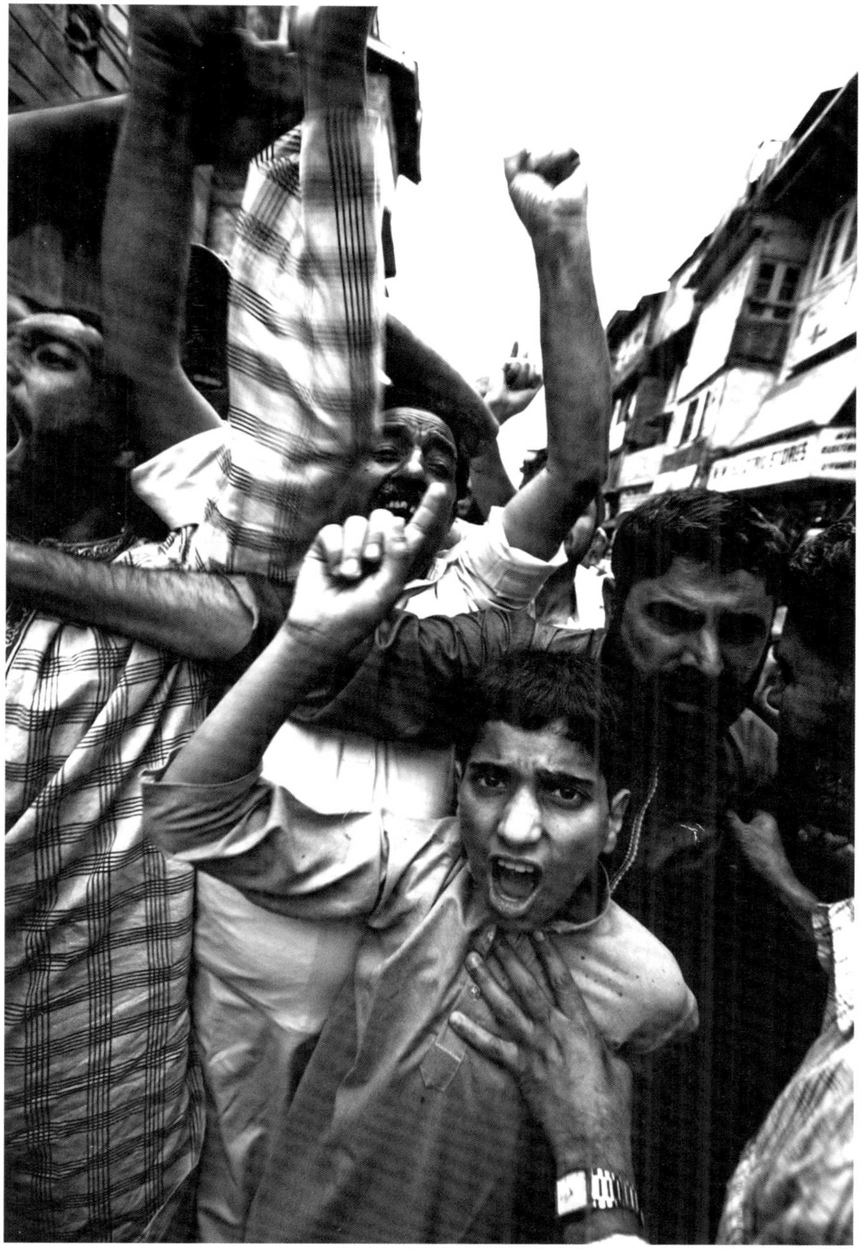

JKLF, which is now more of a political front than a militant organisation. People of all ages can be found in this gathering

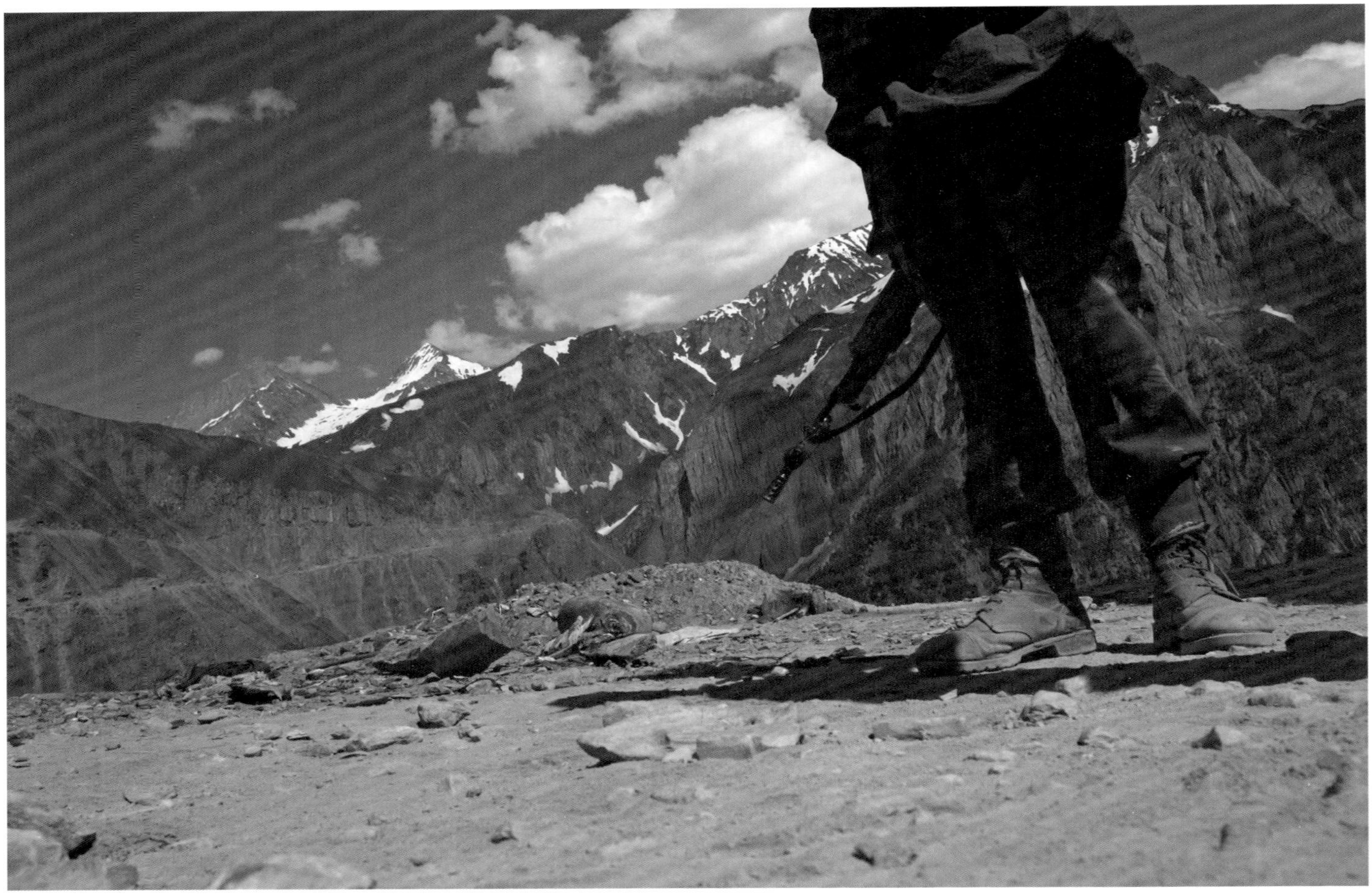

Paradise, patrolled by the Indian Army

ACKNOWLEDGEMENTS

I am a photojournalist and my work involves taking pictures and narrating stories through images. But this body of work, packaged and published as a book, has been a task in itself. Numerous thanks and appreciations are in order for making this impossible.

To start with. my editors of the magazines I worked for: Sanjoy Narayan from *Business Today*, Sandipan Deb from *Open*, and Neena Haridas from *Marie Claire*. All three, former editors of the magazines, allowed me to travel freely in the Valley which helped me immensely in my understanding of the place.

My buddies were the best of companions during some of the dark trips: Moinak Mitra, Priyamvada Kaushik, Nirad Seth and Nayanima Basu were fellow travellers during the coverage. Rahul Pandita has a special place. We experienced the pall of the curfew nights in dark hotel rooms, with the sounds of firing and explosions in the background. Another friend Tauseef from French news agency *AFP* never failed to comfort me with hot tea and local buns, during power shortages in the Valley on chilly winter nights.

Friends in the Valley: Suhel Bukhari, Raheel Khurseed, Tabish Naseer, Dilnaaz Boga, Imran, Danish Ismail, Fayaaz Kabali, Uzma Falak, Muzameel Jaleel, Zubair Dar, Captain Karan, Dirk, Gilles, Andrea Splalinger, Dar Yasin, Jawed, and many more who wish to remain anonymous—I call them: A,B and C—my heartfelt thanks to all.

Special mention goes to driver Ali Md, my local guardian out there. Without him I may not have lived to tell my story. Aizaj from News X channel watched over me relentlessly at the hospital, taking care of my calls while I got treated for an injury in a riot at Soura. Post this injury the wonderful couple Nirmala and Roshan Sharma, parents of a friend, took care of me at Abi Guzar their home. Many thanks to all.

This book is an extension of my 'Kashmir As I See' exhibition of photographs at Visual Arts Gallery, India Habitat Centre, New Delhi, June 2011. I thank Dr Alka Pande, its Curator, for all her support. I also thank my picture agency, Zuma Press and Wostok Press for circulating these images worldwide.

I wish to thank my friend from JNU, Happymon Jacob, for writing such a fitting and illuminating introduction to this book. Thanks to my friends from the French Embassy, Jeremie Roberts and his wife Shinuna Karume, for introducing me to Happymon. I sincerely thank my publishers Bikash D Niyogi and Tultul Niyogi for accepting my book idea and editor Jayalakshmi Sengupta for her inputs in finally shaping this book. Many thanks are also due to my photographer friend Ed Kashi and authors, Pankaj Mishra and Arif Jamal, for readily critiquing my book.

My wife Nayanima Basu, who has been to many trips with me to the Valley needs a special mention. She rushed to the Valley in 2010, totally surprising me, when I lay injured. Ali Md had managed the curfew pass for her. My heartfelt thanks to my father, Animesh Basu Thakur, for teaching me photography, and encouraging me to take it up seriously. I thank my mother and mother-in-law for supporting my bohemian life and appreciating every image I clicked, and finally, my father-in-law, who travelled the globe, but unfortunately, did not live to see Kashmir.

Thanks to all those who understood my madness for photography and my urge to travel, and finally many thanks to the admirers and readers of this book. Without you this mission would have been incomplete.